Acknowledgements

Author acknowledgments
We have been lucky enough to work with an enthusiastic and professional team of people at Cambridge University Press who have helped us produce this book. Our thanks go to Karen Momber, Dilys Silva, Robert Vernon, Caroline Thiriau, and Kate Hansford, who have all played a part in shaping the course. Kate in particular has made a major contribution to the *Advanced* book. Verity Cole and Andrew Reid have worked with great expertise and care to edit the material and take it to its published form. Linda Matthews has organised production schedules with her usual efficiency. Michael McCarthy has advised on the course as a whole, particularly on the use of corpora in the material. We would also like to thank the Corpus team at Cambridge University Press, and Claire Dembry in particular, for their help in accessing the academic corpus.

Martin would like to thank Ann, Suzanne and David for their endless patience and support.

Craig would like to thank Steven Shuttleworth for ongoing support during the writing of this book.

Publisher acknowledgements
A special thanks to Dr Karen Ottewell at the University of Cambridge Language Centre for reviewing the material so thoroughly and helping us to organise the lectures and to all the lecturers who allowed us to film them delivering lectures and the seminar for the book: Professor David Crystal; Dr Clare Lynch; Professor Guido Rings and Professor Dr John Spencer.

We would like to thank all the reviewers who have provided valuable feedback on this project: Jon Carlise, Philip Herdina, Simon Kinzley, Sylvia Maciaszczyk, Maggie McAllinden, Tatyana Polina, Tisa Rétfalvi-Schär and Lisa Zimmerman.

We would also like to thank the students who participated in the interviews which appear in the Lecture skills units: Youness Bouzinab, Karthik Depuru Mohan, Diana Kudaibergenova, Max Reibman and Fotis Vergis.

Text and photo acknowledgements
The authors and publishers acknowledge the following sources of copyright material and are grateful for the permissions granted. While every effort has been made, it has not always been possible to identify the sources of all the material used, or to trace all copyright holders. If any omissions are brought to our notice, we will be happy to include the appropriate acknowledgements on reprinting.

John Wiley and Sons for the article on pp. 11-12 'Academic success and the international student: research and recommendations' by Charles F. Abel (2002) taken from *New Directions for Higher Education* © John Wiley and Sons; Article on p. 16 "Does Media Literacy Work? An Empirical Study of Learning How to Analyze Advertisements" from *Advertising & Society Review*, published December 2004 by Advertising Educational Foundation. Reproduced with permission of Advertising Educational Foundation, www.aef.com; Graph on p.19 © Copyright [2011] by ESOMAR® - The essential organisation for encouraging, advancing and elevating market research worldwide. This paper first appeared in [ESOMAR Asia Pacific Conference 2010 – Eyes on Asia], published by ESOMAR; World Advertising Research Center Limited for the chart on p. 20. Reproduced with permission; Article on pp. 21-22 "Ethics and Advertising" from *Advertising & Society Review/ ADText*, published October 2007 by Advertising Educational Foundation. Reproduced with permission of Advertising Educational Foundation, www.aef.com; Extract on pp. 27-28 from *The Oxford Handbook of Innovation* by Fagerberg, J., Mowery, D. C. & Nelson, R. R. (Eds.) (2005). Published by Oxford University Press; Extracts on pp. 42-43 taken from 'The politics of plants' by Emma Frow, *Food Security*, Feb 1 2009. Copyright © 2009, Springer; Paul Collier for the article on p. 49 'Can biotech food cure world hunger? Put aside prejudices', *New York Times*, 26 October 2009. Reproduced with permission of Paul Collier; Dr Vandana Shiva for the article on p. 50 'Can biotech food cure world hunger? The failure of gene-altered crops' *New York Times*, 2 August 2011. Reproduced with permission of Dr Vandana Shiva; Adapted article on pp. 55-56 'Laptop use in higher education' taken from 'Assessing laptop use in higher-education classrooms: The Laptop Effectiveness Scale (LES)' by Lauricella, S. & Kay, R. (2010). *Australasian Journal of Educational Technology*, reprinted with permission; Jones and Bartlett Learning for Extract 3 on p. 61 adapted from 'How we work: the paperless office' by J. Harrington, *Technology and Society* 2009. Published by Jones and Bartlett. Reproduced with permission; Extract on p. 71 taken from *The power of Culture for Development*. Published by UNESCO; Fig. 4 on p. 76 'Public understanding of, and attitudes toward, scientific research: what we know and what we need to know' taken from *Public Understanding of Science* by Miller, J. D © 2004. Reprinted by Permission of SAGE; Extract on pp. 83-84 'Where does the time go? A diary approach to business and marketing students' time use' by Sarath A. Nonis, Melodie J. Philhours and Gail I. Hudson, *Journal of Marketing Education*, 8 Jan 2006. Reprinted by Permission of SAGE; Michael Saren for the text on p. 98-99 *Marketing Graffiti: The view from the street*, Butterworth-Heinemann 2006; Daragh O'Reilly for the text on pp. 99-100 'Book review: Marketing graffiti: the view from the street' taken from *European Journal of Marketing* 2007; Extract on p. 106 'Chinese children's perceptions of advertising and brands: an urban rural comparison' by Kara Chan, *Journal of Consumer Marketing* 2008. Reproduced with permission of Emerald Group Publishing Limited; Extract on p. 110 *Forensic Science (2nd edn.)*

by Jackson, A. R. W. & Jackson, J. M.Pearson 2008. Reproduced with permission of Pearson Education Limited; Text 1 on p. 118 'Crime trends through two decades of social changes in Spain' by Elisa Garcia-España, taken from *Crime, Law and Social Change*, Jan 1 2010. Copyright © 2010, Springer Science+Business Media B.V; Text 2 on p. 118 *Crime in England and Wales 2009/10. Findings from the British Crime Survey and police recorded crime* (3rd edn.) Edited by J. Flatley, C. Kershaw, K. Smith, R. Chaplin and D. Moon. Licensed under the Open Government Licence v1.0; World Advertising Research Center Limited for the charts on p. 119. Reproduced with permission; Extract on p. 127 'The wider family' taken from *Sociology* by Nicholas Abercrombie. Published by Polity Press 2004. Reproduced with permission; Lena Edlund and Aminur Rahman for the extract on p. 133 'Are children better off in nuclear or extended families?' taken from *Household Structure and Child Outcomes: Nuclear vs. Extended Families – Evidence from Bangladesh* by Lena Edlund and Aminur Rahman. Reproduced with permission; Extract on pp. 134 – 135 adapted from 'Family change and community life: An empirical investigation of the decline thesis in Australia' by Jody Hughes and Wendy Stone, Volume 42, Issue 3. Copyright © 2006. Reprinted by Permission of SAGE; Extract on pp. 139-142 'The Big Bang – A Hot Issue in Science Communication' by Martin Griffiths, Senior Lecturer of Astronomy at University of Glamorgan, and Carlos Oliveira, taken from *Communicating Astronomy with the Public Journal* 2010. Reproduced with permission; Extract on p. 171 'Please may I have a bike? Better yet, may I have a hug? An examination of children's and adolescents' happiness' by Lan Nguyen Chaplin taken from *Journal of Happiness Studies*, Jan 1 2008. Copyright © 2008, Springer; Extract on pp. 172 *The relationship between teacher attitudes and skills and student use of computers in northern schools*' by Greschner, K. J. (2003). Unpublished Master of Education thesis, University of Saskatchewan, Saskatoon, Canada.

The Cambridge Advanced Learner's Dictionary is the world's most widely used dictionary for learners of English. Including all the words and phrases that learners are likely to come across, it also has easy-to-understand definitions and example sentences to show how the word is used in context. The Cambridge Advanced Learner's Dictionary is available online at dictionary. cambridge. org. © Cambridge University Press, Third edition & 2008, reproduced with permission.

Development of this publication has made use of the Cambridge English Corpus (CEC). The CEC is a computer database of contemporary spoken and written English, which currently stands at over one billion words. It includes British English, American English and other varieties of English. It also includes the Cambridge Learner Corpus, developed in collaboration with the University of Cambridge ESOL Examinations. Cambridge University Press has built up the CEC to provide evidence about language use that helps to produce better language teaching materials.

The publisher has used its best endeavours to ensure that the URLs for external websites referred to in this book are correct and active at the time of going to press. However, the publisher has no responsibility for the websites and can make no guarantee that a site will remain live or that the content is or will remain appropriate.

The publishers are grateful to the following for permission to reproduce copyright photographs and material:

Key: l = left, c = centre, r = right, t = top, b = bottom

Alamy/©Science Photo Library for p28(r), /©Richard Osbourne for p49, /©Pictorial Press Ltd for p77(r), /©Alan Edwards for p116, /©Mike Harrington for p138(l); Getty Images/©Panoramic Images for p46, /©Stockbyte for p126; istockphoto/©Rene Mansi for p17; Masterfile for pp26, 31, 47, 101, 128; Oxford University Press/©Corbis/Lebrecht Music & Arts for p96; Pulvermacher Galvanic Company. Electricity, Nature's Chief Restorer: Pulvermacher's Electric Belts &C.; Self-applicable for the Cure of Nervous and Chronic Diseases Without Medicine. Cincinnati, O.: The Company, [ca. 1890]. Special Collections, University of Delaware Library, Newark, Delaware; Science Photo Library for p77(l); Science Photo Library/©NASA/JPL-Caltech// UCLA for p138(r); Shutterstock/©Pedro Salaverria for p28(l); UNESCO/©Francisco Monteiro, 2010 for p71(t), /©Michel Ravassard for p71(bc); UNICEF©/NYHQ2006-2046/Pablo Bartholomew for p71(b)

We have been unable to trace the copyright of the photograph on p98 and would welcome any information enabling us to do so.

Picture Research by Hilary Luckcock.

Designed and produced by Wild Apple Design, www.wildappledesign.com
Video production by Phaebus, and Phil Johnson.
Audio production by Leon Chambers.

Cambridge
Academic
English

An integrated skills course for EAP

Student's Book

Advanced

Martin Hewings and Craig Thaine

Course consultant: Michael McCarthy

CAMBRIDGE

CAMBRIDGE UNIVERSITY PRESS
Cambridge, New York, Melbourne, Madrid, Cape Town,
Singapore, São Paulo, Delhi, Mexico City

Cambridge University Press
The Edinburgh Building, Cambridge CB2 8RU, UK

www.cambridge.org
Information on this title: www.cambridge.org/9780521165211

First published 2012
Reprinted 2013

Printed in Italy by L.E.G.O. S.p.A.

A catalogue record for this publication is available from the British Library

ISBN 978-0-521-16521-1 Advanced Student's Book
ISBN 978-0-521-16527-3 Advanced Teacher's Book
ISBN 978-0-521-16524-2 Advanced Class Audio CD
ISBN 978-0-521-16531-0 Advanced DVD
ISBN 978-1-107-60715-6 Advanced Class Audio CD and DVD pack

Introduction

Who is the course for?

Cambridge Academic English is for anyone who needs English for their academic studies.

It is an integrated skills course, which means that at each of the levels you will develop your abilities in reading, writing, listening and speaking in an academic context. In your class there will probably be students studying or hoping to go on to study many different subjects. With this in mind, *Cambridge Academic English* includes topics and texts that will be of interest to students from all disciplines (subject areas), and teaches language and skills that will be of use to students working in all subjects. However, some parts of the course also help you to develop abilities relevant to your particular area of study.

This book, *Student's Book: Advanced*, is aimed at students who may already have begun their academic studies. It will also be of interest to non-native English-speaking academics who need to present and publish in English. If you are familiar with the Common European Framework of Reference (CEFR) proficiency levels, *Student's Book: Advanced* is likely to be most useful to Proficient Users at level C1 and above. *Student's Book: Intermediate* is aimed at students who need to improve their English significantly in order to guarantee success in higher education and are Independent Users at level B1 and above. *Student's Book: Upper Intermediate* is aimed at students who will soon be starting undergraduate or postgraduate studies and are Independent Users at level B2 and above.

How is the book organised?

The introductory unit, *Academic orientation*, introduces you to some of the skills you will need to develop to be successful in higher education: being an independent learner, and adopting good study strategies. Many students using *Student's Book: Advanced* will go on to do their own research, and the unit also introduces you to research proposals and research projects.

The *Student's Book* is organised into integrated skills and lecture skills units:

• **Integrated skills units 1–10 (with separate Audio CD)**

Ten units are organised around a broad topic of interest and help you develop your skills in reading, speaking, listening to and writing academic English. Each of these units ends with a *Grammar and vocabulary* section where you will learn about language of particular importance in academic communication. Cross references in the margins point to the further information and practice exercises which can be found in the *Grammar and vocabulary* section of that unit.

◀)0.1 The separate Class Audio CD includes all the recordings needed for the listening and speaking sections. It gives focused listening practice, and will also help you develop strategies for participating in tutorials and group work.

• **Seminar skills units A–B and Lecture skills units C–E (with separate DVD)**

After every two integrated skills units there is either a *Seminar skills* unit or a *Lecture skills* unit to help you develop skills in taking part in seminars and listening to lectures. For this course, seminars and a variety of lectures were recorded at the University of Cambridge, and a separate DVD accompanies the *Student's Book* containing clips of these seminars and lectures, and of students talking about their experience of studying in English at university.

A.1 Extracts have been used in the seminar and lecture skills units to help you understand, for example, how lecturers use language, visual information, gesture and pronunciation to present content and show how they are organising the lecture.

What kind of language does the course teach?

Cambridge Academic English uses authentic academic texts. The texts you will read are taken from the kinds of textbooks and journal articles that your subject tutors might recommend you to read.

You may find these challenging at first but you will learn strategies in the course to help you to cope with them. We believe that working with authentic texts in EAP is the best way of preparing to read them during your academic course of study.

The lectures you will watch are delivered by experienced lecturers and researchers. In many colleges and universities around the world you will be taught in English by some tutors who are native English speakers and others who are non-native English speakers. To help you prepare for this, both native and non-native English-speaking lecturers have been included in this course.

The vocabulary focused on in the course has been selected for being of particular importance in academic writing, reading, lectures and seminars. In choosing what to teach we have made use of the Academic Word List compiled by Averil Coxhead (see www.victoria.ac.nz/lals/resources/academicwordlist/ for more information). This list includes many of the words that you are likely to encounter in your academic studies.

What are the additional features?

Each unit contains the following additional features:

 The *Study tip* boxes offer practical advice on how you can improve the way you study.

 The *Focus on your subject* boxes encourage you to think about how what you have learnt applies to your own subject area.

 Corpus research boxes present useful findings from the CAEC (see below).

- The *Word list* at the back of the Student's Book covers key academic words essential for development of academic vocabulary.

- For each level of the course, a full-length version of one of the lectures from the DVD is available online. This gives you the opportunity to practise, in an extended context, the listening and note-taking skills that you develop in the *Lecture and seminar skills* units. The video and accompanying worksheets are available for students at www.cambridge.org/elt/academicenglish.

To make sure that the language we teach in the course is up-to-date and relevant, we have made extensive use of the Cambridge Academic English Corpus in preparing the material.

 What is the Cambridge Academic English Corpus (CAEC)?

The CAEC is a 400-million-word resource comprising two parts. One is a collection of written academic language taken from textbooks and journals written in both British and American English. The second is a collection of spoken language from academic lectures and seminars. In both parts of the corpus a wide variety of academic subject areas is covered. In addition to the CAEC, we have looked at language from a 1.7-million-word corpus of scripts written by students taking the IELTS test.

Conducting our research using these corpora has allowed us to learn more about academic language in use, and also about the common errors made by students when using academic English. Using this information, we can be sure that the material in this course is built on sound evidence of how English is used in a wide variety of academic contexts. We use the CAEC to provide authentic examples in the activities of how language is used, and to give you useful facts about how often and in what contexts certain words and phrases are used in academic writing.

We hope you enjoy using *Cambridge Academic English* and that it helps you achieve success in your academic studies.

Martin Hewings and Craig Thaine

Contents

Seminar skills B *Page 66*	**Preparing for seminars**	**Seminar skills**	**Listening**	**Follow up**
	Working in groups Understanding task instructions	Giving a feedback presentation Organising a group presentation Introducing a group presentation	Creating an effective presentation	Giving a mini-presentation
Unit 5 **Culture, science and society** *Page 70*	**Reading**	**Listening and speaking**	**Writing**	**Grammar and vocabulary**
	Preparing to read Identifying the main points Understanding meaning in context Vocabulary building: formal and informal verbs Reading in detail Evaluating websites	Giving opinions in presentations Presentation practice	Using primary and secondary sources Writing practice Writing up research: writing an introduction	Complex noun phrases 1 Classifying nouns Compound adjectives Specialist terms: collocation Language-announcing goals in research paper introductions
Unit 6 **Ways of studying in higher education** *Page 82*	**Reading**	**Listening and speaking**	**Writing**	**Grammar and vocabulary**
	Reading efficiently Practice in reading efficiently Understanding the relationship between research findings Vocabulary in context: movement up and down Vocabulary building: dependent prepositions Reading in detail	Presenting and explaining results in charts Presentation practice	Choosing between paraphrase and quotation Quotation conventions Writing up research: the literature review Writing practice	Complex noun phrases 2 Producing compound nouns *as*-clauses: referring to the work of others *of which*: expressing ideas efficiently
Lecture skills C *Page 94*	**Preparing for lectures**	**Listening**	**Language focus**	**Follow up**
	Thinking about the content of lectures Understanding introductions	Understanding detailed points; making notes Understanding the main point	Recognising quotes Recognising examples that support key points	Responding to questions posed in a lecture Lecture structure
Unit 7 **Marketing and consumers** *Page 98*	**Reading**	**Listening and speaking**	**Writing**	**Grammar and vocabulary**
	Evaluating academic texts: a book review Vocabulary building 1: understanding complex noun phrases Vocabulary building 2: word families Reading in detail	Conclusions and recommendations Presentation practice	Organising information in sentences Writing up research: the Methods section	Irregular plural nouns Noun + passive verb combinations in Methods sections Using *it*-clauses to organise Information Word families in texts Problem words: *adopt* and *adapt*
Unit 8 **Criminology** *Page 110*	**Reading**	**Listening and speaking**	**Writing**	**Grammar and vocabulary**
	Making predictions Vocabulary building 1: adjectives Vocabulary building 2: verbs Reading in detail Understanding plagiarism	Dealing with questions in presentations Presentation practice	Organising information in texts Writing up research: the Results section Writing practice	Problem words: *comprise, be composed of, consist of, constitute, make up, include* Classifying phrases Problem–solution phrases Word order in *as*-clauses

Lecture skills D *Page 122*	**Preparing for lectures**	**Listening**	**Language focus**	**Follow up**
	Thinking about the content of lectures Vocabulary for the context	Practice in gist and detailed listening 1 Recognising lecture introductions Recognising lecture styles Practice in gist and detailed listening 2	Understanding lecture structure	Further listening practice
Unit 9 **Families and** **relationships** *Page 126*	**Reading**	**Listening and speaking**	**Writing**	**Grammar and vocabulary**
	Understanding the writer's opinion Inferring the meaning of words Vocabulary building: word families Reading in detail Understanding figures	Your relationship with your supervisor Formality and politeness in arranging meetings	Writing a critique Writing up research: the Discussion section	Collocation: evaluative language in critiques Hedges Problem words: *tendency, tend, trend* Comparing results in Discussion sections
Unit 10 **Communicating** **science** *Page 138*	**Reading**	**Listening and speaking**	**Writing**	**Grammar and vocabulary**
	Following the argument in a long article	Working with your supervisor: ending a meeting	Writing practice Editing your work Writing up research: the Abstract	Punctuation: colons and semi-colons Conditional expressions
Lecture skills E *Page 150*	**Preparing for lectures**	**Listening**	**Language focus**	**Follow up**
	Discussion on culture Vocabulary for the context Understanding slides and predicting content	Practice in gist and detailed listening	Signposting language Referring to diagrams	Further listening What happens in lectures

Academic orientation

- Being an independent learner
- Adopting good study strategies
- Finding information about research projects
- Writing a research proposal

This unit introduces some of the skills you will need to develop in order to be successful in higher education. It also looks at what is involved in beginning a research project.

1 Being an independent learner

1.1 Students at most universities are expected to be independent learners. Tick the sentences below which describe characteristics of this type of learner.

Independent learners:
1 make choices about what courses to study within a programme.
2 set their own short- and long-term learning goals.
3 leave assignment writing until the last minute.
4 know who to ask for help in case of difficulty.
5 know where to find information they need.
6 use the library, online information and other resources effectively.
7 wait for their tutor to tell them what to read.
8 identify areas where they are weak and need to do further work.
9 can conduct an investigation on a particular topic with limited guidance.
10 accept what they read in textbooks and on websites as facts.

1.2 a Choose two of the characteristics of an independent learner that you think you already have, and two that you need to develop. How might you develop the weaker characteristics?

b In pairs or small groups, compare your answers.

1.3 ◀) 0.1 Listen to Max talking about differences in being a student on an undergraduate and then a postgraduate programme.
1 In which programme was he expected to study more independently?
2 What particular differences between the programmes does he mention?

Note: The amount of independent study you are expected to do may also depend on the subject you are studying. For example, science students often spend a lot of time doing supervised study in the laboratory and are given much of the information they need in lectures, while arts students often have less-structured study programmes and are expected to read more widely.

Max Reibman is from the United States. He is now studying for a PhD in History at a British university.

2 Adopting good study strategies

2.1 An international student, who will shortly go to university in an English-speaking country, has asked you what study strategies to use in order to achieve academic success.
1 Work in pairs or small groups and suggest, based on your experience, at least three pieces of advice.
2 Share your ideas with the class.

2.2 **a** You are going to read extracts from an article about academic success. Study this chart from the article, where recommendations are made. Is any advice you talked about in 2.1 mentioned?

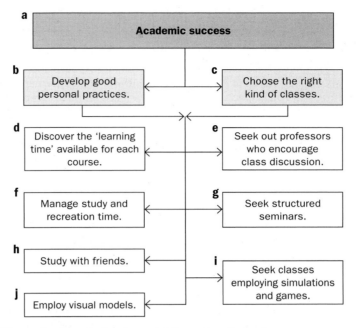

Note: In the United States, 'professor' refers to any full-time university teacher.
In the UK, a professor is a teacher of the highest rank in a university.

b In these extracts from the article, the writer reports research on which his recommendations are based. Read the extracts (1–5) below and match them with sections of the chart (a–j).

1 Research indicates that after exposure to between ten and twenty minutes of continuous lecturing, learning falls off rapidly. Luckily, several teaching practices counter this tendency. First, look for professors who ask rhetorical questions every ten minutes or so (Weaver and Cotrell, 1986) and who reinforce material by asking for nonthreatening forms of participation such as a show of hands or volunteer speakers with examples confirming or countering the material (Hunter, 1983).

2 Gage and Berliner (1992) argue that models provide "accurate and useful representations of knowledge that is needed when solving problems in some particular domain" (p.314). Specifically, they found that students who study models and conceptual maps before a lecture may recall as much as 57 percent more of the conceptual information than students who do not study and discuss such maps and models.

3 Available learning time depends on the calendar established by the university for each semester and the time allotted by professors for covering various topics in each class during the semester. Perseverance refers to the student's intensity and focus on academic content during the allocated learning time. Carroll's (1963) study suggests that all else being equal, the more time you spend on a course and the better you focus on the material, the more successful you will be.

4 Although informal and less-structured classes are employed to stimulate engagement in American classrooms, the research mentioned earlier indicates that these practices may impede international student learning. In addition, international students are often unaccustomed to frequent testing and have more experience taking essay-oriented examinations.

5 Research indicates that classroom atmosphere and especially the quality and degree of faculty–student interaction in American universities trouble international students (Craig, 1981; Edwards and Tonkin, 1990). These findings reflect the fact that most international students are accustomed to listening and learning rather than speaking in class. International students should therefore consider seeking out professors who lecture well.

Abel, C. F. (2002). Academic success and the international student: research and recommendations. *New Directions for Higher Education*, 117, 13–20.

2.3 **Does the evidence reported in these extracts match your own experience of academic study? In pairs, discuss whether you agree or disagree with Abel's recommendations for academic success. Do you think any are impractical?**

3 Finding information about research projects

Many undergraduate and postgraduate students have to undertake a research project as part of their programme and write this up in a dissertation or thesis (a long piece of writing, normally considerably longer than an essay). The terms 'dissertation' and 'thesis' are used differently in different parts of the world. In British universities, 'dissertation' often refers to undergraduate work and 'thesis' to postgraduate work (as in the website below). In the United States, 'dissertation' refers to the work submitted for a doctorate (PhD).

3.1 **Universities are providing an increasing amount of information online. As an independent learner, you should make sure you know what is available. Look at the university website on page 13 and decide where you can find answers to questions about writing a dissertation. Match questions 1–10 below to options a–c.**

a on this part of the website
b probably on another part of the same website
c probably not on this website

1 What are the sections of a typical dissertation?
2 What are the advantages and disadvantages of using interviews and questionnaires in my research?
3 Should I pay the people who answer my research questionnaire?
4 Does my dissertation have to follow my initial plan exactly?
5 What is the deadline for handing in my dissertation?
6 Where should I include ideas for further research?
7 How do I avoid plagiarism?
8 How much help will my supervisor give me?
9 What shall I include in the introduction?
10 Where can I find a list of possible topics for my dissertation?

Companion for Undergraduate Dissertations
Sociology, Anthropology, Politics, Social Policy, Social Work and Criminology

Contents

knowledge and understanding, and show you the areas that need further thought and research.

It is useful, therefore, to write the proposal and to retain it for reference and revision. It helps to attempt such an abstract even if your supervisor has not suggested that you write one. However, practice varies, and your supervisor will advise you on how to proceed. As you continue to write the main chapters of the work, you may find that your initial plan has changed. This means that when you have completed the chapters that form the main body of your dissertation you can return to the proposal and revise it as much as you need, to form the introduction.

It is highly advisable to draft a plan of the dissertation. There is a lot in common between different dissertations regarding the structure and although you do not need to stick slavishly to a standard plan, such a plan is very helpful as a template to impose some order on what may seem an unmanageable task. Here is an indicative structure that might help you with your initial plan.

Dissertation structure

Section	Section information
Introduction	The field of study, the research question, the hypothesis (if any) or, more generally, the research question that is to be investigated. It should also include a summary of the contents and main arguments in the dissertation.
The Literature Review	Usually, this comes immediately after the introductory chapter. This may be more than one chapter, but should certainly be written in sections. This should include previous work done on the field of study and anything that you consider to be relevant to the hypothesis or research question and to its investigation. It will include a large number of references to the literature in your chosen area.
Methodology	This section should include an account of the research questions and/or hypotheses to be investigated, relevant methods of investigation and an argument for why you think these methods are the most appropriate ones for the question and for your circumstances. You should consider the benefits of your chosen method as well as identifying any disadvantages and how you overcame them. Ethical issues and the ways in which you dealt with them should be noted. This section should also discuss any variations from the original fieldwork plan, and should conclude with a reflection on the experience of doing fieldwork.
Findings	This section should present the main findings of your research together with an account of the strengths and weaknesses of your data relative to your research question/hypothesis. You may also wish to include an evaluation of any difficulties you encountered in collecting and analysing data, together with an assessment of how this affected your plan of research.
Evaluation	Here you can provide an assessment of whether and how well you were able to answer your research question and/or confirm/reject your hypotheses.
Discussion	This chapter must relate the findings to theoretical/policy discussion in your literature review. You should NOT introduce any new literature at this stage.
Conclusions and recommendations	An overall assessment of what you found out, how successful you were and suggestions for future research.

Available at www.socscidiss.bham.ac.uk/s11.html

🎓 **Focus on your subject**

Try to find a website which gives advice on writing dissertations or theses in your subject at your level of study. Look first for information from your university (i.e. where you are studying or plan to study). If this is not possible, search for a website from another university. Does it give you advice on what sections should go into the dissertation? Are there any differences between these and the sections suggested on the website in 3.1?

---

4   Writing a research proposal

Unlike a taught Master's degree, an MPhil (Master of Philosophy) is usually awarded for the successful completion of a research project written up in a dissertation or thesis.

Youness Bouzinab is from Belgium. He is now studying for an MPhil in Assyriology (the study of ancient Iraq) at a British university.

4.1   a   **You are going to listen to Youness talking about his research proposal. He has included the following parts. Decide the order you expect them to be in the proposal.**

  · Research questions
  · Methods
  · Conclusion
  · Outline of previous research

b   0.2   **Listen to Youness and check your answers.**

c   0.2   **Listen again. What is the main way his research is different from work done by other researchers?**

d   **Why it is important to include a statement in a research proposal (and in the final dissertation) saying how your work is different from previous research? Share your ideas with the class.**

e   **Think of one piece of research that you are familiar with from your own subject. In pairs, take turns to explain how it is different from previous research.**

1 Advertising and critical thinking

Reading

1 Reading critically

A critical reader questions the information and points of view presented by the writer in a text. An uncritical reader simply accepts what is said in a text as correct.

1.1 **Answer these questions and then discuss your ideas in pairs.**

1 Why is it important to be able to read critically in your academic studies?
2 In your previous academic studies, were you expected to read critically?

1.2 **a You are going to read critically two extracts on the topic of the consumer society. Before you read, discuss what 'consumer society' means to you.**

b Read Extract A and then discuss questions 1–6 below.

Extract A

The social value of brands

The rise of the consumer society is frequently blamed for many ills but rarely praised for its principal social contribution: generating the wealth that pays for and sustains social progress. Long-term improvements in health, education, living standards and opportunities depend on wealth creation. Strong economic growth goes hand-in-hand with strong, recognisable brands: no brand, no way to create mass customer loyalty; no consumer loyalty, no guarantee of reliable earnings; no reliable earnings, less investment and employment; less investment and employment, less wealth created; less wealth created, lower government receipts to spend on social goods (see Figure 4.1). This is the most basic, and arguably the most valuable, social contribution that brands make.

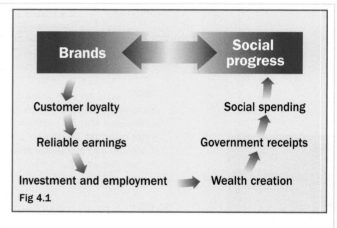
Fig 4.1

Gibbons, G. (2009). The social value of brands. In R. Clifton, et al. (eds) *Brands and branding* (2nd edn) London: Profile Books.

1 Does the title of the publication tell you anything about the writer's position?
2 What general position does the writer take in the extract?
3 What claims are made that lead the writer to this position?
4 Does the writer provide any supporting evidence for claims?
5 What alternative positions are there and does the writer acknowledge these?
6 Are you persuaded that the writer's position is correct?

c Go through questions 1–6 from page 14 again to read Extract B critically.

Extract B

Consumer culture

We cannot ignore the disadvantages of a consumer society. The freedom of the individual consumer has limited the freedom of the community. The society that has fed, clothed, and housed people has also damaged the environment and created more trash than any other society in history. Perhaps the most worrying aspect of a consumer society is that our options for addressing its problems seem to be narrowing. Most people, for example, are deeply concerned about the ecological damage caused by consumption, but the response to it has been channelled into individual consumer choices. People do not agonize over different government and community-based solutions; instead, they agonize over whether they should use paper or plastic bags at the grocery store. The truth is that neither choice makes much difference given the current institutional structures, but the consumer approach to solving problems cannot change institutional structures or even talk about communal solutions.

Goodman, D. J. (2004). *Consumer culture*. Santa Barbara, CA.: ABC-CLIO.

1.3 Is it necessary to read all academic texts critically? What text types do you <u>not</u> need to read critically? Discuss your ideas with a partner.

2   Preparing to read

An abstract is a short summary of a journal article, thesis, etc. found at the beginning.

2.1 You are going to read an extract from a journal article. Before you do, read the first line of its abstract below. What do you think are the aims of the research reported in the article?

Abstract

Many school districts are implementing media-literacy programs in high schools that teach about the advertising production process and introduce students to techniques for critically analyzing media messages.

3   Note-taking

  Study tip
There are a number of common note types: tabular notes (notes organised in a table); diagrammatic notes (notes connected by lines – key words may be put in boxes); and linear notes (notes written as ordinary text – underlining, etc. may be used to show text organisation, key words, and so on). Choose the most useful type for each text you read.

3.1 Read the extract on page 16 and add to these notes.

➤ *is defined as*
G&V **2, p24**

➤ *In using*
G&V **1, p24**

➤ *affect vs effect*
G&V **3, p25**

Does media literacy work?
An empirical study of learning how to analyze advertisements.

In an increasing number of secondary classrooms, print and TV ads are used by teachers as texts to be formally analyzed and studied. Educational practices like this are commonly identified as *media literacy*, which is defined as an expanded conceptualization of literacy that includes print, audio, visual, and electronic messages from contemporary culture (Kress, 2002). In using advertising texts
5   in the classroom, teachers emphasize the skills of analyzing and evaluating ads to identify the message purpose, target audience, point of view and persuasive techniques used. Often, there is a focus on the social, political, economic, and historical contexts in which media messages reflect and shape culture (Buckingham, 2003).

Occasionally, as part of media literacy education, students also learn about the pre-production,
10   production, and post-production processes involved in the creation of advertising messages (Young, 1990; Singer, Zuckerman & Singer, 1980). While it may be common for students enrolled in media production or marketing electives to learn about advertising production processes, it is far less common for students to gain this information in the context of their high-school English coursework. Potter (1998) points out the importance of knowledge structures in building critical
15   analysis skills when it comes to analyzing advertising, but empirical research has not yet examined the impact of increased knowledge of advertising production processes, as it may affect critical thinking skills in responding to advertising messages.

However, there is only limited evidence that shows that learning about advertising and discussions about advertising in school can reduce children's vulnerability to advertising appeals and increase
20   their ability to produce counter-arguments in response to advertising. For example, Christenson (1982) developed a three-minute video about advertising and showed it to children ages six to 12, finding that children who viewed the video were more aware of commercials and expressed less trust in commercials in general. Roberts, Christenson, Gibson, Mooser and Goldberg (1980) evaluated short films that were made to show children how television ads use various techniques
25   to persuade. They found that heavy-viewing children who were initially most susceptible to commercials were most influenced by the films.

While older children and teens may have more knowledge about advertising, they also may not necessarily employ critical thinking skills in response to advertising, or have more skepticism about advertising in general. Boush, Friestad and Rose (1994) measured middle school students'
30   knowledge of advertiser tactics and effects and their skepticism of advertising. Tactics included the use of celebrities, music, humor, cartoons, product comparisons, product demonstrations, and depictions of target audience. They found increased knowledge about advertiser tactics over a nine-month period, but no increase in advertising skepticism. They note:

> Improving students' understanding of the way advertising works may have more potential for
35   > creating discerning consumers than has changing students' general attitudes. Exhortations
> to 'not believe everything you see on TV' are, therefore, less likely to produce changes in the
> processing of advertising claims than is a more careful analysis of advertisements that lays
> bare the persuasive device. (p. 172)

In evaluating the literature on advertising and children, Young (1990) criticizes the validity
40   of research that has used superficial measures of children's skepticism, including responses to attitude statements using Likert-type scales. Even young children are aware of the social desirability of attitudes opposing advertising, he claims. Instead, Young argues that knowledge about the tactics used by advertisers to persuade, and skills like being able to understand the purpose and function of a media message, are key components needed to acquire critical thinking
45   skills about advertising.

Hobbs, R. (2004). Does media literacy work? An empirical study
of learning how to analyze advertisements. *Advertising and Society Review*, 5.

3.2 **Work in pairs and evaluate each other's notes. Check that the notes:**
- include all the main points;
- make a distinction between main and secondary points;
- show connections between information.

3.3 **Based on what is said in the extract, discuss what further research do you think is needed on the question 'Does media literacy work?'.**

4 Vocabulary in context: compound nouns

 Study tip
Compound nouns (e.g. target audience) express information in a concise way and are very common in academic writing. One way to try to understand them is to 'unpack' the compound noun using a longer explanation.

Target audience ...
this probably means the audience (the readers, listeners, or viewers) that a particular medium, for example, TV or radio, wants or tries to get.

> *Producing compound nouns*
>
> Unit 6 G&V 2, p92

4.1 **Work in pairs. Look up any words you don't know in these compound nouns from the text in 3.1. Explain in detail what each compound means.**
1. advertising texts (line 4)
2. media literacy education (line 9)
3. media production (line 12)
4. high-school English coursework (line 13)
5. critical analysis skills (line 14)
6. advertising production processes (line 16)
7. advertising messages (line 17)
8. product demonstrations (line 31)

5 Inferring relationships between sentences

Sometimes, writers signal the relationship between sentences using a sentence connector (a word or phrase that links two sentences). At other times, the reader has to infer the relationship between a sentence and what has come before.

5.1 **Find the sentences in the text in 3.1 which include these extracts. What sentence connectors do the sentences begin with? What meanings do they have?**
1. ... Christenson (1982) developed a three-minute video ... (line 21)
2. ... Young argues that knowledge about ... (line 42)

5.2 **Find the sentences which begin with these extracts. Explain the relationship between the sentences and what comes before. For example, does 1 contradict, exemplify or add to what came before it?**
1. Boush, Friestad and Rose (1994) measured ... (line 29)
2. Tactics included the use of ... (line 30)

6 Nominalisation

In academic writing, we often prefer to use a noun rather than a related verb or adjective form. In this process of nominalisation, *we talk about things or concepts (with nouns) rather than actions, events and characteristics (with verbs and adjectives).*

6.1 **a Complete the sentences with a noun phrase related to the words in brackets. Use nouns from the same family as the <u>underlined</u> words.**

1 ... students also learn about the processes involved in *the creation of advertising messages*
(how advertising messages are <u>created</u>) (line 9)

2 Potter (1998) points out _____ in building critical analysis skills.
(how <u>important</u> knowledge structures are) (line 14)

3 Boush, Friestad and Rose (1994) measured _____ and effects, and _____. (what middle-school students <u>know</u> about advertiser tactics; how <u>skeptical</u> they were of advertising) (line 29)

4 Improving _____ may have more potential for creating discerning consumers. (what students <u>understand</u> about the way advertising works) (line 34)

b Check your answers in the text in 3.1.

c Can you suggest reasons why nominalisation is common in academic writing?

7 Reading in detail

7.1 **a Reword this sentence, replacing the three phrases in bold with one word. You may need to make changes to word order. Check your answer in the text in 3.1.**

> Occasionally, [...] students also learn about the processes **before production, during production** and **after production** involved in the creation of advertising messages ... (line 9)

b Why is 'Singer' repeated in this reference?

> ... Singer, Zuckerman & **Singer**, 1980 ... (line 11)

c What type of course is 'elective'?

> ... students enrolled in media production or marketing **electives** ... (line 11)

d When we refer back to ideas in a previous part of the text, do we prefer to use *this* or *that* in academic writing? For example, would we use *this information* or *that information*? (Check your answer in line 13.)

e What do you notice about word order in the phrase in bold below?

> Improving students' understanding of the way advertising works may have more potential for creating discerning consumers **than has changing students' general attitudes** ... (line 34)

f Why do you think inverted commas are used in this extract?

> Exhortations to 'not believe everything you see on TV'... (line 35)

⊙ *Research shows that in the written academic corpus, the most frequent adverbs that come before less/more common are* much *and* far. *What other adverbs often combine with less/more common?*
1 _much_   2 _far_   3 sig_____ly   4 sl__ly   5 con_____ly   6 som___at
7 ra___er   8 subs_____ly
Divide the adverbs you have written into two groups, one meaning 'a lot' (less/more common) and the other meaning 'a little' (less/more common).

8 Pros and cons of group work

Group work takes place in an increasing number of academic courses. It is important to develop skills and to acquire useful language that will help you participate successfully in this kind of learning.

8.1 **In 9.1, you are going to listen to extracts from a discussion by a group of marketing students on brand preferences. Before you listen, read these ideas about group work and discuss which you agree with more.**

Text 1

> Students learn best when they are actively involved in the process. Researchers report that, regardless of the subject matter, students working in small groups tend to learn more of what is taught and retain it longer than when the same content is presented in other instructional formats. Students who work in collaborative groups also appear more satisfied with their classes.

Gross Davis, B. (1993). *Tools for teaching.* San Fransisco: Jossey-Bass.

Text 2

> Some students feel that class time is best spent hearing from the instructor (who's the authority) rather than working with students who, they believe, know as little as themselves. Others may feel that they have succeeded thus far on individual effort, and don't want to be encumbered by other students with different histories of success or different working methods. And some students are simply shy and unaccustomed to sharing their work with their peers.

Stanford University Newsletter on Teaching (1999). Cooperative learning: students working in small groups. *Speaking of Teaching*, 10, 2.

8.2 **In pairs, discuss these questions.**

1 What experience of group work have you had in your academic studies so far?
2 Based on this experience, what other advantages and disadvantages of group work can you think of?

9 Getting an opportunity to speak in a group discussion

Because it can be difficult to make a contribution to group work at the right time, it is useful to learn phrases that help you to take a turn in the discussion.

9.1 (◄) **1.1** **Listen to an extract from a group discussion, in which Ken talks about the chart below. Why did he choose it? What limitation does he mention?**

Brand preferences by product category and nation in China, Q4 2009

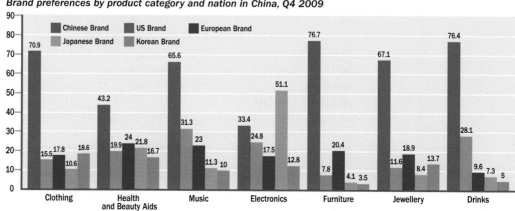

Schultz, D.E. & Block, M.P. (2010). *Relevant Pieces to the Chinese Media Puzzle. ESOMAR.*

9.2 a ◀) **1.2** **Now listen to six extracts from the group's discussion of the chart and complete the gaps.**

   1 Can I just _come in here_? Yeah, I think it's interesting …
   2 Can I just _____ _____ _____ _____ _____ said about clothing?
   3 Can I just _____ _____ _____ _____ _____ made a while ago?
   4 Can I _____ _____ _____ ?
   5 Can I just _____ _____ _____ _____ _____ said earlier?
   6 Can I just _____ _____ _____ _____ ?

   b **Which phrases in 9.2a introduce a point relevant now (N) in the discussion? Which make a point relevant to something said before (B)?**

9.3 a **Work alone. Look at the chart on page 19 in more detail and make a note of other interesting findings and possible explanations.**

   b **Work in small groups and discuss your ideas. Try to use phrases in 9.2a to get an opportunity to speak.**

9.4 **Work in new groups. Repeat the steps in 9.3 using the chart below.**

Global ad spend by medium, 2009

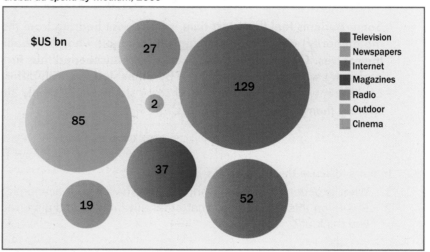

Adstats: Global advertising spend

Writing

10 Writing a summary

Being able to produce summaries of what you have read is an important skill used in writing many kinds of academic text, including essays, research proposals and research reports.

10.1 **After a seminar, you have been given an essay with the title 'Discuss the influence of advertising on consumer behaviour'. You decide to include a short section on the ethics of advertising. Follow the steps below.**

   1 Read the text on page 21 for general meaning. (In this text, look first at the headings. How do they relate to each other? What main points are made under each one?)
   2 Read the text again in more detail. Guess or look up any important-seeming words which you don't understand.
   3 Underline the main points and other important information in each section/paragraph which are relevant to your essay.
   4 Write notes on these main points. This is done for you in the first part of the text.

Ethics and advertising

Ethics and culture

The world of advertising has its own set of stories about the good and the bad, truth and dishonesty. This unit focuses on truth and deception in advertising and on the ethical dilemmas of those who produce advertising. These stories show that in advertising, just as in the world at large, there are not only clear instances of good and bad behaviors but also a vast grey area that lies between these extremes – an area where ethical decisions must be made on a daily basis.

> some clear cases of
> good (ethical) ads vs
> bad (unethical) ads
> but many ads in the
> grey area between

False advertising

In ancient Rome, the Latin expression *caveat emptor*, "let the buyer beware," warned buyers of unscrupulous sellers. It remains a good dictum today, but it is much less likely that a seller would be telling outright lies about a product than sometimes occurred in the past. As recently as the early 1900s, advertising was still largely unregulated (by either government or advertising standards) and sellers were pretty much free to make whatever claims they could get away with. Patent medicines were among the worst offenders. The claims in such ads were not only often outrageous but frequently completely false. For example, the claims of the electric belt ad shown below have no basis in fact. Rather, they represent the boastful proclamations of the seller.

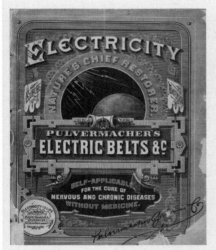

Fig 13.8 This ad claims that electricity cures nervous and chronic diseases. (c. 1890)

Today, such patently false claims are highly unlikely in national advertising. Not only are there both governmental and industry-based standards that regulate what can be said in ads, but the force of negative publicity that would surround an outright lie, if discovered, would have severe or fatal repercussions for the company making the claims.

> in the past, sellers
> could lie about
> products
> vs
> today much less likely
> ← (i) govt & industries
> regulate ads,
> (ii) negative publicity
> for companies that lie

Deceptive advertising

Claiming that a product can do something that it cannot is a clear-cut case of deception. Saying that a package is one and one-half times bigger than another (if it is!) is a clear-cut case of telling the truth. But in the real world of advertising, the issues are seldom so clearly demarcated. Is it deceptive, for example, to say that Big Macs and Whoppers taste great without also saying that too many of them can make you fat, raise your cholesterol, or increase your sodium intake above healthy levels?

The public want and expect advertising to be truthful, but exactly what does this mean in practice? Does it mean saying that a new car can get you from New York to California in style is insufficient? For the ad to be truthful, does it also need to say that driving cars adds to environmental pollution and that you might get hurt or killed in an accident along the way? Does "honest" advertising require that some products (like prescription drugs, for example) need to make fuller disclosures about possible side-effects than do ads for hamburgers and cars?

Disguised advertising

Ads that purport to be something else – a letter that looks like it is from the government, an ad in a newspaper or magazine that masquerades as news, or nowadays a blog or website that is packed with ads – are familiar techniques in contemporary marketing and advertising. Consumers know they should be skeptical of suspicious looking letters and unusually printed "stories" set in a typeface similar to articles.

The internet and trade journals are full of advice to companies who want to break through contemporary advertising clutter. The advice is simple: do it *online*. It does not take long to find a blog on a subject that interests you, but it does take a while to figure out just what is an ad and what is not. Product mentions (like product placement in the movies) are rampant. This new area of advertising is so slick and often so subtle that the ads move in unannounced. Are these online devices merely good business strategy in the digital age, or do they deceive consumers by their lack of disclosure that they are actually commercial announcements and publicity?

O'Barr, W. M. (2007). Ethics and advertising. *Advertising and Society Review* 8, 3.

10.2 Use your notes to write a summary of the main points in 150–200 words. Use your own words as far as possible. Include additional information (such as examples) only when necessary, to make what you are saying clearer.

> As O'Barr (2010) has pointed out, it can be difficult to draw a distinction between what is ethical and what is unethical in advertising. In the past, he suggests, …

10.3 a You are going to compare summaries with their original paragraphs to identify strategies for changing language. Match phrases 1–4 in the text to summarising strategies a–d.

a reword a phrase
b change clause to adverb
c use a synonym
d change a verb form (here, a consequence of changing the verb from *cause* to *result in*)

Another criticism is that advertising **1** <u>causes</u> people **2** <u>to buy</u> products or services **3** <u>that they do not need</u>. The defenders acknowledge that the whole reason to advertise the product or service is to persuade consumers to purchase the right products.

4 <u>Another</u> <u>common criticism of advertising</u> is that it perpetuates stereotyping, the process of categorizing individuals by predicting their behaviour based on their membership in a particular class or group. The problem, critics say, is that advertisements often portray entire groups of people in stereotypical ways, for example, showing only women as homemakers and elderly people as senile. These advertising stereotypes can reinforce negative or undesirable views of these groups, and this can contribute to discrimination against them.

> A number of criticisms of advertising have been made (Lee and Johnson, 2005). For example, some have argued that advertising **¹results in** people **²buying** products or services **³unnecessarily**. **⁴Advertising is also often criticised** for presenting groups of people in stereotypical ways (for example, elderly people as confused or forgetful), and this can encourage negative perceptions of the group.

Lee, M. & Johnson, C. (2005). *Principles of advertising: a global perspective* (2nd edn). Binghampton, NY: The Haworth Press.

b Find other examples of strategies a–d and other strategies in the example below. Then compare ideas with a partner.

Should products that can have harmful effects, like tobacco and alcohol, be advertised at all? Many advertising agencies respond in the affirmative. They back up their decision by saying that it is not an agency's responsibility to decide which products should be advertised and which should not. Rather, their reasoning goes: if it's legal to sell it, it's okay to advertise it. By contrast, there are other agencies and a handful of famous advertising men and women who refuse tobacco or alcohol accounts on ethical grounds. They do not want to be associated with the social ills of products that appear to be as harmful as these.

> Advertisers are divided on whether they should advertise harmful products such as tobacco and alcohol (O'Barr, 2007). Some refuse to, because they do not want an association with the problems that such products can cause. Others are willing to advertise them, arguing that they should not be responsible for prohibiting the advertising of legal products.

O'Barr, W. M. (2007). Ethics and advertising. *Advertising and Society Review* 8, 3.

10.4 Look again at the summary you wrote in 10.2. Can you improve it by using strategies from 10.3?

> 🎓 Focus on your subject
>
> Take a paragraph or two from an academic text in your subject (e.g. a textbook or journal article) that you are currently reading. Write a short summary, following strategies from 10.3.

11 In-text referencing conventions

In your academic writing, it is very important that you acknowledge the source of the words and ideas where these are neither your own nor common knowledge. You will learn about conventions for in-text referencing in this unit.

11.1 Look at this extract from a student's essay on the impact of advertising on child behaviour. Are in-text references 1–10 correct (✓) or incorrect (✗)? Where they are incorrect, correct them or explain what is wrong.

1 ✗ date needed, e.g. (Lee, 2010)

→ *In-text references*

Appendix 1, p168

It is now well established that food promotion influences children's food preferences and their purchasing behaviour **1** (Lee). For example, a study of primary school children by **2** Teresa Cairns (2006) found that exposure to advertising influenced which food they said they liked. A more recent study showed that labelling on a vending machine had an effect on what was bought by secondary school children **3** Willis (2012). A number of studies have also shown that food advertising can influence what children eat **4** (e.g. Barry, 2011, May 2010, White, 2010). One, for example, showed that advertising influenced a primary class's choice of daily snack at playtime **5** (May, P, 2010). However, it is more difficult to establish whether a link exists between food promotion and obesity **6** (Levin, Advertising in focus, 2008), although some studies have attempted this by using the amount of television viewing as a measure of exposure to television advertising **7** (e.g. Marks, 2006, in Allen, 2008). They may have established a link between television viewing and diet, obesity and cholesterol levels, but as **8** Alvin 2010 has pointed out, it is impossible to say whether this effect is caused by the advertising itself or other factors. One study tried to resolve this problem by taking a detailed diary of children's viewing habits **9** (Collins, 2011), showing that the more food adverts they saw, the more snacks and calories they consumed. In summary, while the literature does suggest that food promotion influences children's diet in a number of ways, 'incontrovertible proof of a link simply isn't attainable' **10** (Petersen, 2012, page 13).

> 🎓 Focus on your subject
>
> It is important that you become familiar with the in-text referencing conventions used in your subject. If you are not given information about these on your course, follow the conventions used in a leading journal in your subject.

Grammar and vocabulary

Grammar and vocabulary
- -ing clauses with prepositions and conjunctions
- Prepositions after passive verbs
- Problem words: affect vs effect

1 -ing clauses with prepositions and conjunctions

In academic writing, we often begin a sentence with a preposition or conjunction (e.g. after, before, by, on, while) followed by an -ing clause, to give information about the purpose, cause, time, etc. of the event in the main clause that follows.

> **In using advertising texts in the classroom**, teachers emphasize the skills of analyzing and evaluating ads.

(= 'the purpose of using advertising texts is to emphasize …')

> **By not adopting a more liberal trade policy**, the United States failed to set an example to others.

(= 'the result of not adopting a more liberal policy was that the United States failed …'. Note that we put not before the -ing form.)

> **On coming to power**, SWAPO announced an ambitious programme of educational expansion.

(= 'when they came to power, SWAPO announced …')

1.1 Match sentences 1–6 with a–f and then write a new sentence beginning with the word given.

1 A more efficient larger firm was created.
2 I will review the literature.
3 He became president.
4 The two groups were compared.
5 She doesn't deny that there is discrimination in the workplace.
6 They start school in September.

a Bright (2009) contends that it is not older workers who are a particular target.
b He made education the main priority of his government.
c The merger reduced costs.
d Children are immunised against tetanus and measles.
e I will outline the methods used in the research.
f Both quantitative and qualitative data were used.

1 _c_ By *creating a more efficient larger firm,*
    the merger reduced costs
2 ___ After _____
3 ___ On _____
4 ___ In _____
5 ___ While _____
6 ___ Before _____

The implied subject of the -ing clause should be the same as the subject in the main clause.

> In using advertising texts in the classroom, …

*Teachers use advertising texts, so '**teachers**' is the subject of the -ing clause.*

> … teachers emphasize the skills of analyzing and evaluating ads.

*'**teachers**' is the subject of the main clause.*

1.2 In pairs, decide whether these sentences are correct or incorrect and suggest improvements to the incorrect ones.

1 On starting school, the researchers examined children's achievement.
2 In conducting the research, I became aware of the limitations of the method.
3 After watching the video, students answered ten questions.
4 While recognising that the results may not be generalisable to all businesses, managers should have a working knowledge of accounting.

2 Prepositions after passive verbs

Many verbs commonly used with the passive voice are usually followed by a particular preposition.

> Educational practices like this are commonly identified as media literacy, which **is defined as** an expanded conceptualisation of literacy …

2.1 What prepositions are most common after these passive verbs?

> ~~as~~ at in into of on to with

1 be defined/known/regarded + _as_
2 be applied/attributed/related + _____
3 be associated/correlated + _____
4 be comprised/made up + _____
5 be included/involved + _____
6 be divided/translated + _____
7 be based/centred + _____
8 be aimed/estimated + _____

2.2 Complete these sentences with the correct preposition or verb form. (Try to do this without looking back at the list in 2.1.)

1 The total cost of the project was estimated _at_ nearly $2 billion.
2 This chapter is _____ into three sections.
3 Japan's high saving rate has been attributed _____ several factors, including less access to consumer credit and cultural factors.
4 Health expenditure per capita is negatively correlated _____ health inequality.
5 Since the late 1940s, France has been widely _____ as the leader of European integration.
6 Policy debates in modern Britain are often _____ on the assumption that care for the elderly has been taken over by the state.
7 This protein is involved _____ the development of the growing brain.
8 The book is comprised _____ 12 chapters.
9 A straight line can be _____ as a curve of infinite or very large radius.
10 Only one of her novels has so far been _____ into English.

3 Problem words: *affect* vs *effect*

3.1 Complete rules 1–8 with examples a–h.

> **affect**
> - usually a verb (/ə'fekt/) meaning to influence someone or something, or to cause them to change. **1** _f_
> - sometimes a noun (/'æfekt/) meaning a feeling or emotion that influences what you do or think. **2** __
>
> **effect**
> - usually a noun (/ɪ'fekt/) meaning the change or event that happens as a result of an influence. **3** __
> - sometimes a verb (/ɪ'fekt/) meaning to make something happen. **4** __
> - Note these phrases which are common in academic writing (look them up in your dictionary to check their meaning):
>   in effect **5** __
>   take effect **6** __
>   come/put into effect **7** __
>   to good effect **8** __

a The Amsterdam Treaty **took effect** on May 1, 1999.
b Weather patterns have a significant **effect** on people's beliefs about the evidence for global warming.
c Smaller firms can also use marketing **to good effect** to gain more clients.
d Indicators of negative **affect**, such as depression and hopelessness, typically increase dramatically throughout the teen years.
e Improvements in relations between senior management and more junior staff are needed to **effect** change in teaching and learning.
f ~~Increased knowledge of advertising production processes may **affect** critical thinking skills.~~
g It is difficult to see how their recommendations could be **put into effect** in practice.
h From 1996 until 2001, there was, **in effect**, a civil war in the country.

3.2 Rewrite the words and phrases in bold using *affect*, *effect* or a phrase from the box in 3.1.

1 The main ~~impact~~ of the new law was to increase insurance claims. _effect_
2 Privatisation of the telecommunications industry was announced in January 1982 and **carried out** two years later. _____
3 The number of components made of plastic was increased in order to **bring about** a saving in weight and cost. _____
4 The rise in student fees **begins** at the end of the year. _____
5 With three senior army officers in the cabinet, the government was **in practice** controlled by the military. _____
6 It was felt that distractions in the classroom might **have an adverse influence** on children's concentration, so interviews were conducted in an adjoining room. _____
7 Fathers who were more aggressive toward their partners displayed lower positive **feelings** toward their infants. _____
8 Illustrations are used **in a way that works well** in the book to explain processes which are often very complex. _____

> ☉ *Research shows that in academic writing, the most common adverb before* affect *is significantly (e.g.* Poverty **significantly affects** *infant mortality).*
> *What are the next most common?*
>
> 1 _significantly_
> 2 adv _____ ly
> 3 dir _____ ly
> 4 neg _____ ly
> 5 str _____ ly

2 Innovation and invention

Reading

1 Lectures, note-taking and follow-up reading

You will often be expected to follow up a lecture with further reading. This may be to gain more details about topics dealt with in the lecture, or to fill gaps in your understanding of what was covered.

1.1 a **As part of a Business Studies course, you attended a lecture with the title *Innovation and invention*. You found it hard to follow, but you noted down as much as you could. Work in pairs and discuss how these phrases used by the lecturer might be connected to the topic of innovation and invention.**

- market knowledge
- breakthrough
- commercialisation
- diffusion
- entrepreneur
- facilities

> *innovation* noun /ɪnəʊˈveɪʃən/ [C or U]
> (the use of) a new idea or method
> *the latest **innovations** in computer technology.*

> Market knowledge should inform an invention: there's no point in coming up with a new product if nobody needs it.

Study tip

If you find a lecture difficult to understand, note down key words or phrases, which the lecturer might repeat or highlight in slides. Also, note down points you think you need to research more. After the lecture, find out the meaning of these words or phrases and more information about these points in recommended texts.

b On a handout given to you by the lecturer, you noted down questions on this slide to research later. After the lecture, you find a recommended textbook for more information. Read the extract below and make notes in answer to your questions.

Innovation and invention

- different but connected
- often a delay between the two
- a process, not an event

> What's the difference?

> What's the relationship between them?

> Why is there a delay?

> What does this mean?

What is innovation?

An important distinction is normally made between invention and innovation. Invention is the first occurrence of an idea for a new product or process, while innovation is the first attempt to carry it out in practice. Sometimes, invention and innovation are closely linked, to the extent that it is hard to distinguish one from another (biotechnology for instance). In many
5 cases, however, there is a considerable time lag between the two. In fact, a lag of several decades or more is not uncommon (Rogers 1995). Such lags reflect the different requirements for working out ideas and implementing them. While inventions may be carried out anywhere, for example in universities, innovations occur mostly in firms, though they may also occur in other types of organizations, such as public hospitals. To be able to turn an invention
10 into an innovation, a firm normally needs to combine several different types of knowledge, capabilities, skills, and resources. For instance, the firm may require production knowledge, skills and facilities, market knowledge, a well-functioning distribution system, sufficient financial resources, and so on. It follows that the role of the innovator, i.e. the person or organizational unit responsible for combining the factors necessary (what the innovation
15 theorist Joseph Schumpeter called the "entrepreneur"), may be quite different from that of the inventor. Indeed, history is replete with cases in which the inventor of major technological advances fails to reap the profits from his breakthroughs.

Long lags between invention and innovation may have to do with the fact that, in many cases, some or all of the conditions for commercialization may be lacking. There may not be
20 a sufficient need (yet!) or it may be impossible to produce and/or market because some vital inputs or complementary factors are not (yet!) available. Thus, although Leonardo da Vinci is reported to have had some quite advanced ideas for a flying machine, these were impossible to carry out in practice due to a lack of adequate material, production skills, and – above all – a power source. In fact, the realization of these ideas had to wait for the invention and
25 subsequent commercialization (and improvement) of the internal combustion engine. Hence, as this example shows, many inventions require complementary inventions and innovations to succeed at the innovation stage.

➤ to the extent that
G&V 2, p36

➤ well-functioning
G&V 3, p37

➤ his breakthroughs
G&V 1, p36

Another complicating factor is that invention and innovation is a continuous process. For instance, the car as we know it today is radically improved compared to the first commercial
30   models, due to the incorporation of a very large number of different inventions/innovations. In fact, the first versions of virtually all significant innovations, from the steam engine to the airplane, were crude, unreliable versions of the devices that eventually diffused widely. Kline and Rosenberg (1986), in an influential paper, point out:

> it is a serious mistake to treat an innovation as if it were a well-defined homogenous
35   thing that could be identified as entering the economy at a precise date – or becoming available at a precise point in time. The fact is that most important innovations go through drastic changes in their lifetimes – changes that may, and often do, totally transform their economic significance. The subsequent improvements in an invention after its first introduction may be vastly more important, economically, than the initial
40   availability of the invention in its original form.
> (Kline and Rosenberg 1986: 283)

Thus, what we think of as a single innovation is often the result of a lengthy process involving many interrelated innovations.

Fagerberg, J., Mowery, D. C. & Nelson, R. R. (eds) (2005). *The Oxford Handbook of Innovation*. Oxford: Oxford University Press.

c **Work in pairs and compare notes. Make any necessary changes.**

d **Work in pairs and decide which of these recent innovations has had the greatest impact. Can you think of other important recent innovations?**

the solar cell   anaesthetics   the credit card   the internet   the mobile phone

 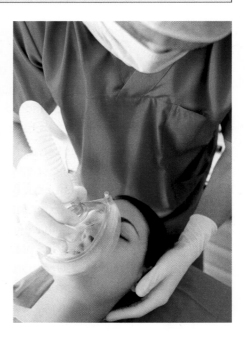

Writing

7 Writing summaries from multiple sources

In many of the academic texts you write, you will need to summarise information you have found from a number of sources.

7.1 a You have been asked to write an essay with the title 'Choose a recent invention and outline its social and economic impacts'. You have decided to focus on the mobile phone. You want to include a paragraph on its impact in developing countries and have found the following extracts from a number of sources. First, follow steps 1–4 in Unit 1, 10.1 for extracts A–D. As an example, in A, the main points are underlined and notes on these points are included.

Extract A

The <u>past decade</u> has seen a <u>rapid expansion of mobile telephony in developing countries</u>. In 2006, it was estimated that 56% of individuals in low-income countries were covered by one or several mobile networks, and 22% actually subscribed to such services, up from virtually zero at the end of the 1990s. With <u>less than 5% of the population having access to a landline phone, mobile phones have made telecommunications available for the first time to hundreds of millions of people</u>, either through the ownership of personal handsets or as users of rented phones in public access points.

> *mobile phone use – substantial increase – since 2000*

> *landlines inaccessible for vast majority – so mobiles have made telecoms available to many for first time*

Barberousse, G., Bernard, T. & Pescatori, V. (2009). The economic impact of the development of mobile telephony: results from a case study in Haiti. *Private Sector Development*, 4, 26.

Extract B

Mobile communications have a particularly important impact in rural areas, which are home to nearly one-half of the world's population and 75% of the world's poor (World Bank 2007). The mobility, ease of use, flexible deployment and relatively low and declining rollout costs of wireless technologies enable them to reach rural populations with low levels of income and literacy. An important use of mobile phones in rural areas is to access market information. TradeNet, a Ghana-based trading platform, allows users to sign up for short message service (SMS) alerts for commodities and markets of their choice and receive instant alerts for offers to buy or sell when anyone else on the network has submitted an offer by mobile phone. In India, access to market information through mobile phones has allowed fishermen to respond faster to market demand and has increased their profits (Jensen 2007).

Khalil, M., Dongier, P. & Qiang. Z.W.C. (2009). *Overview. Information and Communications for Development 2009: Extending Reach and Increasing Impact.* The World Bank, p 4.

Extract C

> However, all these positive impacts must not obscure the problems posed by the mobile phone industry in developing countries. One particular problem is that mobile phone services represent a major expense item in the budgets of the poorest households which may then be inclined to reduce expenses for their basic needs (education, health, food, clothing).

Lefilleur, J. (2009). Lessons-learned from this issue (What are the economic and social impacts of the mobile phone sector in developing countries?). *Private Sector Development*, 4, 31.

Extract D

> The main unprompted impact identified by the surveys related to easier contact with family and friends. In both Tanzania and South Africa, many people move away from their home to find work, and mobile phones are now an important means of keeping in touch with families. A number of respondents also used mobile phones to contact schools and universities. For example, mobile phones are used by the students in Kwa Phake, to correspond with various tertiary institutions such as UNISA (University of South Africa). Instead of having to travel to these institutions they can easily access information they need using a mobile phone.

Vodafone (2005). *Africa: The Impact of Mobile Phones.* The Vodafone Policy Paper Series, 3, March 2005, p 49.

b **Now write a summary which includes information from all four extracts in no more than 150 words.**

There has been a substantial increase in the use of mobile phones in developing countries since 2000 (Barberousse et al., 2009). …

c **Compare your summaries in pairs and make any necessary improvements.**

8 Reference lists

At the end of every academic text you write, you will normally be expected to give a reference list (i.e. a list giving details of all the books, articles, websites, etc. that you mentioned). It is important to become familiar with the conventions used in writing reference lists. Note that some people use the term 'bibliography' to mean reference list. However, this can also mean a list of publications on a particular subject, not necessarily publications that you have read or mentioned.

➤ *Reference lists*

Appendix 2, p168

8.1 a **Look at the reference list on page 35 from a student's essay. What type (1–13) is each source (A–M) in the reference list?**

1 book with a single author
2 book with two or more authors   2
3 edited book
4 publication without a named author
5 article in a journal
6 paper in an edited book
7 article in a magazine or newspaper

8 unpublished dissertation
9 handout from a lecture
10 article in an online publication
11 article in a journal; originally printed, but found online
12 article in an online reference source
13 information or statistics from a government or other organisation online

References

A Baumol, W., Litan, R., & Schramm, C. (2007). *Good capitalism, bad capitalism, and the economics of growth and prosperity.* Yale University Press.

B Block, James., & Wagner, Mark. (2006). Necessity and opportunity entrepreneurs in Germany: Characteristics and earnings differentials. *MPRA Paper no. 610.* Retrieved 2 November 2011 from http://www.mpra.ub.uni-muenchen.de/610/

C Carayannis, E. G & Campbell, D. F. J. (eds) (2006). *Innovation networks and knowledge clusters.* Westport, CT: Greenwood.

D Caliendo, M., F. M. Fossen, & A. S. Kritikos (2009). Risk attitudes of nascent entrepreneurs – new evidence from an experimentally validated survey. *Small Business Economics,* 153–167.

E Davidsson, P. (2004). Researching entrepreneurship. New York: Springer.

F European Fair Trade Association (2010). *Fair Trade Yearbook 2010.* Retrieved 11 February 2011 from http://www.european-fair-trade-association.org/Efta/yb.php.

G Innovation. (n.d.). In *Wikipedia.* Retrieved 21 May 2011 from http://en.wikipedia.org/

H OECD (2010). *SMEs, Entrepreneurship and Innovation.* Paris: Organisation for Economic Cooperation and Development.

I Rauch, A., Wiklund, J., Lumpkin, G. T., & Frese, M. (2009). Entrepreneurial orientation and business performance: An assessment of past research and suggestions for the future. [Electronic Version]. *Entrepreneurship: Theory & Practice,* p. 761.

J Peters, M. (2010). *Innovation and invention.* MBA lecture notes, 2009/10, Southport University, Business School.

K K. Roback (2006), Medical device innovation – The integrated processes of invention, diffusion and deployment. Unpublished PhD. Linköping, Sweden: Linköping University.

L Samuelson (2009). Advances in total factor productivity and entrepreneurial innovation. In Z. J. Acs, D. Audretsch, & R. Strom (eds) *Entrepreneurship, growth and public policy.* Cambridge: Cambridge University Press.

M Woolridge, A. (2009, March 14). *Global heroes: A special report on entrepreneurship.* The Economist, 1–19.

b **Find any mistakes in the reference list and discuss ways to correct them.**

Grammar and vocabulary

Grammar and vocabulary
- Using gender-neutral language
- Complex conjunctions
- Adjective compounds with *well-, ill-, poorly*

1 Using gender-neutral language

In your academic communication, avoid using gender-specific language. For example, avoid the use of man *where it refers to people in general (that is, both men and women). Also avoid suggesting that a particular job or role is filled only by men or by women when it might be filled by either. This is important because gender-specific language can imply (usually) male superiority, or reflect an unequal status in society. Try to use gender-neutral language instead. Make sure that you are consistent in a particular piece of writing. For example, if you use* she/he *to refer to a male or female student, don't change to* he/she.

1.1 a Work in pairs. Look at sentences 1–11 below and decide whether they are inappropriate because they contain gender-specific language. Check your answers by looking in Appendix 3 on p169.

1 What consequences do they have for the way a teacher approaches his job and his training?
2 Ernest Miller Hemingway was born in 1899 at Oak Park, a highly respectable suburb of Chicago, where his father, a keen sportsman, was a doctor.
3 Throughout history, man has affected the natural environment, often in a destructive way.
4 One of the basic elements contributing to the urban housing problem is the difference in goals of landlords and their tenants.
5 In *The Climates of the Continents*, we have a book which should be of interest, not only to the student of climate and the factors which determine it, but also to the man in the street.
6 The daily life of a small shopkeeper struggling to survive had little in common with that of a prosperous businessman employing a number of workers.
7 Harkness and Waldfogel (1997) calculate the pay ratios for women with children compared to the average man.
8 Quite sophisticated equipment and trained manpower are required.
9 Bowles (2001) observed that his findings supported earlier research results.
10 In the intensive-care unit, it is imperative that the nurse must not allow her attention to wander from the patient.
11 Before entering the market, each consumer decides, on the basis of his income, tastes and alternative opportunities, the maximum price he will pay.

b In pairs, suggest improvements to sentences 1–11.

c Here is a quotation from Prasad (1967) you would like to report in an essay you are writing. How would you deal with the gender-specific language that it includes?

'From the age of seven to 12 years, […] [t]he child is greatly attached to his house, yet he is partly influenced by his school and school-mates.'

2 Complex conjunctions

Conjunctions link words, phrases, or clauses in a sentence. Some conjunctions consist of a single word (e.g. after, while, because*), and others are phrases consisting of more than one word (e.g.* to the extent that*). These phrases can be referred to as 'complex conjunctions'. Many complex conjunctions are common in academic writing.*

2.1 a Read the definitions of these complex conjunctions. Then choose the correct options in sentences 1–6.

to the extent that to a particular degree or stage, often causing particular results
in that because
so that used before you give an explanation for the action that you have just mentioned
in such a way that used before you say that a particular action, situation, etc. causes the result that follows
in order that with the aim of achieving something
in the event that used before you say what will happen – usually something unpleasant – in a particular situation

1 We asked teachers to select a friendship group of around six pupils from each class *to the extent that / in order that* participants would feel comfortable with each other during the group discussion.
2 The sentence structures in (6a) and (6b) are similar *in order that / in that* both include a complex conjunction.
3 During end-of-life care, family members often suffer most because they may be called on to make decisions *in the event that / in such a way that* the patient cannot.

4 Obesity is a medical condition in which body fat has accumulated to *the extent that / so that* it may have a negative effect on health.

5 The apparatus comprised a computer with a colour monitor and a keyboard which was covered *in the event that / in such a way that* only the space bar and enter key were exposed.

6 Participants from all three age groups were asked to complete the same tasks *so that / in that* data collected could easily be compared.

b Match ideas 1–6 with ideas a–f. Then connect them in one sentence using complex conjunctions from 2.1a.

1 the capital J and the lower-case j are alike
2 it is important to use classroom technology regularly
3 stone houses are rarely damaged in floods
4 equipment may need to be modified
5 the small-group discussion activities were designed
6 response rate falls below 40%

a a second round of questionnaires will be distributed
b they both look like a hook
c small children can successfully use it
d benefits and limitations can be analysed
e all students were able to contribute to the discussion
f they need to be completely rebuilt

1 + b   The capital J and the lower case j are alike in that they both look like a hook.

3 Adjective compounds with *well-, ill-, poorly*

A noun phrase + relative clause can often be expressed more efficiently using an adjective compound + noun phrase.
a distribution system that functions well
→ a well-functioning distribution system
(well-functioning = *adjective compound*;
distribution system = *noun phrase*)

3.1 Look again at the text on pages 27–28. Find another *adjective compound + noun phrase* example and write its *noun phrase + relative clause* equivalent.

3.2 Express sentences 1–6 more efficiently by rewriting the section in bold with an *adjective compound + noun phrase* with a similar meaning. Use a prefix from A and the past participle form of a verb from B.

A	B
well- ill- poorly	conceive manage define document time pay

1 There are numerous **examples supported with a lot of written evidence** of racial discrimination in the workplace.

2 Berg (2011) points out that good teaching cannot make up for a **curriculum that is not sensible.**

3 Even if they complain a lot about rules, younger teenagers tend to find security within **limits that are clearly explained** about family and personal behaviour.

4 An **announcement made at the wrong moment** of a huge pay rise for the company's chief executive provoked protests among the workforce.

5 Preschool teachers **do not earn very much** compared to professionals with similar qualifications.

6 The study looks at soil quality on **farms that were not organised in a good way.**

⊙ *Research shows that the most common* well-, ill-, *and* poorly *adjectives in the corpus of academic writing are:*
- well-known, well-defined, well-established, well-formed, well-founded
- ill-defined, ill-formed, ill-posed, ill-fated, ill-equipped
- poorly differentiated, poorly educated, poorly paid, poorly developed
Make three sentences relevant to your own subject using adjectives from each list.

Seminar skills A

Preparing for seminars
· Seminars and lectures
· Good business language

Listening
· Practice in gist and detailed listening

Seminar skills
· Understanding new terms
· Understanding the tutor's instructions
· Understanding tutor feedback

Follow up
· Further listening

Preparing for seminars

1 Seminars and lectures

As part of a course focusing on business communication, you will watch and listen to extracts from a seminar given by Dr Clare Lynch.

Clare Lynch

1.1 **Work in pairs. Discuss what you think the differences are between seminars and lectures. Think about:**

a size of the student group.
b interaction between the tutor and students.
c manner of the tutor.
d contributions from students.
e amount of explaining the tutor does, compared to the amount of questioning.
f opportunities for students to discuss ideas.

2 Good business language

2.1 **In the seminar, you will watch the tutor explain what makes good business writing. Predict which features she will identify as good business language.**

1 a It tries to be impersonal and objective.
   b It tries to communicate directly with the reader.
2 a It uses more verbs.
   b It uses more nouns.
3 a It is generally more concrete and straightforward.
   b It can sometimes be abstract and complex.

2.2 **Which sentence uses more appropriate business language (e.g. for an advert)? Give reasons, using the features from 2.1.**

a We have the expertise and ability to deliver IT solutions that allow for your personalisation.
b We are experts who can solve your IT problems.

Listening

3 Practice in gist and detailed listening

3.1 **a** (▣ **A.1**) **Watch an extract from the seminar and answer the questions.**

a Which features of business language from 2.1 does the tutor talk about?
b What is the tutor's opinion of a lot of business writing?

b **Were any of your ideas about seminars from 1.1 mentioned?**

3.2 (A.2) **Watch the first part of the extract again. Complete the notes.**

- business language (b.l.) = body (e.g. flabby, skeletal, **1**_____)
  (e.g. we are of the opinion of = we **2**_____)

- abstraction in business language ➔ people try to **3**_____ **4**_____
  abstract noun = thing you **5**_____ **6**_____
  (e.g. advice, **7**_____, **8**_____)

- business language attracts abstract nouns ➔ easy to **9**_____, **10** over-_____

- abstract nouns come from **11**_____ & **12**_____
  (e.g. available ➔ availability; reduce ➔ **13**_____)

- abstract noun = skeleton ➔ give **14**_____, necessary
  BUT too many means writing ossified, i.e. **15**_____ & **16**_____

- verbs – language has **17**_____, is dynamic, **18**_____ writing forward

Study tip
Seminars often begin with an input stage like the one you have just seen. In contrast to a lecture, in a seminar you can ask the tutor about a key point you have not understood after the input stage. Tutors will often invite questions of this nature. However, many seminars can have quite a relaxed, fluid atmosphere and students may feel free to ask questions at any time.

3.3 (A.2) **In this extract, the tutor gives examples of abstract business writing. Watch again and find examples of:**

a   a padding (or filler) verb.
b   eight suffixes that indicate abstract nouns.
c   abstract business expressions, as well as an improved version suggested by students.
d   a Latinate verb.
e   an Anglo-Saxon verb phrase.

4   Understanding new terms

4.1 **You watched the tutor provide the key input in the seminar. What do you think will happen next? Discuss these possibilities and give reasons.**

Students will:
a   repeat the key information back to the tutor.
b   share examples that include abstract language.
c   rewrite some examples of business language that are too abstract.
d   write a company profile from notes provided by the tutor, trying to avoid abstract nouns.

4.2 (A.3) **Watch the next extract and discuss the questions.**

a   Were your predictions from 4.1 correct?
b   In this part of the seminar, the tutor introduces a new term. How does she explain its meaning?
·   She says the term in a variety of different example sentences.
·   She provides a definition, similar to one found in a dictionary.
·   She compares it to familiar words with a similar suffix.

Seminar skills

5 Understanding the tutor's instructions

5.1 ▣A.3 The tutor sets up the task using a variety of instructions. Put phrases a–h in order and then watch and check your answers.

a the next exercise _____
b it's entitled 'Curing Nounitis' _____
c that would be great _____
d OK, do you want to _____
e do you know what I mean by 'nounitis'? _____
f take a look at _____
g again, some real-life examples of business language _____
h so if you could cure these examples of 'Nounitis' _____

5.2 **a** **The tutor could have given her instructions as follows. Look at the examples in 5.1. What language does she use instead of the phrases in bold?**

a Could you please **do** the following exercise on 'nounitis'?
b **Do you understand** 'nounitis'?
c Could you **rewrite the examples**?

b **Discuss whether the tutor's language is more or less direct than the examples in 5.2a.**

> **Study tip**
> *In seminars, tutors are not always directive in the way they set up activities. This is often because a seminar is seen as a collaborative learning context in which a tutor facilitates rather than instructs. It also suggests that tutors expect their students to be more independent.*

6 Understanding tutor feedback

In the next extract, the tutor gives feedback on the 'Nounitis' task. Students have rewritten the following text using more straightforward language.

> We have the willingness and capacity to close this transaction in the most rapid and effective manner and we are confident in our ability to deliver a solution that will be acceptable to all parties.

The tutor gets answers from three groups.
Group 1: two students wearing black pullovers
Group 2: two students wearing red pullovers
Group 3: three students, with the middle student wearing a grey sweatshirt

6.1 **a** ▣A.4 **Watch the extract without sound and focus on body language and facial expressions. With which groups does the tutor do the following?**

a She nods affirmatively, but steps back. She has a mostly neutral look, but seems to be questioning students. She turns to address the whole group to make a point.
b She looks uncertain. She has a questioning look and nods in a negative way. She smiles awkwardly and raises an eyebrow.
c She moves towards the group and maintains her position. She gestures with her arm towards the group. She nods in an affirmative way and gestures towards the group.

b **Which group do you think:**

a has a problem with their answer?
b has an answer which is quite good, but needs some changing?
c has a good answer?

c **Which adjective best describes her overall manner with each group?**

a cautious   **b** encouraging   **c** uncertain

d ▣A.5 **Watch the clip again, this time with sound. Were your ideas correct?**

6.2 **Look at these examples of giving feedback. Choose the example that you think is more appropriate (a or b) and give reasons.**

1 **indicating there is a problem**
a I'm not sure I entirely agree with your ideas.
b Oh, so that was your answer? Maybe.

2 **showing that an answer is almost correct**
a It's not 100% correct.
b I like what you say in the first part of your answer, but perhaps in the second part you could …

3 **showing that an answer is correct**
a Yes.
b I like that, yes, it works.

6.3 **a** ▓ A.6 **Listen and complete the phrases the tutor uses to give feedback to each group.**
Group 1
I think you had _____ there. Yeah.

Group 2
I think you're trying _____ cancel something.

Group 3
Close, yeah, I mean _____ sure you got …

b **Which examples do you think are direct? Which are more indirect?**

6.4 **a** ▓ A.7 **Watch the end of the extract, where the tutor gives her version of the text. She makes a comment which is not part of the definition. This is known as an aside. Which expression does she comment on?**
a close this transaction
b deliver a solution

b **How does she signal the aside? Choose the correct option.**
a Her intonation falls in the middle of her dictation and again for the aside.
b Her intonation stops in the middle of a rise and she pauses. She pauses again at the end of the aside.

6.5 ▓ A.7 **Watch again and write down the tutor's version. She provides two different endings.**
We're willing …

ending 1: _____
ending 2: _____

 Study tip
In seminars, tutors often give indirect feedback on tasks that focus on the content of students' answers. This approach to feedback aims to be more interactive and exploratory in nature. It is more common than feedback that simply confirms or denies the accuracy of an answer.

Follow up

7 **Further listening**

7.1 ▓ A.8 **Listen to Youness talk about his experience of seminars.**
a What helped give him confidence?
b How did he try to contribute to seminars?
c Did tutors have high expectations of the students in the seminar group?

Youness

3 Facing challenges

Reading

1 Following the writer's argument

1.1 **In preparation for a tutorial on world politics, your tutor has given you this handout. Work in pairs and follow steps 1 and 2. Then share your ideas with the class.**

Issues in current world politics

Over the next few weeks, we are going to look at some of the most important challenges facing global decision-makers today: food security, energy security, climate change and pollution. In preparation for next week's tutorial, work with a colleague and:

1 discuss what you understand by each of these four terms

2 put them in order of importance for decision-makers.

In the tutorial, we'll begin by talking about your ideas.

1.2 **a** **After the tutorial, your tutor asked you to read the following article:**
Frow, E. et al. (2009). The politics of plants. *Food security*, 1, 17–23.

Before you read the abstract, predict what the article will be about.

b **Now read the abstract below and check your predictions. To which of the four challenges in 1.1 does the article seem to be most relevant?**

➤ *in relation to*
G&V **1, p52**

➤ *Items in lists*
G&V **2, p52**

Abstract

1 Food security is not a new concern, but has taken on new dimensions in recent years. **2** Here we position food security in a broader context in relation to the use and management of global biomass resources, and specifically the push to develop a "bio-based economy". **3** We note a growing focus on plants as a source of innovative solutions to complex problems including food security, energy security, climate change and global environmental health. **4** However, we also note that plants are a renewable but finite resource, and propose that renewed enthusiasm for plants is resulting in an increasingly complicated "politics of plants", as competition for limited land and biomass resources intensifies – the clash between food security and energy security over biofuels being an obvious example. **5** Plants are a common thread across many policy domains including agriculture, energy, environment, health, and industry, and as such we suggest that they might provide a focal point for joined-up thinking and governance. **6** We identify this broader picture as an important backdrop for discussions regarding food security and from our proposed framework, develop a number of recommendations for further investigation.

Keywords: Bioeconomy – Biofuels – Biotechnology – Food security – Plant science – Research policy

c **Look at the abstract again and answer the questions.**

1 What verb is used in sentences 3 and 4 to indicate that the authors are describing the present situation?

2 What language is used in sentences 5 and 6 to indicate that the authors are making proposals for the future?

d **Many journal abstracts, like this one, list keywords from the article. What purpose do you think these have? Check that you understand the keywords in this article.**

1.3 a **Work in pairs. What does the prefix *bio-* mean in the keywords in the abstract? Scan the article extract below to find more words with *bio-* and try to work out their meaning.**

Plants and the bio-based economy

Plants are the bedrock of food and energy production. The management of plants, as a link between the economy, human health and the environment, is in many ways taken for granted, particularly in developed nations. However, the critical position of plants has been increasingly recognized in recent years, largely through policy-level attention
5   to the concept of the 'knowledge-based bioeconomy' (OECD 2006; European Commission 2005). Although working definitions differ, in a bioeconomy the raw materials and basic building blocks for food, energy, industry, growth and well-being are derived from biological, renewable resources (mainly plants and microorganisms). Arguably, humans have always had a bioeconomy, being largely dependent on biological resources for
10   nourishment, clothing, shelter, and so on – even the fossil fuel economy obtains energy from 'ancient sunlight'. However, current thinking emphasizes the use of cutting-edge science and technology to support the transition away from a petroleum-based economy to one dependent on bio-renewables (European Plant Science Organization 2005). As noted by the European Commission (2005), 'although plants are not most people's idea of
15   high technology, much of the knowledge-based bioeconomy is firmly rooted in the plant sciences' (p.11).

Plants are thus capturing the interest of businesses, researchers and policymakers worldwide. Although plant science research suffered in terms of profile and funding in the 1980s and 1990s, the possibilities being opened up by modern biotechnology are
20   leading to renewed enthusiasm – and funding to match. For example, the knowledge-based bioeconomy is a cross-cutting theme in the European Commission's latest round of research funding (the €1.75 billion Framework Programme Seven, FP7). From cellulosic bioethanol to large-scale "biorefineries", some of the impending applications for plants extend far beyond their traditional uses.

25   As potentially environmentally sustainable commodities, the enthusiasm for plant-derived products is understandable. Tantalizingly, they might offer a way out of the zero-sum game between economic growth and environmental protection (World Commission on Environment and Development, 1987). In principle, a deeper understanding of plants and other living systems could allow us to better manage the earth's resources for both
30   environmental and economic ends. But are we likely to reach such a win-win situation? The re-valuing of plants in terms of their technological potential is exposing tensions among the many different systems to which plants contribute. Demand for land, water and biomass resources is intensifying, with consequences (notably, higher food prices) that are being felt by all. If current developments are anything to go by, the politics of
35   plants will quickly become increasingly complicated.

Frow, E. et al. (2009). The politics of plants. *Food security*, 1, 17–23.

> *being*
> G&V 3, p53

b Scan the article extract again to find words with these definitions.

1 the main thing on which something else is built or based: be_____ck

2 obtained from something else: de_____ed

3 the change from one form or type to another: tr_____ion

4 substances or products that can be traded, bought or sold: com_____es

5 problems caused by opposing aims or influences: te_____ns

6 becoming greater, more serious or more extreme: int_____ing

1.4 **Look at these notes summarising the main steps in the authors' argument. Read the extract again carefully and complete the notes below with information a–j. Compare answers in pairs.**

> Although **1** _____f_____, **2**_____.
> **3**_____, but **4**_____.
> As a result, **5**_____, and **6**_____.
> **7**_____. But for this to happen, **8**_____.
> However, **9**_____. In consequence, **10**_____.

a businesses and researchers are becoming more interested in plants

b the importance of plants in the 'knowledge-based economy' is becoming increasingly recognised

c a re-evaluation of the technological potential of plants may also lead to conflicts of interest over land, water, etc.

d people have always been dependent on biological resources

e we need to know more about plants and other living systems

f the relationship between plants and health, the environment, etc. has been widely taken for granted

g the politics of plants is rapidly becoming more complex

h the development of environmentally sustainable plant-derived products would allow both economic growth and environmental protection

i more money is being put into research in plant science

j new technological developments are enabling the change from a petroleum-based economy to a bioeconomy

2 Vocabulary in context 1: focusing and evaluative adverbs

Many adverbs are used in academic texts to indicate the writer's attitude. For example, <u>focusing adverbs specify or focus on an event</u> in some way, while <u>evaluative adverbs</u> indicate the writer's <u>opinion on a fact or event</u>.

2.1 **a Replace the ideas in bold with an adverb with a similar meaning. (Make any other necessary changes.) Compare your answers with the extract in 1.3a. Were there any differences?**

> arguably   increasingly   particularly   potentially

1 The management of plants [...] is in many ways taken for granted, **mostly** in developed countries. (line 1)

2 **Although some people might disagree, we think that** humans have always had a bioeconomy ... (line 8)

3 Plant-derived products **may in the future be** environmentally sustainable .... (line 25)

4 If current developments are anything to go by, the politics of plants will quickly become **more and more** complicated. (line 34)

b Which *are* of these *is a* focusing adverbs and which are evaluative adverbs?

c Can you find other focusing adverbs or evaluative adverbs from the text in 1.3a?

3 Vocabulary in context 2: adjective compounds

➤Adjective compounds
Unit 2 G&V 3, p37

An adjective compound is a combination of two or more words that functions as an adjective. The words in an adjective compound may or may not be hyphenated (e.g. part-time, recently formed).

3.1 a Complete the hyphenated adjective compounds in these sentences.

> ~~joined~~ based edge level petroleum derived large zero

1 We suggest that plants might provide a focal point for _joined_ -up thinking and governance.
2 The critical position of plants has been increasingly recognized in recent years, largely through policy-_____ attention to the concept of the knowledge-_____ 'bioeconomy'.
3 Current thinking emphasizes the use of cutting-_____ science and technology to support the transition away from a _____-based economy to one dependent on bio-renewables.
4 From cellulosic bioethanol to _____ -scale "biorefineries", some of the impending applications for plants extend far beyond their traditional uses.
5 The enthusiasm for plant-_____ products is understandable [... they] might offer a way out of the _____ -sum game between economic growth and environmental protection.

b Check your answers in the abstract and the extract.

c Work in pairs. Find more hyphenated adjective compounds in the texts and try to explain their meanings using the context, your own knowledge or a dictionary.

4 Reading in detail

4.1 a What does *Here* refer to in this example?

> **Here** we position food security in a broader context ... (abstract, sentence 2)

b *As such* is often used as a sentence connector with the meaning 'because something has the characteristics described...' or 'as this name or description implies ...'.

> ... **as such,** we suggest that they might provide a focal point for joined-up thinking and governance. (abstract, sentence 5)

However, it is often used incorrectly. In which of these examples is it used correctly?

1 Nutrition is a science, and **as such**, the results of analyses conducted by nutrition experts should be taken seriously.
2 Playing video games leads to inactivity during the day, and **as such**, children burn few calories.

c Find the phrase in bold in the abstract. Explain what it refers to.

> We identify **this broader picture** as an important backdrop for discussions ... (abstract, sentence 6)

d Why is 'a' included in this in-text reference?

> ... von Braun 2007**a**.

e Why is the first mention of *politics of plants* in inverted commas, and why are there no inverted commas around it in the other sentence?

> ... enthusiasm for plants is resulting in an increasingly complicated **"politics of plants"** ... (abstract, sentence 4)
>
> ... the **politics of plants** will quickly become increasingly complicated ... (extract, line 34)

f Can you suggest how a 'working definition' is different from a 'definition'?

> Although **working definitions** differ... (extract, line 6)

> ☉ When working *has the same meaning, other common collocations in the academic corpus are:*
> · working hypothesis
> · working knowledge
> · working title

4.2 The article was written in 2009. Can you think of any examples in which the 'politics of plants' has influenced countries or regions since then? Share your ideas with the rest of the class.

5 **Working with colleagues: problem solving**

In many subjects, students are asked to work together in small groups to solve problems. In this section you will practise language for discussing problems.

5.1 Work in small groups to discuss the following scenario. Include in your discussion stages a–d below.

a Describe the possible causes of the problem.
b Suggest possible responses.
c Speculate on the outcome of these suggested responses.
d Agree on a recommended response.

> *You live in a beautiful city set in a valley surrounded by mountains. The city has become prosperous, with industries being set up on the outskirts and offices in the city centre. Most people are wealthy enough to own one or more cars. Unfortunately, in recent years the number of cases of respiratory diseases such as asthma has increased rapidly and the problem has become so severe that large numbers of people – particularly well-off families with children – are moving to other parts of the country. Discuss this problem and come up with one recommended response that the city government should prioritise.*

5.2 a ◀) 3.1 **Listen to a group of students discussing the same scenario. Did you suggest the same responses?**

b **Listen again and complete extracts 1–10 in the table below.**

a	Describe the possible causes of the problem	**1**	I suppose _it could be_ **that** all the cars …
		2	Yes, that's a possibility. _____ **also** the industry …
		3	I think **the most** _____ **the problem is** the location …
b	Suggest possible responses	**4**	… to start with. // Well, _____ **would be** to build …
		5	… not the best answer. // _____ **if** tighter controls …
		6	… to the cars – _____ **could** encourage people …
c	Speculate on the outcome of these suggested responses	**7**	… from their cars. // _____ **difficult**, though. …
		8	… a possibility, but **if they** _____ **be that** the industries …
		9	… a lot recently. // **I'm not** _____ **to help much** if they keep …
d	Agree on a recommended response	**10**	… perfect in itself, but **it looks like** _____ **that encouraging** the use of …

5.3 **Work in small groups. Discuss the problems in these scenarios and suggest responses. Follow the steps and use language from the table.**

1

One of the effects of climate change is a rise in sea levels around the world. You live in a small coastal town that has existed in the same place for hundreds of years. The town is quite poor, being dependent almost entirely on fishing, although your country as a whole is wealthy. Over the last few years, the sea levels appear to have risen. During high tides, low-lying parts of the town regularly flood.

2

You live on an island with a population of about one million. The island is prosperous, exporting fish, agricultural products and a number of minerals used in computers and mobile phones. However, the island is heavily dependent on imported oil and petroleum for energy for its power plants, in cars, etc. at a time when the cost of oil and petroleum is increasing rapidly because world stocks are reducing.

Writing

6 Understanding instructions in essays and other assignments

*Some essay titles and other assignments – for coursework or in examinations – include an instruction phrase which tells you what kind of answer you should give. Most instruction phrases ask you to do one of three things: **describe** one or more topics; present one or more positions on a topic and **argue** in support of one of these; or show how two or more topics are **related** by indicating how they are similar or different.*

6.1 a **How would your answers to the following assignment questions from the field of marketing be influenced by the different instruction phrases? Discuss your ideas in pairs.**

1 Describe the ways in which marketing managers use the media to achieve their marketing objectives.

2 Discuss the ways in which marketing managers use the media to achieve their marketing objectives.

3 To what extent do marketing managers use the media to achieve their marketing objectives?

b **Do the same with these pairs of assignment titles from other subjects.**

1 a A wide range of methods exists for delivering drugs into the human body. Using examples, outline why there are so many options.

b A wide range of methods exists for delivering drugs into the human body. Using examples, evaluate these options.

2 a Ageist language is often also sexist language. Explain why this might be so.

b 'Ageist language is often also sexist language.' Discuss.

3 a Critically evaluate the ways in which political parties try to manipulate the media and affect the political agenda in a country you are familiar with.

b In what ways do political parties try to manipulate the media and affect the political agenda in a country you are familiar with?

4 a Compare and contrast two alternative models of change within business organisations.

b Summarise two alternative models of change within business organisations.

5 a Assess the environmental benefits of recycling. Give examples of the energy reductions achieved by recycling paper, aluminium and iron.

b Illustrate the environmental benefits of recycling. Give examples of the energy reductions achieved by recycling paper, aluminium and iron.

6.2 a **Complete these points with instruction phrases from 6.1.**

- **Description** instruction phrases include: _____

- **Argument** instruction phrases include: _____

- **Relationship** instruction phrases include: _____

b **What other instruction phrases do you know? Add them to 6.2a.**

6.3 a **Work in pairs. Choose one of the assignment titles in 6.1 and make notes of a brief outline for an essay answering the question.**

b **Report your outline to another pair of students, explaining how you have responded to the instruction phrase in the title.**

7 Developing an argument in an essay

A typical argumentative essay has the following parts.

An introduction: *this gives the background, says what the different views are on the topic, includes a statement of your position on the topic, and may outline how the essay is to be organised.*

A body: *this makes claims in favour of or in opposition to each view, and provides evidence in support of these claims.*

A conclusion: *this summarises the different views and reinforces your position by saying which side of the argument you think is stronger*

7.1 A challenge you discussed on page 42 was food security: the availability of food and access to it. Some people have suggested that the use of genetically modified (GM) foods can help overcome this problem. In a later tutorial, you are given the following essay title: 'Genetically modified (GM) foods are necessary to end world hunger.' How far do you agree with this statement?

a Working in small groups, share what you already know about GM foods and decide how far you agree with the statement.

b Your tutor has suggested that you should read the following texts as a starting point in reading for your essay. In them, the writers give their views on GM foods. Identify the main claims made by the writers and then decide an order that would be suitable for the essay body. Work individually and then compare in pairs.

Text A

The debate over genetically modified crops and food has been contaminated by political and aesthetic prejudices: hostility to US corporations, fear of big science and romanticism about local, organic production.

Food supply is too important to be the plaything of these prejudices. If there is not enough food, we know who will go hungry.

Genetic modification is analogous to nuclear power: nobody loves it, but climate change has made its adoption imperative. As Africa's climate deteriorates, it will need to accelerate crop adaptation. As population grows, it will need to raise yields. Genetic modification offers both faster crop adaptation and a biological, rather than chemical, approach to yield increases.

Opponents talk darkly of risks but provide no scientific basis for their amorphous expressions of concern. Meanwhile, the true risks are mounting. Over the past decade, global food demand has risen more rapidly than expected. Supply may not keep pace with demand, inducing rising prices and periodic spikes. If this happens, there is a risk that the children of the urban poor will suffer prolonged bouts of malnutrition.

African governments are now recognising that by imitating the European ban on genetic modification, they have not reduced the risks facing their societies, but increased them. Thirteen years, during which there could have been research on African crops, have been wasted. Africa has been in thrall to Europe, and Europe has been in thrall to populism.

Genetic modification alone will not solve the food problem: like climate change, there is no single solution. But continuing refusal to use it is making a difficult problem yet more daunting.

Collier, P. (2009, October 26). Can biotech food cure world hunger? Put aside prejudices. *New York Times*. Retrieved August 2, 2011 from http://roomfordebate.blogs.nytimes.com/2009/10/26/can-biotech-food-cure-world-hunger/

Text B

Food security over the next two decades will have to be built on ecological security and climate resilience. We need the real green revolution, not a second 'Green Revolution' based on genetic engineering.

Genetic engineering has not increased yields. Recent research by Doug Gurian-Sherman of the Union of Concerned Scientists, published as the study 'Failure to Yield', has shown that in a nearly 20-year record, genetically engineered crops have not increased yields. The study did not find significantly increased yields from crops engineered for herbicide tolerance or crops engineered to be insect-resistant.

The International Assessment of Agricultural Science and Technology for Development, carried out by 400 scientists over four years, has also concluded that genetic engineering does not hold much promise. Instead, small farms based on principles of agri-ecology and sustainability produce more food.

That is why I am so disappointed that the Gates Foundation, in its global development program, is supporting the use of genetically modified crops in Africa.

Green revolution technologies and strategies, reliant on monoculture and chemical fertilisers and pesticides, have destroyed biodiversity, which has in many places led to a decline in nutrition output per acre.

As I have shown in my book, 'Soil, Not Oil', industrial systems of food production are also a major contributor to greenhouse gas emissions and climate change. Industrial monocultures are more vulnerable to climate change, since they reduce soil organic matter which is vital for moisture conservation and resilience to drought.

The claim by the genetic engineering industry, that without genetically modified food we cannot respond to climate change, is simply false. Climate-resilient traits in crops have been evolved by farmers over centuries. In the community seed banks that I have helped create through the Navdanya movement, we have seeds for drought resistance, flood resistance and salt tolerance. This is the biological capital for the real green revolution.

The gene giants are now pirating and patenting the collective and cumulative innovation of Third World farmers. Patent monopolies on seed cannot create food security. They can only push small farmers into debt.

The green revolution that we are building through Navdanya is based on conserving biodiversity and conserving water while increasing food production per acre. What we need is biodiversity intensification, not chemical intensification. What we need is to work with nature's nutrient cycles and hydrological cycle, not against them. It is time to put small farmers, especially women, at the heart of this process.

Vandana, S. (2009, October 26). Can biotech food cure world hunger? The failure of gene-altered crops. *New York Times.* Retrieved August 2, 2011 from http://roomfordebate.blogs.nytimes.com/2009/10/26/can-biotech-food-cure-world-hunger/

7.2 **Consider why your tutor said that the texts should only be a 'starting point' for your reading. What other types of texts should you read? What other information would you search for?**

8 Style in academic writing

8.1 The texts in 7.1 are from the *New York Times*. Work in pairs and identify features of style in Text B that are unlikely to appear in research articles published in academic journals, and that would also be inappropriate in most of the academic assignments you write.

➤ *Writing in academic style*

Appendix 4, p170

8.2 Using the guide to academic style in Appendix 4, improve these sentences from a student's essay on food security. Work individually and then compare suggestions in pairs.

1 Everyone knows that an insufficient food supply causes food insecurity.

2 Worldwide, up to two billion people regularly face food insecurity! (FAO, 2003).

3 Vast amounts of food are destroyed by rats, mice, etc.

4 If a disease breaks out, this can destroy entire crops.

5 Globalisation leads to continued food insecurity and poverty in rural communities.

6 Smallholder farmers have an important role to play in getting rid of hunger and poverty.

7 You can find further details of the World Food Summit of 2009 in Jackson (2011).

8 The big problem is not food production, but food distribution.

9 People who rent a farm rather than own it haven't got a lot of incentive to improve the land.

10 It seems to me that farming does not receive the attention it deserves.

11 It is outrageous that so many people are overweight in developed countries, when so many people in developing countries go hungry.

12 People can be considered to be food-secure when they don't live in fear of hunger or starvation.

🎓 **Focus on your subject**
The acceptability of 'I' in academic writing seems to vary from subject to subject. As you read journal articles in your subject, note whether 'I' is used and, if it is, what contexts it is used in.

Grammar and vocabulary

Grammar and vocabulary
· Complex prepositions
· Items in lists
· *being*

1 Complex prepositions

Some prepositions consist of one word (e.g. in, between*).
Complex prepositions can consist of:*
- *two words (e.g.* regardless of)
- *three words (e.g. _____)*
- *or four words (e.g.* with the exception of).

1.1 **Find a three-word complex preposition in the final paragraph of the text on page 43 and write it in the space above.**

1.2 **Sentences 1–12 include a two-, three-, or four-word complex preposition. The last word of each is missing. Complete them, using a dictionary to help you.**

| for   from   of   on   to   with |

1 Fees at private schools can vary widely depending $\overset{on}{\wedge}$ the status of the school.

2 Our findings are broadly in line previous research (Arber, 1993; Vindras, 2000).

3 The children built shapes with ten cubes that were identical except their colour.

4 Figure 8.1 lists procedures to be followed by tutors in the event an emergency in the laboratory.

5 The recent government policies have increased differences among groups with regard income and wealth.

6 In general, the teachers felt that, apart a few exceptions, descriptive statistics do not pose particular learning problems.

7 A memory-image – as distinct a daydream, for instance – is a visualisation of what was actually witnessed.

8 The family, as I define it here, comprises a husband and wife, with or without never-married children, irrespective their age.

9 Subjects completed the two relevant questionnaires along several other, unrelated experimental tasks.

10 The results from this study indicate that, contrary expectations, a large majority of test-takers had either high familiarity (50%) or moderate familiarity (34%) with computers

11 Recent analysis suggests that the daily temperature range has decreased as a result urbanisation.

12 Employees believed that they owe their employer certain contributions (e.g. hard work, loyalty) in return certain benefits (e.g. high pay, job security).

1.3 **Complete these sentences with complex prepositions from 1.2.**

1 Acts of war, including war crimes and crimes against humanity are regarded as _____ terrorism.

2 The young shrew develops rapidly, and by the time it is three weeks old it appears much like its mother _____ its smaller size.

3 The term 'social revolution' may have different meanings, _____ the writer.

4 In the next section, data is presented graphically _____ an analysis of the results.

5 The main objective of the scheme was to provide financial support to farmers _____ crop failure during the drought.

6 Members of society usually acquire culture during early childhood, _____ where they live.

7 The two groups were balanced _____ gender (six male patients, six female patients).

8 These differences are _____ predictions from Rubin, Schrauf and Greenberg's (2003) model and strengthen support for that model.

9 Cox and Alm (2011) argue that, _____ conventional wisdom, the United States is at the peak of its economic well-being, with more opportunity for more people than at any other time in its history.

10 Thirty-five undergraduate students at the university participated in the research _____ a gift voucher.

11 Of the eight people who were injured in the explosion, three died later _____ their injuries.

12 The bird is now almost extinct in the wild, _____ a few isolated pairs in south Asia.

2 Items in lists

2.1 **Work in pairs. Compare the list in sentence 1 (from the abstract on page 42) and sentence 2 (from a student's essay). What is wrong in sentence 2? Can you correct it?**

1 [There is] a growing focus on plants as a source of innovative solutions to complex problems, **including food security, energy security, climate change and global environmental health.**

2 The country faces a number of serious problems, such as **unemployment, to get rid of racial discrimination, and crime is increasing.**

2.2 Complete each sentence with the information listed in brackets. Use the same grammatical form for each item in the list.

1 North et al. (2000: 263) found that adolescents listen to and play pop rather than classical music for a number of reasons including: _____

_____

_____

(enjoying music – to be creative – relief from boredom – the reduction of loneliness)

2 Schools are expected to work towards goals such as: _____

_____

(an increased level of attendance – improving punctuality – to arrange work experience – a record of achievement should be prepared for each student)

3 Demographic factors were recorded, including:

_____

_____

(how old they were – what was their gender – whether they were married – how many years they had been in full-time education)

4 The following threats from environmental hazards can be recognised: hazards to people, including

_____

(dying – getting injured – to suffer disease – mental stress); hazards to goods, including

_____

(to damage property – economic loss); and hazards to the environment, including

_____

(loss of flora and fauna – polluting)

3 *being*

The word being *has a number of uses in academic writing. Here we look at two important ones.*

1 It is used to give an explanation of something.

Arguably, humans have always had a bioeconomy, *being* largely dependent on biological resources for nourishment, clothing, etc. (= *because they are ...*)

Not being able to find a job as a research chemist, she went into teaching. (= *because she wasn't able to ...*)

2 After words such as besides, despite, without, *and* while, *it forms a clause with an adverbial meaning (giving information about causes, results, etc.).*

Despite being (= *although it is*) of great concern in its own right, we see food security as deeply embedded in the debate over plant resources in general.

Note that the clauses can usually be reversed.

She went into teaching, **not being** able to find a job as a research chemist.

3.1 Rephrase the bold part of these sentences using *being*.

1 The plant's leaves are unusual **because they are almost square in shape.**

_____

2 **Because they were part of such a large organisation,** staff felt they had no role in decision-making.

_____

3 Argon, **because it is a gas**, is not present in molten lava.

_____

4 **Because Portuguese was her native language,** she found it easy to settle in Brazil.

_____

5 **Because I am not a statistician,** I am unable to evaluate their claims.

_____

3.2 Write four new sentences relevant to your subject using structures with *being* from 3.1.

3.3 Complete these sentences with the information in brackets and *being*. Also use *besides*, *despite*, *without* or *while*.

1 The book provides information that is clear ...

_____

_____

(the information is not too technical)

2 A total of 33 percent of participants described themselves as fat ...

_____

_____

(33 percent of participants who described themselves as fat were underweight)

3 The public demands first-class education ...

_____

_____

(the public is unwilling to pay higher taxes for first-class education)

4 Vegetables are best in the growing season, ...

_____

_____

(vegetables are also cheaper in their growing season)

5 Some materials allow much of the light that falls on them to pass through the material ...

_____

_____

(the light is not reflected)

6 ... South Africa was comparatively late in introducing television broadcasting.

_____

_____

(South Africa is the most economically advanced country in Africa)

4 IT in education and business

Reading
- Preparing to read a research article
- Checking predictions
- Producing slides from texts
- Vocabulary in context 1: recognising the relationship between pieces of research
- Vocabulary in context 2: noun/verb + preposition
- Reading in detail
- Reasons for referencing

Writing
- Using evidence
- Writing up research: a research proposal

Listening and speaking
- Presenting professionally
- Introducing presentations
- Presentation practice

Reading

1 Preparing to read a research article

You have been asked to read a research article with the title 'Assessing laptop use in higher-education classrooms: The Laptop Effectiveness Scale (LES)', and to give a presentation of what you have read to your tutorial group.

1.1 Before you read part of the article, work in pairs. Look at Table 1 and answer the questions.

a   Can you identify three patterns of laptop use?

b   Do you find any of the percentages surprising? Can you suggest possible explanations?

c   Do the figures reflect your experience of using a laptop in a classroom?

Table 1: Frequency of in-class activities by Canadian university students, 2007 (n=177)

In-class activities		Percentage of class time				
		0%	1–25%	26–50%	51–75%	76–100%
Academic	Taking notes	2%	8%	15%	34%	40%
	Academic activities	3%	9%	20%	31%	37%
Non-academic	Using email	12%	41%	31%	10%	5%
	Instant messaging	8%	32%	24%	17%	14%
	Watching movies	89%	6%	4%	0%	1%
	Playing games	63%	24%	11%	1%	1%

1.2 a In your presentation, you are going to deliver information from the literature review in the article. First, check that you understand these words from the text. Match the words (1–6) to the definitions (a–f).

1	asynchronous	a	to make something less harmful, unpleasant or bad
2	collaborative	b	not occurring at the same time or speed
3	ubiquitous	c	harming or damaging
4	distracting	d	causing loss of attention
5	mitigate	e	involving two or more people working together for a purpose
6	detrimental	f	seeming to be in all places

➤ The literature review

Unit 6, 10 p89

A literature review is an important part of a research article and of most other academic texts which present original research. It gives a description and evaluation of previous work that is relevant to the study.

b   **Work in pairs and predict ways in which these words might be used in the text to talk about laptop use in higher-education classrooms.**

2 Checking predictions

2.1 Read the literature review on pages 55 and 56 and check the predictions you made in 1.2b.

Laptop use in higher education

A number of themes have emerged regarding the use of laptops in higher education, including general use, communication, student attitudes toward learning, student achievement and distractions. Each of these will be discussed in turn.

General use

Researchers have examined how students use laptops for learning. For example, Demb, Erickson and Hawkins-Wilding (2004) found that 16% of overall laptop use involved typing papers and notes. Arend's (2004) work showed that out of class, work such as writing papers, using software programs, searching the internet, and completing group projects constituted the bulk of laptop use. McVay, Snyder and Graetz (2005) added that students reported using their laptops an average of five hours per day, with 36% of that time being spent on academic activities.

Communication

Students report that using a laptop to communicate with faculty via email is generally gratifying (Mitra & Steffensmeier, 2000), and that with email, they communicate with faculty more often and more freely (Arend, 2004). Traditional office hours are being replaced with email communication (Dickson & Segars, 1999; Reynolds, 2003), as students can ask brief questions of faculty without having to meet in person. This asynchronous communication allows for greater flexibility for students and faculty, and also provides faculty with an electronic record of student advising and counselling (Partee, 1996). Brown and Pettito (2003) suggest that email is becoming ubiquitous in that, 'a majority of academic communities are presuming that students and faculty communicate via email' (p. 26).

Email communication in education is not limited to faculty–student interactions. Demb, et al. (2004) suggest that laptops offer students the opportunity to engage in peer-to-peer communication via email, chat rooms, bulletin boards and instant messaging. This kind of mobile communication, including multimedia messaging, web access, email and voice/text messaging, provides short learning activities that are attractive to students and foster collaboration (Shih & Mills, 2007). Gay, Stefanone, Grace-Martin and Hembrooke (2001) suggest that within a collaborative learning environment, students working in groups recognise and use social communication for the exchange of information, and that wireless connections increase the ability for students to collaborate whenever and wherever they want.

Although email and instant messaging technologies suggest increased communication among faculty and students, use of these communication tools is potentially detrimental in the classroom. Grace-Martin and Gay (2001) found that recreational email and instant messaging are among the primary uses of wireless laptops by students, while Crook and Barrowcliff (2001) suggest that recreational use of email and instant messaging in class can be distracting to students. Some attempts at quantifying the time spent on non-academic communication and social distraction have been made, such as Barak et al. (2006), who found that 12% of students used their laptops for non-learning purposes such as web surfing or social emailing. Crook and Barrowcliff (2001) also found evidence of recreational laptop activity, arguing that the self-reported work:play ratio in student interviews was 30%:70%.

Student attitudes toward learning

Jones (2002) found that a majority of college students own computers and wireless devices and believe that internet use has enhanced their learning experience. Similarly, alumni who participated in an undergraduate laptop program agreed that portable computers were beneficial in their college careers (Finn & Inman, 2004). Mitra and Steffensmeier (2000) found that students who used laptops preferred taking classes where they could use the computer. Despite the affinity for using the computer, student satisfaction is higher when students report using the laptops for academic purposes (McVay, Snyder & Graetz, 2005).

A number of studies have reported that students believe that laptops make learning 'easier' (Barak et al., 2006; Mitra & Steffensmeier, 2000; Hyden, 2006; Weaver & Nilson, 2005). This may be an extension of the notion that modern students have grown up with technology, and the progression to having the 'convenience of a personally configured computer [that] students naturally use as a life tool' (Brown & Pettito, 2003, p. 27). Caudill (2007) suggests that by carrying a personalised device, students can quickly and easily access the resources they need.

Student achievement

Zucker (2004) argues that increasing student achievement is the most important goal for adopting 1:1 computing, and that studies focusing on student learning deserve a high priority. Results from studies measuring the efficacy of laptops on student achievement, though, are mixed. Demb et al. (2004) found that for about two-thirds of students, the laptop computer made a significant difference in study habits, with students reporting that the laptops helped with classroom assignments, email, communication and research.

► *communication …
provides*

G&V **1, p64**

► *Crook and Barrowcliff
(2001) suggest …*

G&V **2, p65**

9 Writing up research: a research proposal

For undergraduate or postgraduate students, a research proposal is an outline of the research project they intend to undertake for their dissertation or thesis. Although there can be variation across subjects and institutions in the organisation of research proposals and their parts, many research proposals have a similar format. Following the title, which gives an indication of the topic of the research, they are often divided into the five or six sections outlined below.

9.1 **Work in pairs. Think of three reasons why students are usually asked to write a proposal before starting their research. Share your ideas with the class.**

9.2 **Complete section headings 1–6 in the table with information from the box.**

~~Introduction~~	Timescale	Ethical considerations
Methods	References	Aims and objectives

Sections of a typical research proposal

Section headings	General purpose of section	Elements in the section will say ...
1 Introduction	to say why you want to do the research	7
2	to say what exactly you want to do in the research	
3	to say how you are going to do the research	
4	to show that you will conduct your research in an ethical way	
5	to show how you will complete your research by the deadline for submission	
6	to acknowledge the sources you have referred to in the research proposal	

9.3 **Read the list of elements (1–17) that are found in a research proposal. Add them to the table. Sometimes there is more than one element for each section.**

1 what your research will contribute to the field

2 why the topic is important

3 how your research will conform to the ethical codes of your institution

4 how you will analyse the data

5 by what date you will finish each section

6 how your research relates to what has been done so far

7 ~~what general area you will be working in~~

8 what theoretical approach you will use

9 how you will collect the data

10 what you hope to find out in the research

11 what sources you have mentioned, including full bibliographical details

12 how you will select the data

13 what research questions or hypotheses you will address in the research

14 what work has and has not been done on the subject so far in a brief literature review

15 how you will manage issues such as anonymity of subjects and confidentiality of data

16 why you have chosen a particular method or methods

17 how you came to be interested in the topic

> 🎓 Focus on your subject
> Try to find either: information from your institution or department about writing a research proposal in your subject; or online advice (perhaps from a university website) on how to write a research proposal in your subject.
> Compare the information in the table in 9.2 with what you discover about writing research proposals in your subject. Note any differences and report these to the class.

Listening and speaking

10 Presenting professionally

As well as expecting a high standard of slides, academic audiences expect presentations to be given in a professional way.

10.1 **Look at these presenters. What advice would you give to help make their presentation more professional? Share your ideas with the rest of the class.**

11 Introducing presentations

11.1 (◄)) **4.1** **Listen to the introductions of three presentations on the applications of IT in business and education. For each one, answer the questions.**

  a   What kind of opening information does the speaker use before introducing the specific topic: background, a quotation, or statistics?

  b   What specific topic will the speaker talk about?

  c   How many main sections will the presentation have?

  d   What will be the subject of each section?

11.2 **What does the speaker say to introduce the topic and indicate how the presentation will be divided? Complete the table.**

	Introducing the topic	Dividing up the presentation
1	... business is conducted. And **what I _____ today is** one aspect of this ...	... online. **I'll _____ parts.** **First, _____ about** some of the experiences ... ... the lessons learned. **After that _____** look to ...
2	... a traditional university environment. **In my _____ look at** the experience ...	... an online course. **First _____ going to** provide some information ... they're following. **Second,** _____ consider whether ... and past experiences. _____, I'll suggest ...
3	... as these figure suggest, **my** _____ **at** the problems ...	... with telecommuting. **The first _____ is** outline some of the ... the hidden administrative expenses, **and _____** look at ... between employees. **In the _____** I want to present ...

12 Presentation practice

12.1 a   **Work in pairs. You have been asked to give a short presentation with the title 'Will the paperless office ever arrive?'. Share ideas on the following two questions, using information from the extracts on page 61 and your own ideas.**

  1   What are the advantages of the paperless office?

  2   Why has the paperless office not yet happened?

  b   **Prepare two or three slides to introduce your presentation on the topic.**

  c   **Give the introduction to your presentation to the class. As you do, try to use some of the language you heard in 11.1. Think about what you discussed in 10.1.**

Grammar and vocabulary

Grammar and vocabulary
- Subject–verb agreement
- Tense choice in reporting verbs
- Common prefixes in academic writing

1 Subject–verb agreement

In a sentence, the verb should agree with the subject; that is, a singular subject should be followed by a singular verb and plural subject by a plural verb. After a complex subject (common in academic writing) the verb must agree with the main noun in the subject.

Agreement after a complex subject

1.1 a Study this example sentence from the text on page 55.

main noun in the subject   *subject underlined*

This (kind) of mobile communication, including multimedia messaging, web access, email and voice/text messaging (provides) short learning activities that are attractive to students and foster collaboration (Shih & Mills, 2007).

verb related to the subject

b In sentences 1–8, underline the subject. Then circle the main noun in the subject and the verb related to it. If the verb does not agree with the main noun in the subject, correct the verb.

1 Student comments about unhelpful behaviour was consistent with the inclusion of non-academic communication behaviours.
2 The demand for a learner to be physically at a computer and physically connected via some kind of cable to a network means that learning locations were constrained.
3 The only potential drawback to the use of personal digital assistants (PDAs) are their lack of processing power relative to a laptop computer.
4 Reliable and valid scales assessing the impact of laptops during class has not been developed.
5 Research outcomes reported in Attewell's (2005) summary of the 2001 MLearn project suggest that the use of mobile learning may have positive contributions to make in a number of areas.
6 Evidence based on student comments indicates that the LES may need to be expanded to include more specific examples of academic and non-academic use.
7 Some attempts at quantifying the time spent on non-academic communication and social distraction has been made, such as Barak (2006).
8 Identifying the level of academic activity in laptop-based classes is critical to improving the quality of instruction offered.

Study tip

When you proofread your assignments, make a point of checking agreement between complex subjects and verbs. You can't always rely on the grammar check on your word processor to help you with this.

Agreement after quantifying phrases

1.2 Use the rules in the table to choose the correct form of the verbs in sentences 1–14.

After …	
• *any of, none of, the majority of, all (of), some (of)* + uncountable noun • *one of* + plural noun / pronoun • *the number of* + plural noun • *every, each* + singular noun or a co-ordinated noun (*x* and *y*) • *everyone, everybody, everything* (and similar words beginning *any-, some-,* and *no-*) • a measurement, amount of quantity	use a singular verb
• *any of, each of, either of, neither of, none of* + plural noun / pronoun	use a singular verb (although a plural verb is possible in less formal contexts)
• *a / the majority of, a number of, all (of), some (of)* + plural noun / pronoun	use a plural verb
• a complex subject in which the first noun is a percentage, a fraction, or a proportion	the verb agrees with the noun closest to the verb

1 The majority of research on language teaching *has/have* focused on English.
2 It is worth noticing that approximately 70% of the responses *was/were* from women.
3 The number of universities offering foreign language courses *has/have* declined in the last ten years.
4 Each of these procedures *has/have* advantages and limitations.
5 A number of studies *has/have* shown that aspirin can help reduce deaths from heart disease.
6 Table 3 shows that only one in ten of the population now *works/work* in agriculture.
7 5.5 metres *was/were* the average distance between trees in the forest.
8 Some of the findings *suggests/suggest* that as many as 70% of children's television shows *contains/contain* violent content.
9 In the experiment, each participant *was/were* given four problems to solve.

10 Johnson (1999) and Sims (2000) are less useful because neither of these studies *uses/use* country-level data.

11 One of the people who started the computer revolution *was/were* John Von Neuman.

12 The majority of cases of eating disorders *begins/begin* to develop during adolescence.

13 Not everyone *agrees/agree* that aboriginal peoples in North America used ecosystems in a sustainable manner.

14 Obtaining responses was complicated by the fact that about a quarter of the sample *was/were* residing abroad.

2 Tense choice in reporting verbs

2.1 **Underline the reporting verbs in these extracts from the text on page 55. What do you notice about the tenses used?**

1 Researchers have examined how students use laptops for learning.

2 Demb, Erickson and Hawkins-Wilding (2004) found that 16% of overall laptop use involved typing papers and notes.

3 Crook and Barrowcliff (2001) suggest that recreational use of email and instant messaging in class can be distracting to students.

> It is not easy to give reliable rules for which tense to use with reporting verbs, as there can be considerable variation from publication to publication and from author to author. However, here are some guidelines.
>
> **present simple:**
> · to make a generalisation
> · to present a previous finding as accepted or as a fact
>
> **past simple:**
> · to report a claim or finding from a single piece of previous research
>
> **present perfect:**
> · to refer to a general area of investigation
> · to make a general statement about what previous researchers have done or found

2.2 **Find a journal article from your subject or a related area which includes a literature review using the author–date referencing system (see Appendix 1 on page 168). Underline all the reporting verbs and note their tenses. Do the guidelines above help explain why particular tenses were chosen?**

3 Common prefixes in academic writing

3.1 **a Which prefix matches each section of the table?**

co inter multi out pre trans

1 _____	active dependent personal related	4 _____	break come lying weigh
2 _____	determined -existent judge -war	5 _____	education exist -occur operation
3 _____	-border formation national plant	6 _____	dimensional disciplinary lateral tasking

b Replace the underlined part of sentences 1–12 using a word from 3.1a. Make any other changes that are necessary. Use the prefix in brackets in 1–6.

1 The study involved a team of <u>researchers from many different subjects</u> from across the world. (multi) *multidisciplinary researchers*

2 She argues that the use of mixed-ability pairs has a very positive <u>effect</u>. (out)

3 The success of teaching <u>girls and boys in the same classrooms</u> in state schools led to its introduction into the private sector. (co)

4 It was felt that the benefits of using a computerised language test would <u>be greater than</u> any problems associated with it. (out)

5 Commercial forest exploitation for timber is largely controlled by wealthy <u>companies that operate in several countries</u>. (trans)

6 The problems of disease and malnutrition <u>have an effect on each other</u>. (inter)

7 People tend to <u>form an opinion of</u> others from their dress and appearance before hearing what they have to say.

8 It can be difficult to differentiate between anxiety and depression because these disorders tend to <u>be found together</u>.

9 Surgeons are now able to <u>move</u> entire faces and hands <u>from one person to another</u>.

10 Rabinovitz (2010) looked at the behaviour of online American college students <u>doing more than one thing at the same time</u>.

11 Bankoff (1993) has found an association between the establishment of satisfying <u>relationships with other people</u> and academic achievement.

12 There is little incentive for voters to go to the polls if the outcome is <u>already arranged</u>.

Seminar skills B

Preparing for seminars
· Working in groups
· Understanding task instructions

Seminar skills
· Giving a feedback presentation
· Organising a group presentation
· Introducing a group presentation

Listening
· Creating an effective presentation

Follow up
· Giving a mini-presentation

Preparing for seminars

1 Working in groups

As part of a course focusing on business communication, you will watch more extracts from the seminar led by Dr Clare Lynch. In this second part of the seminar, students work in groups to prepare and then give a short presentation.

1.1 Work in pairs. Think of an experience you have had working in a group or team (not necessarily associated with study). Discuss the positive and negative aspects of working with other people.

1.2 a Often in seminars, you need to work in groups. Discuss which idea (1–6) is the least useful idea for working successfully in groups.

1 Roles and tasks should be divided evenly amongst group members.
2 Participate actively in the task that you are working on, and ensure you make a complete contribution.
3 Be sensitive to group members who may be shy or lacking in confidence. Encourage them to contribute, without being too forceful.
4 Determine whether everyone in the group has a responsible attitude, and question students who you think lack commitment to the task.
5 Let everyone in the group share their opinions and, even if you disagree with another person's opinion, acknowledge their point of view and be prepared to compromise.
6 Be flexible about the approach to a task and try to fit in with other people's way of working, even if it is different from your own.

b What other ideas can you think of for working in groups?

2 Understanding task instructions

2.1 a In the first extract, the tutor will set a task. Predict the correct order of these steps.

a She explains the nature of the texts in the handout.
b She outlines the nature of the task.
c She divides students into three teams.
d She makes suggestions about how to approach the task.
e She hands out the texts to be used in the tasks.
f She allocates different texts to different teams.

b (B.1) Watch the extract to check your predictions.

2.2 a (B.1) Read this summary of the task. There are six mistakes. Watch the extract again and correct them.

OK, so all together there are six extracts and I have to read only three extracts that are aimed at investors. Some of the extracts are good, but others are too formal. I need to understand which are the formal extracts by underlining the verbs. I should do this on my own and then present my ideas to other students in my team.

b **Complete the tutor's instructions.**

> **1** _____ is to get you to look at some more business language. And
> **2** _____ divide you into teams of three. **3** _____
> maybe that's a good team. Maybe four here and then five there.

c **Choose the best description of the purpose of the language in 2.2b.**
1 To provide key information about the activity.
2 To signal that an instruction will follow the expression or word.

 Study tip
Sometimes, instructions for more complex activities and tasks are more difficult to perceive.
Learn to listen for signals such as pauses or the use of discourse markers (e.g. 'what I'd like to
do', 'so' or 'OK') that indicate that an instruction sequence will follow. If you are not sure what
you have to do, you can always ask your tutor.

2.3 a **The tutor uses slightly different expressions to give instructions. Complete the expressions.**
   a What _____ do …
   b So _____ do …
   c Would _____ do …
   d I'd _____ do …

   b **The tutor uses the following words:** *squiggling* (v), *squiggle* (n), *squiggly* (adj). **What do you**
      think they mean? (It might help to draw to show the meaning.)

   c **What modal verb does the tutor use to indicate that she is making a suggestion about how**
      to do the activity, rather than giving specific instructions?

   d **B.2 Watch and check your answers.**

3.1 **B.3 B.4 Watch two extracts of students working together on their presentation. Which**
   description best describes what they are doing?

   Extract B.3: The students are deciding …
   a … what roles they will have in the task.
   b … how they will carry out the task.

   Extract B.4: The students are trying to work out which …
   c … examples from the texts they will include in the presentation.
   d … adjectives work best for one of the language categories.

3.2 a **B.3 Watch the first extract again.**
   a What does Natasha outline?
   b What does the tutor suggest?
   c How do Natasha and Anton signal agreement?
   d What does Anton point out?
   e What two different expressions does Natasha use to
      make suggestions to the others?

   b **B.4 Watch the second extract again.**
   a The students use a variety of terms to describe the language in the texts. Which word
      below is not mentioned?

   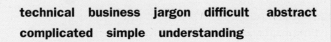
   > **technical   business   jargon   difficult   abstract**
   > **complicated   simple   understanding**

   b Which two words do they agree on?
   c Work in pairs. Can you identify a problem with the way they are carrying out the task?

67

Seminar skills

4 Giving a feedback presentation

4.1 **B.5** Watch five speakers giving feedback on the text-analysis task. **Which aspect of the texts is each speaker mostly talking about?**

a the language _____, _____, _____

b the writer's purpose _____

c the layout of the text _____

4.2 **Each speaker talks about two text extracts. Make notes on what each speaker says. Also note which of the two extracts each speaker prefers.**

	Extract 1	Extract 2	Prefers ...
Speaker 1			
Speaker 2			
Speaker 3			
Speaker 4			
Speaker 5			

5 Organising a group presentation

5.1 **Work in pairs. What is a good way to organise a group presentation? Put these steps in order.**

a Take turns to explain and outline key points from your task, and hand over clearly by introducing the next speaker.

b Summarise the keys points made in the presentation.

c Introduce the topic, and the group.

d State the outcome or result of the task.

e Provide an overview of the presentation and briefly describe the task process.

f Give examples and refer to any visual information (charts. diagrams, graphs, etc.)

5.2 a **The following examples come from the presentation extracts you have seen. Which step in 5.1 do they illustrate?**

Let's turn to something else ...

Moving to the third question ...

As to the fourth part ...

b **Match these examples to other steps from 5.1. Some examples can be used more than once.**

1 What we worked out was ... _____

2 We approached these exercises by ... _____

3 So in summary we'd say ... _____

4 We all looked at a different aspect of ... _____

5 We came to the conclusion that ... _____

6 And we'll all take turns talking about different features ... _____

7 In the final analysis it's fair to say ... _____

8 In this presentation, we'd like to talk about ... _____

6 Introducing a group presentation

6.1 a **B.6** Watch another group introducing their presentation. Complete these sentences.

    a The texts that the students are talking about in their presentation are _____.

    b The texts were written for _____.

    c The reports discuss _____ that the company has lost.

    b **B.6** Watch the extract again. There are strengths and weaknesses in the way this group begins their presentation.

    a What steps from **5.1** do they not follow?

    b Why does the tutor intervene?

    c What do the students do well?

Study tip

When you give group presentations, it helps if you think about not only what you will say but how you will present the information. Following a clear structure will make your presentation easier for your audience to understand. It also helps to use clear signposting language.

Listening

7 Creating an effective presentation

7.1 **B.7** Listen to Karthik talking about the way he tries to create an effective seminar presentation.

    a What three components does Karthik say go into a seminar presentation?

    b What does he keep in mind when preparing his presentation?

    c What suggestion does he make about using PowerPoint?

    d How does he try to overcome the challenge of a presentation?

Karthik

Follow up

8 Giving a mini-presentation

Below are two extracts from the 'Nounitis' task focused on in the first seminar.

> We have extensive experience in each of the above areas, and would not envisage any of them being problematic with regards to closing the transaction in a timely and efficient manner.

> Going forward, our strategic direction for the business remains unchanged. We have strengthened our senior-management team, recruited talented and experienced executives with extensive industry knowledge to move forward our agenda of investing to build competitive advantage with commensurate returns, whilst remaining committed to providing excellent customer service.

8.1 a **Work in small groups. Plan a mini-presentation in which you discuss the style of language used in these two extracts. Follow these steps.**

    a Analyse the extracts using the criteria for clear business language outlined by the tutor.

    b Choose specific examples of appropriate/inappropriate language.

    c Evaluate whether you think these extracts are effective overall.

    b **Plan your feedback presentation. Decide on these points.**

    a Who will introduce and give an overview of your presentation?

    b What will each person say?

    c What written examples do you need to back up your points?

    d Who will summarise your key points?

    c **Give your presentations to the class.**

5 Culture, science and society

Reading

1 Preparing to read

1.1 You recently attended a tutorial on the impact of culture on development. Work with a partner to discuss what you think these terms (used in the tutorial) mean.

cultural heritage	cultural industries	cultural tourism

1.2 a At the end of the tutorial, your tutor asked you to write an essay with this title: 'How can culture enhance the development process?' It was recommended that you begin by reading a UNESCO publication, *The power of culture for development*.

Note: The mission of the United Nations Educational, Scientific and Cultural Organization (UNESCO) is 'to contribute to the building of peace, the eradication of poverty, sustainable development and intercultural dialogue through education, the sciences, culture, communication and information' (www.unesco.org).

Check that you understand these phrases.

empowerment	marginalise	reconciliation	stewardship	social cohesion

b Work in pairs and suggest ways in which culture can help achieve development and social cohesion. Share ideas with the class.

2 Identifying the main points

2.1 a Read the extract from the UNESCO publication on page 71 and make notes on the headings below.

> ways in which culture can enhance economic development
> .
> .
> .
>
> ways in which culture can enhance social cohesion and stability
> .
> .
> .

b Work in pairs and compare notes. Make any necessary improvements to your notes.

Culture: a vehicle for economic development

Cultural industries: Culture is a powerful global economic engine generating jobs and income with a value of US$1.3 trillion in 2005. Global cultural industries account for more than 7% of global GDP. During the 1990s, the cultural industries grew at an annual rate twice that of service industries and four times that of manufacturing in OECD countries
5 (2009 UWR). However, infrastructure investments are needed in the South to enhance and support cultural industries.

Cultural tourism: Cultural tourism comprised 40% of global tourism revenue in 2007. Heritage, especially UNESCO World Heritage sites, produces revenues from visits, sale of local crafts, music and cultural products generating employment for communities.
10 International tourism represented approximately 10% of the EU's GDP in 2004 (2009 UWR).

Traditional livelihoods: Culturally embedded livelihood practices help retain local knowledge and generate employment while enabling local economic development. These may vary from building crafts to agriculture and natural resource management.

15 **Opportunities for economic growth through micro-enterprises:** Cultural goods and services often need low capital investment by building on materials and skills available within the community. The successes of micro-credit enterprises that benefit women have been especially valuable.

Cultural infrastructure and institutions: Universities, museums, cultural centres,
20 cinemas, theatres, craft centres and other such institutions are significant generators of employment and revenues. A museum such as Tate Modern is estimated to bring in revenues of over £100 million to London every year.

➤ materials and skills available in the community
 G&V 1, p80

➤ other such institutions
G&V 2, p80

Culture: a vehicle for social cohesion and stability

Mutual appreciation of diversity among cultures creates positive and constructive engagement. Dialogue promotes mutual understanding, knowledge, reconciliation
25 and peace, which are essential for social stability.

Reconstructive force of culture: Intercultural dialogue brings peace and possibilities of reconciliation in the event of conflicts. Following a disaster, culture in all its forms helps communities reconstruct their disrupted lives and restore psychological well-being.

Symbolic force of cultural heritage: Culture is a wellspring of hope, enabling a
30 deep sense of belonging.

Social cohesion through cultural tourism: Cultural heritage not only generates income, but also builds social cohesion, mobilising communities around its care and management. Cultural festivals enhance dialogue.

Empowerment of women: Intercultural dialogue, with its focus on the respect of
35 difference rather than standardisation, empowers women by acknowledging their role as both 'value carriers' and 'value creators'. Women in local cultures carry the responsibility of interpreting cultural forms, practices and their meanings, as well as transmitting them to new generations. Women are also empowered by an acknowledgment of difference and reinforcement of their identities.

40 **Safeguarding** distinctive cultural forms and the processes of their production contributes to strengthening the social capital of a community and creates a sense of stewardship and trust in public institutions.

Notes:
Tate Modern is a gallery of modern art.
'Social capital' refers to connections within
and between groups of people.

UNESCO (2010). *The Power of Culture for Development*. Paris: UNESCO

2.2 a Look again at the phrases in 1.2a. What have you learned about them from reading the extract?

b Were any of the ideas you thought of in 1.2b <u>not</u> mentioned?

2.3 Think of other examples, in a country you know, where culture has been a vehicle for economic development or social cohesion and stability. Report these to the class.

3 Understanding meaning in context

Study tip
Many words have more than one meaning. When you find a new word in a text and look it up in your dictionary, make sure you know which meaning is used in the text.

3.1 Which of the two dictionary meanings is closest to the meaning used in the text?

> **generate** (line 1)
> **1** to produce energy in a particular form
> **2** to cause something to exist

> **credit** (line 17)
> **1** a method of paying for goods or services at a later time
> **2** praise, approval, or honour

> **vehicle** (headings)
> **1** a machine used for transporting people or goods on land
> **2** a way of achieving, producing or expressing something

> **appreciation** (line 23)
> **1** when you recognise or understand that something is valuable or important
> **2** an increase in the value of something

> **restore** (line 28)
> **1** to bring back into use something that has been absent for a period of time
> **2** to return something or someone to an earlier good condition or position

4 Vocabulary building: formal and informal verbs

➤ *Writing in an academic style*

Appendix 4, p170

4.1 a Replace the informal verbs in bold in these extracts with a more formal verb beginning with the letters in brackets.

1 Following a disaster, culture ... helps communities ... **get back** psychological well-being. (res-) (line 27) *restore*
2 ... infrastructure investments are needed in the South to **make** cultural industries **better**. (enh-) (line 5)
3 Culturally embedded livelihood practices help **hold on to** local knowledge ... (ret-) (line 12)
4 The successes of micro-credit enterprises that **are good for** women have been especially valuable. (ben-) (line 17)
5 Mutual appreciation of diversity among cultures **builds up** positive and constructive engagement. (cre-) (line 23)
6 Women in local cultures carry the responsibility of interpreting cultural forms and **passing** them **on** to the new generations. (tran-) (line 36)

b Check your answers in the text on page 71.

5 Reading in detail

5.1 **a How would you say this extract aloud?**

> US$1.3 trillion (line 2)

b Points of the compass (north, south, east and west) are usually written in lower-case letters. Why does *South* have a capital letter here?

> the **South** (line 5)

c What does *that of* refer to?

> twice **that of** service industries (line 4)

d What does *such institutions* mean?

> and other **such institutions** (line 20)

➤ *Specialist terms: collocation*

G&V **4, p81**

e The text includes a number of phrases about money. Using a dictionary, can you explain the difference between the words in bold?

> 40% of global tourism **revenue** (line 7)

> low capital **investment** (line 16)

> The successes of micro-**credit** enterprises (line 17)

> Cultural heritage not only generates **income** (line 31)

6 Evaluating websites

6.1 Work in pairs. Read the extract below from a university library booklet, giving advice on using sources and referencing, and discuss the questions.

> It is important to refer only to authoritative sources of information that you have found on the internet. The internet provides documents that can be data for research and it also provides documents that you can use to develop your own argument. In both cases it is important only to use authoritative sources of information. This means checking the credentials of the author and the website.

a Which of these two meanings of 'authoritative' is the one used in the extract?
   · having the ability to control people or situations
   · containing complete and accurate information, and therefore respected
b Would you consider the UNESCO extract on page 71 to be authoritative?
c Why is a warning given about internet-based sources of information?
d Do you think online encyclopedias are authoritative sources that can be referred to in your academic writing?

6.2 a Match the criteria for judging whether websites are authoritative (a–h) to the questions (1–16).

a text type ____, ____
b author affiliation and credentials ____, ____
c target audience ____, ____
d publishing body ____, ____
e purpose __1__, ____
f writing style ____, ____
g evidence used to support claims ____, ____
h contemporary relevance ____, ____

1 ~~Is the website intended to inform, persuade, or sell something?~~
2 Does the text look more like a scholarly article or a newspaper article?
3 Is the text addressed to specialists in the subject?
4 Does the text provide up-to-date information?
5 Is appropriate information (e.g. statistics) given to provide evidence for what is said?
6 Does the author work at a university or research institution?
7 Is the text written in a balanced, objective way?
8 Is the website produced by a major publisher or organisation recognised in your subject area?
9 Are references or links given to sources of information?
10 What do the following letters on a URL (website address) tell you?

> .edu .ac .com .org

11 Does the author's name appear in the reference lists of textbooks or journal articles you have been recommended?
12 Has the text been peer-reviewed (i.e. evaluated by other academics)?
13 If there are hyperlinks in the website, do these still work?
14 Does the writer use features of informal writing?
15 Has specialised information been simplified for a general readership?
16 Does the website aim to entertain?

b In pairs, compare your answers.

Listening and speaking

7 Giving opinions in presentations

You are going to listen to part of a group presentation. In it, a student considers whether globalisation has a positive effect on culture.

7.1a ◀) 5.1 Listen to the presentation. Decide whether the student agrees or disagrees with the points presented on the slides below.

> **Globalisation and culture: positive impacts**
>
> 1 spreads foreign products and ideas to other cultures
> 2 promotes peace and understanding

> 3 increases cultural diversity
> 4 English as a global language is good for business & tourism
> 5 allows participation in a 'world culture'

b Do you think the student sounds authoritative? Why/Why not?

c (◀) 5.1 Listen again and complete the phrases the speaker uses to give their opinion.

showing agreement	showing disagreement
• I tend _____ this.	• It's _____ that ... but actually ...
• I think they _____ here.	• I have my _____ this.
_____	• _____, it seems to me that ...
_____	• It _____ that ... but in fact ...
_____	_____
	_____
	_____

d Re-order the words in these expressions for giving opinions. Then add them to the table above in the correct column.

1 That's / point / a / fair
2 They / into / don't / to / appear / take / account ...
3 This / I / right / is / think
4 I'm / at / about / this / sure / not / all
5 I'd / this / question / to / like
6 This / be / me / to / to / valid / seems / entirely

7.2 a (◀) 5.2 Listen to these examples.

1 It's certainly the case that globalisation allows people in one country to know more about people in other countries and their ways of life, **but ACtually ↘↗** this doesn't necessarily lead to more peaceful relationships.

2 It might be true that this is good for business and for tourism, but **in FACT ↘↗** it can lead to the loss of local languages.

When we disagree, we often begin by saying that something is partly true before going on to say why it is wrong. The effect is to be less confrontational and therefore more polite. Disagreeing in this way occurs particularly in formal contexts such as academic communication. The phrase that indicates disagreement is typically said with a fall–rising intonation.

b Add an ending to these sentences and then read them aloud to your partner. Make sure you use a fall–rising tone on the phrase in bold.

1 It's often assumed that private education is better than state-funded education, **but PERsonally ↘↗** ... *I think state–funded education has many more advantages for society.*

2 People often say they're happy to pay for better public services, **but in reALity ↘↗** ...

3 Politicians often say that their policies are 'green', **but in PRACtice ↘↗** ...

4 It's sometimes claimed that texting has a bad effect on writing standards, **but in actual FACT ↘↗** ...

5 Some people have said that the dangers of climate change are overstated, **but to MY mind ↘↗** ...

8 Presentation practice

8.1 a **Look at the recording script of the presentation in 7.1a. Make notes on the negative impacts of globalisation on culture.**

b **Prepare a slide which lists these negative impacts.**

c **Give a brief presentation reporting and evaluating the points on your slide. Try to use language from 7.1c and intonation patterns from 7.2a when you disagree.**

Writing

9 Using primary and secondary sources

Primary sources *are original materials (e.g. photographs, maps, historical documents, statistical information, other research data) that have not been interpreted or evaluated by another writer.*
Secondary sources *are texts (e.g. the discussion section of a research article), in which interpretations or evaluations of original materials are given.*

9.1 **Look at six sources related to the way in which some societies view scientists and their work. Which three are primary sources?**

Fig. 4 Public assessment of the benefits and harms of scientific research, 1981–1999

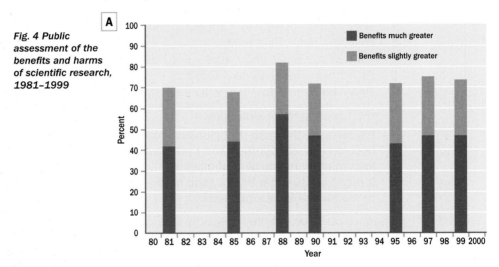

Miller, J. D. (2004). Public understanding of, and attitudes toward, scientific research: what we know and what we need to know. *Public Understanding of Science*, 13, 273–294.

B *'Attitudes toward scientists and engineers'*
In response to the question:
Do you think that a career in science and engineering is a good choice?
(*n*=1,839 British adults)

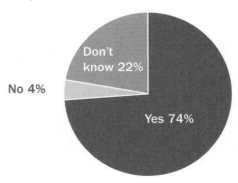

Office of Science and Technology and the Wellcome Trust (2000). *Science and the public: A review of science and communication and public attitudes to science in Britain.* London: Office of Science and Technology/The Wellcome Trust.

C

> A recent survey of public attitudes towards science in Britain uncovered:
>
> > a perception that scientists and engineers are 'not quite like us', that perhaps they operate according to a different moral code, being driven by the desire to discover and create while not necessarily pausing to think about the consequences. (Office of Science and Technology and the Wellcome Trust, 2000)
>
> Overall, then, it might be concluded that: 'the stereotypical image of a scientist is alive and well' (National Science Foundation, 2002). Scientists are seen not to be like ordinary people, and part of this image is unattractive to the public. Although many scientific developments are welcomed, some of their work has little value, and scientists may be unaware of the consequences of their research. Potentially, therefore, they are threatening and dangerous to society.

Hewings, M. (2010). 'Boffins create "Supermouse"': the role of the popular press in creating the public image of scientists and their work. In M.L. Gea Valor, et al. (eds) *Linguistic and Translation Studies in Scientific Communication*, pp. 15-38. Oxford: Peter Lang.

D

> These six Hollywood comedies from 1961 to 1965 project multiple images of the American scientist as an intellectual who is precariously stationed on the margins of acceptable cultural parameters, often socially inadequate and not practically intelligent. The scientists possess varying degrees of control over natural phenomena or even other people, but all are depicted as awkward.

Terzian, S. G. & Grunke, A. L. (2007). Scrambled eggheads: ambivalent representations of scientists in six Hollywood film comedies from 1961 to 1965. *Public Understanding of Science*, 16, 407–419.

E

William Herschel (1738–1822) and Caroline Herschel (1750–1848), astronomers

Pierre Curie (1859–1906) and Marie Curie (1867–1934), physicists

F

> ... in portraying women scientists, Elena (1997) observed that 'it seems that popular misconceptions refuse to yield to more balanced or realistic visions' (p. 276). This was his conclusion after a detailed analysis of the portrayal in film of Madame Curie, one of the 'greatest female superstars of science'. He observed that even with such an exceptional talent: 'Madame Curie's first and best-known film biography ... encapsulates what has become the standard characterisation of women scientists: a research assistant who is permanently subordinate to a male scientist' (p. 276).

Schibeci, R. & Lee, L. (2003). Portrayals of science and scientist, and 'science for citizenship'. *Research in Science & Technological Education*, 21, 177–192.

➤ *best-known*
G&V **3, p81**

🎓 Focus on your subject
In your research, will you work mainly with primary or secondary sources?

77

Grammar and vocabulary

Grammar and vocabulary
· Complex noun phrases 1
· Classifying nouns
· Compound adjectives
· Specialist terms: collocation
· Language-announcing goals in research paper introductions

1 Complex noun phrases 1

In a complex noun phrase, a series of phrases and clauses are used to add information about an initial main noun. These allow a lot of information to be expressed concisely, and so are common in academic writing.

material and skills available within the community
(noun + and + noun + adjective + prepositional phrase)

the successes of micro-credit enterprises that benefit women
(noun + prepositional phrase + relative (that) clause)

a statue discovered in Italy in 1553
(noun + reduced relative clause + prepositional phrase)

1.1 Complete the sentences with a complex noun phrase, using the information in brackets.

1   Michael Faraday, *the 19th-century British scientist who discovered electromagnetism*, also discovered benzene and optical glass.
    (Michael Faraday lived in the 19th century. He was a scientist. He was British. He discovered electromagnetism.)

2   The graves _____
    may be those of foreigners from Anatolia.
    (The graves were found in Knossos. Knossos is in Crete. The graves date to around 1600 BC.)

3   The political revolution _____
    _____ constituted an even more dramatic break with political and social traditions.
    (The political revolution was in France. It began soon after the American Declaration of Independence. The revolution in France was in 1789.)

4   Titanium, _____
    has the highest strength-to-weight ratio of any metal.
    (Titanium was first discovered in England. It was discovered by William Gregor. It was named after the Titans. The Titans are from Greek mythology.)

5   The final death toll _____
    has been estimated to be around 300,000 people.
    (People were killed by the tsunami. The tsunami was in 2004. It was caused by an undersea earthquake. The earthquake was in the Indian Ocean. It measured 9.3 on the Richter Scale.)

1.2 Search the internet to find information about three of the following and write one sentence about each. Include at least one complex noun phrase in each sentence.
· Caroline Herschel
· Luiz Inácio Lula da Silva
· Yuri Gagarin
· arsenic
· cicada
· giant redwood

2 Classifying nouns

At the end of an incomplete list, we often use ... and other (such) ... followed by a classifying noun summarising what kind of items are listed.

Universities, museums, cultural centres, cinemas, theatres, craft centres, and other such **institutions**.

2.1 Complete the sentences with one of these nouns. Use a dictionary to help you.

~~resources~~   characteristics   documents   goods
factors   measures   media   stakeholders

1   The Department of Education was responsible for providing funding for staffing, books, computers, and other *resources*.

2   Government agencies often face a variety of interests whose competing demands continually force policy-makers and managers to balance quality, cost, customer satisfaction, and other _____.

3   The reorganisation of the health service was a collaborative effort between government, doctors, patients, and other _____.

4   The inhabitants of the country were divided by ethnicity, religion, language, wealth and other _____.

5   Factories were opened producing soap, cement, and other _____.

6   Attempts were made to discourage car use by introducing road tolls, higher petrol costs, and other _____.

7   In their campaigns, candidates used TV, radio, newspapers, and other _____.

8   In my investigation of the company, I analysed a sample of letters, reports, memos, and other _____.

3 Compound adjectives

Compound adjectives are often made up of two parts, connected by a hyphen.
Madame Curie's first and **best-known** film biography …

3.1 Match sentence beginnings 1–8 and endings a–h, adding the second part of the compound adjective.

~~reaching~~	called	day	effective
related	risk	standing	term

1 The changes in timber-trading laws had far-
  reaching + c

2 Attention span is important in explaining age-…
  _____

3 Transplantation remains the most cost-…
  _____

4 Chinese students are frequently reported as following the long-… _____

5 The language corpus is large and reflects present-… _____

6 Anthropologists have shown that even so-…
  _____

7 Government spending is a major determinant of short-… _____

8 In our sample of growing businesses, 60% pursued the high-… _____

a … tradition of treating teachers with respect.
b … primitive societies are sophisticated.
c … ~~consequences for Sarawak's forests~~.
d … fluctuations in economic growth.
e … treatment for severe kidney disease.
f … English usage.
g … strategy of diversification.
h … differences in working memory.

4 Specialist terms: collocation

Study tip
As you read texts from your subject, observe and note important words related to particular topics. If some of these words have a similar meaning, check them in a dictionary and note also the other words they commonly combine with.

4.1 The text on page 71 includes words connected with money. Choose the best word for each pair.

investment/income
1 a … now have a greater disposable _____ …
  b … can increase their monthly _____ …

revenue/credit
2 a … the department in charge of _____ collection …
  b … led to a fall in oil _____ …

investment/revenue
3 a … a substantial _____ in agriculture over the period …
  b … has not been successful in attracting _____ …

income/credit
4 a … increased the demand for consumer _____ …
  b … a consequence of the _____ crunch …

5 Language-announcing goals in research paper introductions

5.1 Look at these extracts from research paper introductions. Put the words in order to make expressions announcing the research paper goals.

1 The difference in gesture production may be one source of miscommunication between the two cultures. _____ (study / The / present / purpose / the / of) was to examine cultural influence on gesture production by comparing the amount of gestures produced during conversation in Japanese and English by native Japanese persons living in the United States.

2 To our knowledge, a comprehensive review of the literature specifically studying determinants of children's fruit and vegetable intake has not previously been undertaken. _____ (objective/ present / The / the / of / paper) is to provide a comprehensive review of potential determinants of fruit and vegetable intake in children and adolescents.

3 Thus, these laws are meant to prohibit health insurers from predicting future health problems that do not currently exist, usually on the basis of genetic test information alone, but sometimes also on the basis of family history. _____ (assess / designed / This / is / study / to) how well these laws have accomplished this goal, and whether they have caused any harm.

4 Most of these studies, however, have focused on poverty, not on differences in economic resources across the income distribution, and few have examined the unique contributions of income during early childhood and income during middle childhood. _____ (The / is / investigation / of / this / aim) to improve our understanding of how income in early childhood and middle childhood influences development in middle childhood.

🎓 **Focus on your subject**
Search the internet or use your library to find research papers in your own subject. Scan the introductions and note down other expressions which announce goals. Report these to the rest of the class.

6 Ways of studying in higher education

Reading

1 Reading efficiently

1.1 **A tutorial group has been asked to provide ideas for a webpage with the title 'How to read efficiently in higher education', aimed at students about to begin a university course. Evaluate their ideas (1–12). Cross out three which you think are not good pieces of advice.**

1 Choose a reading speed appropriate to your reading purpose.
2 Try to understand the writer's point of view.
3 Try to understand every word.
4 Have a purpose for reading.
5 Work out how the text is organised, as well as the main purpose of each section.
6 Use a dictionary whenever you find an unknown word.
7 Try to be a critical reader.
8 Make predictions as you go along.
9 Always write notes on the text in your own language.
10 Put texts to read in order of priority from most to least important/urgent.
11 Read important texts at least twice.
12 Guess the meaning of unknown words before looking in a dictionary.

1.2 **Match the suggestions (a–r) on putting advice into practice to the nine pieces of good advice in 1.1. Work individually and then compare answers in pairs.**

a Before reading the text in detail, skim read the text to get an idea of what it is about and how it is organised.
b Highlight or underline evaluative language used by the writer.
c Note down questions that the writer doesn't answer.
d Look at the context around unknown words to try to understand them.
e Think about what information you want to get from the text.
f Consider whether the writer provides evidence to support claims.
g Decide which parts of a text you should read first, and whether you need to read the whole text.
h Quickly skim read parts containing information you already know.
i Read the title and subheadings to get an overall idea of organisation.
j Find statements where the writer gives their position on a topic.
k Try to distinguish between main points and supporting material in each section.
l Consider how the text will help with your current task (e.g. writing an essay).
m Read the text for a second time in more detail.
n Put items on your list of recommended reading in order of importance.
o At the end of each paragraph, think about what might be said in the next.
p When the writer poses a question, consider possible answers before reading on.
q Read important parts slowly and in detail.
r Make a note of words you don't know and check them later.

1.3 **a Work in pairs. Discuss how often you follow the good pieces of advice in 1.1.**

b Which of the suggestions in 1.2 will you follow to help you become a better academic reader? Share your ideas with the class.

2 **Practice in reading efficiently**

As part of a Research Skills module, you have been asked to conduct a small-scale research project on the relationship between how students in your year group spend their time and the marks they get in their course assignments. As a starting point, your tutor has asked you to read an important research paper.

2.1 a **Work in pairs. Read the title below of the paper. Can you work out the general content from the title?**

> # Where does the time go?
> ## A diary approach to Business and Marketing students' time use

b **What information would you hope to find in the paper to help you with your research project?**

2.2 a **Before you read the literature review from the paper, make sure you understand the following words and phrases.**

freshman	grade point average (GPA)	determinant	median
rule of thumb	proverbial	plausible	beg the question

b **How will you approach the text when you read it for the first time? (Think about the advice given in 1.2.)**

c **Now read the text.**

1 How much time is a college student expected to devote to study outside of class for each credit hour he or she is taking? Although the answer can vary from course to course, student to student, and institute to institute, the rule of thumb is two to three hours per credit hour per week (Young 2002). This proverbial standard, however, may have fallen away as recent research has consistently shown that students spend much less time studying. In fall 1987, the Higher Education Research Institute at University of California, Los Angeles' Graduate School of Education and Information Studies found that 47% of freshmen spent six or more hours per week outside of class on academic work during their senior year in high school. In 2003, this had dropped to 34% (Higher Education Research Institute, 2003). In an investigation of 239 students taking math courses, Cerrito and Levi (1999) found that the median study time for students enrolled in intermediate algebra and college algebra courses was 49 minutes or less and for precalculus, 80 minutes. Clearly, these statistics indicate that the time spent studying by most students is dramatically below the time-honored rule of thumb. [5] [10]

➤ *student behavior*
G&V 2, p92

➤ *Available research focused on this issue*
G&V 1, p92

2 Spending less time studying begs the question, then, of what difference this change in student behavior makes in terms of educational outcomes. Available research focused on this issue has provided mixed results. Pascarella and Terenzini (1991) found the study habits of college freshmen to relate significantly to their first-year cumulative grade point average (GPA)[2] and Lahmers and Zulauf (2000) found that a one-letter-grade increase in quarter GPA was associated with a 40-hour increase in weekly study time. More recently, Young, Klemz, and Murphy (2003) showed that effort and time spent studying influenced learning performance. Mouw and Khanna (1993), however, did not find study habits to significantly improve the explanatory power of first-year cumulative GPA. Similarly, Schmidt (1983) did not find any relationship between time spent studying outside of class and student learning. Most recently, Ackerman and Gross (2003) found that students with less free time to study had a significantly higher GPA than those with more. [15] [20]

3 There is mounting evidence that student study time is decreasing, and research also indicates that a growing number of students work, and the number of hours these students work each week is increasing (Curtis & Lucus 2001). Thirty-nine percent of college freshmen work 16 or more hours per week, an increase of 4% since 1993 (Gose 1998). In terms of the relationship between time spent working and academic performance, once again, available empirical evidence has been mixed. Working more hours per week has been positively related to GPA (Strauss & Volkwein 2002), and on-campus work relevant to students' interests and course also have been associated with higher academic performance (Wilkie & Jones 1994). Bennett (2003) found no relationship [25] [30]

6   Reading in detail

6.1   a   **The writers of the text are from the United States, and they use a number of words and spellings that would be different in British English. Find examples in these extracts and suggest alternatives in British English.**

> In fall 1987, the Higher Education Research Institute at University of California... (line 5)

> ... 47% of freshmen spent six or more hours per week outside of class on academic work during their senior year in high school. (line 7)

> ... what difference this change in student behavior makes in terms of educational outcomes. (line 14)

b   **The word 'moderate' is pronounced differently as a verb and adjective. How would it be pronounced in the extract below? How would it be pronounced as the other part of speech?**

> For example, Barling, Kelloway, and Cheung (1996) found motivation to **moderate** the relationship ... (line 37)

c   **Suggest one-word adverbs that could be used with a similar meaning instead of 'for the most part'.**

> Zuriff (2003) claims that time use ... has been **for the most part** ignored in **empirical investigations**. (line 46)

d   **What are 'empirical' investigations in the extract above?**

> ⊙ *Research shows that in addition to* empirical, *other adjectives commonly used to describe investigations are:*
> · *experimental*
> · *theoretical*
> · *preliminary*
> · *extensive*
> *What are the features of each type of investigation?*

e   **What opinion do the writers express when they start a sentence with 'Clearly, ...'?**

> **Clearly**, there is a need for research that investigates student time use ... (line 53)

> ⊙ *Look at this extract from the article.*
> *... there is a need for **research that investigates** student time use ... (line 53)*
> *Research shows that in addition to investigates, other verbs commonly used to introduce what the research does after the phrase* research that .... *are:*
> 1   ex____nes   2   ad____sses
> 3   f____ses on   4   s____ks to
> 5   co____ers   6   a____s to
> *Can you fill in the gaps?*

Listening and speaking

7 Presenting and explaining results in charts

Figures are often presented in the form of a chart rather than in a table to make them easier for the audience to understand, and to make them more visually appealing.

7.1 a Look at these results (1–3) of a group's research project on how course colleagues spend their time. Decide which chart type from the box would be best to use for the results.

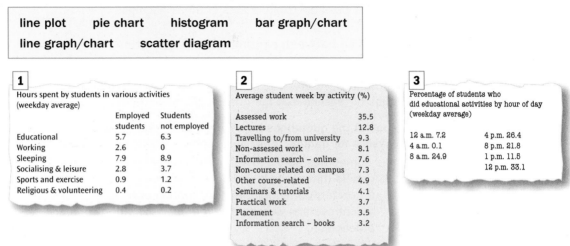

> line plot   pie chart   histogram   bar graph/chart
> line graph/chart   scatter diagram

1

Hours spent by students in various activities (weekday average)

	Employed students	Students not employed
Educational	5.7	6.3
Working	2.6	0
Sleeping	7.9	8.9
Socialising & leisure	2.8	3.7
Sports and exercise	0.9	1.2
Religious & volunteering	0.4	0.2

2

Average student week by activity (%)

Assessed work	35.5
Lectures	12.8
Travelling to/from university	9.3
Non-assessed work	8.1
Information search – online	7.6
Non-course related on campus	7.3
Other course-related	4.9
Seminars & tutorials	4.1
Practical work	3.7
Placement	3.5
Information search – books	3.2

3

Percentage of students who did educational activities by hour of day (weekday average)

12 a.m. 7.2	4 p.m. 26.4
4 a.m. 0.1	8 p.m. 21.8
8 a.m. 24.9	1 p.m. 11.5
	12 p.m. 33.1

b Choose one of the data sets from 7.1a and prepare a chart to be used in a presentation.

7.2 a ◀) 6.1 Listen to a student presenting results from the same survey, using this slide. Which three segments of the chart does she talk about in detail?

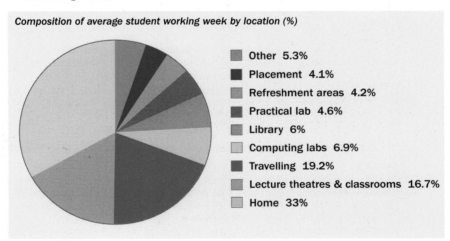

Composition of average student working week by location (%)

- Other 5.3%
- Placement 4.1%
- Refreshment areas 4.2%
- Practical lab 4.6%
- Library 6%
- Computing labs 6.9%
- Travelling 19.2%
- Lecture theatres & classrooms 16.7%
- Home 33%

b ◀) 6.1 Here are some expressions the speaker uses to present explanations of her findings. Put them in the order she mentions them. Listen again to check.

a Maybe this is because … ____
b One reason for this could be that … ____
c It must be, then, that … ____
d A possible explanation for this is that … _1_
e … we felt that a more likely explanation is that … ____
f … it may be that … ____

c Work in pairs and answer the questions.

1 Which expression in 7.2b presents an explanation that the speaker is certain of?
2 Which indicates that one explanation is better than another?
3 What do you notice about the language in the remaining expressions?

8 Presentation practice

8.1 Work in groups of three. Each of you should take one of the sets of data in 7.1a and present it in the following stages. Try to use expressions from 7.2b.

- Explain what your slide shows.
- Highlight two or three particularly interesting or surprising findings.
- Offer possible explanations of these findings.

Writing

9 Choosing between paraphrase and quotation

9.1 At the end of a student's essay, the tutor wrote this comment: 'Good essay, but too many quotations. I'd prefer to see you paraphrase rather than quote because …'. Work in pairs and think of reasons that the tutor might have given.

9.2 Look at the quotations in these extracts from Sociology textbooks. For each decide which of the reasons for quoting (1–4) best explains why the author quotes rather than paraphrases.

It is sometimes better to quote than paraphrase, for example when you are reporting:
1 details that would be hard to paraphrase;
2 a new term or short, clear description used by the original author;
3 a controversial view held by the original author, in order to distance it from your own;
4 a definition.

Extract 1

> Although sociology was born of the modern world – industrialisation, capitalism, the growth of big cities, the rise of democracies, the decline of traditional communities, etc. – it is now finding itself in a world where the features of modernity are accelerating: modernity is speeding up and going faster. It is what Giddens has called 'a runaway world' (Giddens, 1999).

Extract 2

> For some thinkers, these changes have been so extreme as to question the very foundation of sociology. Two French thinkers, for example, have more or less proclaimed the death of sociology and suggested we have moved into a post-modern world. Thus Baudrillard writes that:
>
> > The extreme limit of … possibilities has been reached. It has destroyed itself. It has deconstructed its entire universe. So all that are left are pieces. All that remains to be done is play with the pieces. Playing with the pieces – that is post-modern. (Baudrillard, 1984: 24)
>
> This is an extreme position which will not be adopted in this book.

Extract 3

> The anthropologist Oscar Lewis's particular method focused on a few specific families in Mexico, and the analysis of a 'day' in each of their lives. Of course, his actual familiarity with each family was in no way limited to a day. He 'spent hundreds of hours with them in their homes, ate with them, joined in their fiestas and dances, listened to their troubles, and discussed with them the history of their lives' (Lewis, 1959: 5).

Macionis, J. J .& Plummer, K. (2005). *Sociology: a global introduction* (3rd edn). Harlow: Pearson. (Extracts 1–3)

Extract 4

> According to Robertson (1992, p. 8), globalisation is 'a compression of the whole world, and the intensification of consciousness of the world as a whole … rendering the world as a whole a single place'.

Grieg, A. (2003). Globalisation and social movement. In S. Jureidini & M. Poole (eds) *Sociology: Australian connections* (3rd edn). Crows Nest, NSW: Allen and Unwin.

🎓 **Focus on your subject**

 6.2 Listen to Max (studying History), Karthik (Engineering) and Fotis (Law) talking about the use of quotation and paraphrase in their subject. Who: uses very little quotation; mainly paraphrases; uses both quotation and paraphrase?

Now consider your own subject. Are quotations never, rarely, sometimes or often used? Look at journals in your subject if you are not sure.

10 Quotation conventions

10.1 Complete these pieces of advice (1–8) on using quotation with a word from the box or the number of one of the extracts in 9.2. Work individually and then compare answers in pairs.

> ~~exactly~~   colon   ellipsis   family   indent
> inverted   integrated   reference   source   support

1 When you quote, make sure that you use _exactly_ the same words as in the _____ text.
2 Quotations should _____ what you have said. For example, in extract ___, the quotation illustrates how Lewis's familiarity was not 'limited to a day'.
3 For short quotations, it is usual to continue on the same line and put the quotation in _____ commas; for example, extracts ___, ___ and ___.
4 For longer quotations, start a new line and _____ the quotation; don't use inverted commas (for example, extract ___).
5 A _____ (:) often precedes longer quotations (for example, extract ___).
6 Use an _____ […] to show that you have left a word or more out of the source text (for example, extract ___).
7 Give a _____ for the quotation: _____ name, date, and (usually) page number.
8 The quotation must be _____ grammatically into the text; the grammar of the quotation should match the grammar of what comes before; for example, in extract 4.

> 🎓 Focus on your subject
>
> You may see variations from the layout and punctuation conventions given here. It is important to discover and use the usual conventions in your subject. You may be told about these on your course. If not, follow the conventions used in a leading journal in your subject.

11 Writing up research: the literature review

There are many ways of organising the literature review in your thesis, depending on your subject area (or discipline), the topic of your thesis, the particular purposes of the literature review, the preferences of your supervisor, and so on. What is most important is that you should try to find a logical organisation both for the literature review overall, and within each section.

11.1 Work in pairs. Look at these extracts from the contents pages of theses (1–4). Identify the features (a–d) in each of the thesis outlines.

a   a broad and then a narrower perspective on the topic of the thesis
b   a historical perspective
c   contrasting positions of the topic of the thesis
d   different aspects of the same topic

1

Evaluating the use of L1 in the English-language classroom
by Richard Miles
Chapter 2
Literature Review
2.1 A historical view of the issue
2.2 Support for the Monolingual Approach
2.3 Support for the Bilingual Approach
2.4 The Japanese learner

2

Barriers to the academic achievement of first-year African students at the university of Kwazulu-Natal
by Masello Yvonne Matlala
Chapter Two
Literature review
2.1 Introduction
2.2 International perspectives
2.3 National perspective

3

Inquiry in the classroom:
peer-observation as a form of job-embedded
professional learning
by Alison Strucchelli
Chapter 2
Literature review
1 Learning from the past: a look at traditional forms of professional development
2 Learning for the future: a look at new models of professional development
3 Previous empirical research on peer-observation
4 Chapter summary

4

Project management in cross-border teams: how do United States and India-based managers cope with cultural influences on project management?
by Akshina Ramesh Samtani
Chapter 2
Literature Review
2.1 Culture defined
2.2 Culture and the organisation
2.3 Culture in the global market
2.4 Cultural diversity in cross-border project-management teams
2.5 Why is this study different?

🎓 **Focus on your subject**

On the internet, find a number of theses from your subject area which have literature review chapters. To do this, enter 'Chapter 2 Literature Review' in a search engine.
1 How easy is it to find theses with a chapter called 'Literature review'?
2 How long is each literature review?
3 What might your answers to 1 and 2 tell you about theses in your subject?
4 Use section headings in the literature review (which you might be able to find in the table of contents) to discover how the literature review is organised in each thesis.
5 Look at the opening sentence of literature review chapters. How many of these state the purpose of the chapter? Note down what purposes are mentioned and any language for introducing purposes that may be useful to you.

11.2 a You are going to read a section of a literature review from a journal article about podcasting in higher education and its influence on lectures. First, read the opening sentences of each of the four paragraphs in the section. What order do you think they come in?

a Yet, despite these benefits there are drawbacks to the lecture as a form of teaching.

b According to Edwards, Smith and Webb (2001), lecturing is the main teaching method used in universities.

c Despite the apparent immunity of the lecture to changes over the decades, the development of digital technologies is opening up many possibilities.

d There are several educational advantages to lectures, particularly if they are seen as more than a method of information delivery.

McGarr, O. (2009). A review of podcasting in higher education: Its influence on the traditional lecture. *Australasian Journal of Educational Technology*, 25, 309–321.

b Work in pairs. Discuss what the order of the sentences tells you about how the writer has chosen to organise this part of the literature review.

11.3 Complete the first paragraph of the literature review with sentences a–e below.

Examining the traditional lecture

1__ They note that its dominance has influenced the very architecture of the teaching spaces used, with fixed-point podiums and tiered seating for large numbers of students. The origins of the lecture can be traced back over two millennia. **2__** However, today the lecture remains the most common form of communication in universities: **3__**. **4__** The question has even more relevance today in a digitally rich society with instant access to information in many forms. Yet despite the emergence of various technologies over the centuries, there are numerous reasons why the lecture has remained. **5__**

a Kozma, Belle and Williams (1978) note that its evolution as the main instructional system in European universities emerged in medieval times as the most effective method of transferring information stored in expensive and rare books to large groups of students.

b Kozma et al. (1978) argue that from an economic point of view the lecture is relatively inexpensive; they also note that it has survived the competition of technologies such as television and film because of the relatively low preparation time in comparison to other media.

   c According to Edwards, Smith and Webb (2001), lecturing is the main teaching method used in universities.

   d Forty years ago, Fitzgerald (1968) asked, 'Is there any point in the lecture as a form of university teaching? After all, if information is what the students want, then surely a well stocked library is the answer.' (p. 11)

   e … the established routines that treat lectures as the main medium for communication and education are still strong. Lectures as educational episodes are still likely to represent among the most robust methodologies used by institutions to educate their students. (Moore, Armstrong & Pearson, 2008, p. 18)

11.4 The next section of the review reports literature on podcasting in higher education.

   a **What are the advantages and disadvantages of lecture podcasts, compared with live lectures?**

   b **The table includes notes on relevant literature. Suggest topic areas in which the main findings can be grouped (e.g. how podcasts are listened to). Then decide the best order for these topic areas. Compare your ideas in pairs.**

author(s)	date	research subjects and podcasts used	main findings
Bongey, Cizadlo & Kalnbach	2006	Biology students at college in US; podcasts of recorded lectures	• 70% of students said they had used podcasts • 94% said they preferred actual lecture to the podcast
Copley	2007	undergrad. & postgrad. science students at UK universities; podcasts as supplementary material	• high level of enthusiasm for podcasts (93% wanted greater use of them) • only 13% used podcasts while doing other things
Evans	2008	undergrad. business & management students in UK universities; podcasts as revision material	• 80% listened to podcasts on computer (rather than on mobile device) • students reported podcasts useful for revision
Huntsberber & Stavitsky	2007	students on introductory journalism course at US university; podcasts as revision material	• students had positive view of podcasts but preferred actual lecture to podcast • preference for notes for revision rather than podcasts • notes that there is little research so far on the use of podcasts in higher education
Lazzari	2008	students at Italian university; course in multimedia communication; podcasts as revision material; some podcasts made by students themselves	• 70% of students said they had used podcasts • 94% said they preferred actual lecture to the podcast
Lee & Chan	2007	distance-learning students at Australian university; podcasts as supplementary material	• 89% listened to podcasts multiple times • most preferred to listen to podcasts on computer at home rather than multitasking (e.g. while travelling)

12 Writing practice

12.1 Use the notes to write a literature review for this section of the paper. For each of the topics you identified in 11.4b, introduce the topic, report relevant findings and the context in which they were produced (where appropriate), as well as the sources of your information.

12.2 Look back at the notes you made in 2.4 and write these up as a short literature review in no more than 500 words. Note that you might decide to present the material in a different order from that in the original text.

Grammar and vocabulary

Grammar and vocabulary
- Complex noun phrases 2
- Producing compound nouns
- *as*-clauses: referring to the work of others
- *of which*: expressing ideas efficiently

1 Complex noun phrases 2

1.1 Rewrite the underlined sections as noun phrases, to express the information more efficiently. The main noun in the phrase is given in brackets.

1 <u>Research that is available which has focused on this issue</u> has provided mixed results. (research)
   Available research focused on this issue

2 Their results showed <u>that the relationship between the hours that they studied and the grades that they earned was virtually non-existent</u>. (relationship)

   _____

   _____

3 There is surprising agreement between faculty members and students on <u>how much work is required for students to be successful in courses at university</u>. (amount)

   _____

   _____

4 Young, Klemz and Murphy (2003) found that such simulations actually led <u>to students reporting that they increased the number of hours that they were studying for a class</u>. (increase)

   _____

   _____

5 A study by O'Toole, Spinelli and Wetzel (2000) attempted to determine <u>how congruent the attitudes were by professors who work in business schools and undergraduates who work in business schools about dimensions of learning that are important</u>. (congruency)

   _____

   _____

2 Producing compound nouns

Many compound nouns common in academic writing are formed from two nouns. For example:
student behaviour, learning performance

2.1 Complete the sentences with a compound formed from a noun in A and a noun in B.

A			
community	family	government	information
research	state	time	work

B		
assistants	background	care
interval	intervention	policy
satisfaction	storage	

1 The data was collected by trained _____ _____ and medical personnel.

2 Farmers protested in an attempt to influence _____ _____ on agriculture

3 Contrary to common belief, _____ _____ for the elderly is far more costly than institutional care.

4 Measurement of the _____ _____ between stressed syllables in English speech has not shown the expected regularity.

5 In the 1960s, most researchers studying the learning process accepted that _____ _____ in the brain involved two stages.

6 The most important job factors for _____ _____ were identified as full use of knowledge and skills, and contacts with colleagues.

7 Their research found that people saw themselves as 'working class' because of their _____ _____ rather than their own social circumstances.

8 The economic recession led to demands for much greater _____ _____ in industry.

> **🎓 Focus on your subject**
> The nouns in box A very commonly form the first part of compound nouns in academic writing. Can you find common compound nouns in your subject that begin with some of these words?

3 *as*-clauses: referring to the work of others

It is common in academic writing to refer to the work of others using a reporting verb in an as-clause. These structures with as-clauses are generally used to show agreement with what is being reported.

3.1 a Study these examples from published academic writing and then correct the mistakes in sentences 1 and 2 from students' essays.

As [was] noted by Stinebrickner and Stinebrickner (2004): Despite an increased awareness ...	*as* + (*was*) + past participle + *by* + author(s) (date)
As Haire (2001) has pointed out, there is still surprisingly little research on the effects of colour on human behaviour.	*as* + author(s) (date) + reporting verb

1 As it was found by Levinger (1979), spouses tend to create a more positive image of their marriage than is actually the case.

2 As Willard (2004: 7) has stated that 'only one long vowel is allowed per word'.

b **What is the difference in meaning between these sentences?**

1 As Cameron (2010) has remarked, the misplacement of word stress can cause serious communication difficulties.

2 Cameron (2010) has remarked that the misplacement of word stress can cause serious communication difficulties.

3.2 **Combine two sentences into one using structures with *as* from 3.1a.**

1 The four classic parenting styles are authoritative, authoritarian, permissive, and neglectful. These styles were proposed by Baumrind in 1966.

_____

_____

2 Marker bands were revealed using silver staining. This method was described by Panaud in 1996.

_____

_____

3 Many authors have investigated the idea that better pieces of art are better investments. This idea was first put forward by Pesando (1993).

_____

_____

4 To solve the problems of a particular company, there is a need for specific knowledge of that company. Nelson and Winter have argued this (1982).

_____

_____

5 It is not appropriate to apply findings from research into first-language acquisition to second-language learning. Dornev (1990) has noted this, and others have noted it, too.

_____

_____

4 *of which*: expressing ideas efficiently

Two sentences can sometimes be expressed more efficiently in one, using of which.

Such "learning postponement" is addressed in a study by Dietz, Hofer and Fries (2007). The aim of this study is to somehow relate procrastination to a lack of "daily routines" associated with academic activities.

Such "learning postponement" is addressed in a study by Dietz, Hofer and Fries (2007), **the aim of which** is to somehow relate procrastination to a lack of "daily routines" associated with academic activities.

4.1 **Rewrite two sentences more efficiently as one using *of which* and a word from the box.**

| ~~majority~~ | details | few | outcome |
| significance | understanding | value |

1 In the survey, 12.8% of families were classified as single-parent families. Most of these families were headed by women.
In the survey, 12.8% of families were classified as single-parent families, the majority of which were headed by women.

2 In this section, I will briefly outline the findings from the survey. More information about these findings can be found in the Appendix.

_____

_____

3 Universities provide a service: higher education. It is impossible to quantify what higher education is worth.

_____

_____

4 Only 34% of the sample was female. I will explain why this is important below.

_____

_____

5 The government set up an inquiry into falling educational standards. This inquiry resulted in a new secondary school curriculum.

_____

_____

6 His first paintings date from the early 1850s. Not many of them survive today.

_____

_____

7 The attitudes and policies of employers have only recently received attention. We need to understand these attitudes and policies thoroughly because they are crucial in explaining the experiences of older workers.

_____

_____

Lecture skills C

Preparing for lectures
· Thinking about the content of lectures
· Understanding introductions

Listening
· Understanding detailed points; making notes
· Understanding the main point

Language focus
· Recognising quotes
· Recognising examples that support key points

Follow up
· Responding to questions posed in a lecture
· Lecture structure

Preparing for lectures

As part of a course focusing on sociolinguistics, you will hear a lecture on different varieties of English given by David Crystal, Honorary Professor of Linguistics at the University of Wales, Bangor.

David Crystal

1 Thinking about the content of lectures

1.1 **As preparation for a lecture, you have been asked to think about different varieties of English. Make notes on questions a–d. Then work in small groups and discuss your ideas.**

  a   What different dialects and accents are there in your first language?
  b   What do these variations indicate about the speaker (where they come from, their social status, age, etc.)?
  c   Do some dialects or accents have negative/positive associations?
  d   Is there a variety of your language that is considered 'standard'?

2 Understanding introductions

2.1 **Watch Professor Crystal's introduction and answer the questions.**

  a   He mentions two notices. One directs people to Peterhouse Choral Evensong (a church ceremony). Where does the other notice direct people?
  b   What does he check with the audience?
  c   What does he hope is happening at Evensong?

2.2 **What is the purpose of this introduction? Tick the two best answers.**

  a   To begin the lecture on a humorous note.
  b   To outline what the lecture will be about.
  c   To check that people attending the lecture are in the right place.
  d   To show briefly how religious ceremonies have affected the development of English.

> **Study tip**
> *Many lecturers begin their talks with a short introduction that is not directly related to the topic of the lecture. They may refer to administrative information regarding the lecture, or the course of study, or they might begin with an amusing story to warm up the audience. In the example above, Professor Crystal does both with his comment about the potentially confusing notices for the lecture and the church ceremony.*

Listening

3 Understanding detailed points: making notes

3.1 a **What abbreviations could you use for the following terms used in the lecture?**

  a   English
  b   'Standard English'
  c   non-standard English
  d   dialects

Study tip
Using abbreviations will help you take notes more quickly and efficiently. Because the notes you make will be for your own use, you should work out a system of abbreviations that will work for you. However, it is a good idea to think about this before you attend the lecture rather than during it.

b ▐C.2▌ **Watch and make notes on the key points. Use the abbreviations in 3.1a.**

c **Work in pairs and compare notes.**

4 Understanding the main point

4.1 **Professor Crystal says 'Something has gone horribly wrong'. Complete the summary below.**

misrepresentation   ignored   prioritised   few   use   varieties

In the history of the study of English, dialects and other non-standard **1**_____ of English have been largely **2**_____ . 'Standard English' has been **3**_____, but this has been a **4**_____ because very **5**_____ English-language speakers actually **6**_____ 'Standard English' in their daily lives.

4.2 **Decide if the following statements are true or false, according to the information in the lecture. Correct the false statements.**

a In the past, the study of dialects and varieties of English was deliberately avoided.

b In his book, *A Short History of English*, H.C. Wyld makes no reference to dialects.

c The terms *patois, cant* and *lingo* are more positive ways of describing dialects.

d Linguists have tried to avoid using negative terms for describing dialects.

e It is only recently that 'Standard English' has become a minority dialect.

f 'Standard English' is normally defined by its written form.

g 'Standard English' is never spoken.

h Linguists are interested in rehabilitating 'Standard English'.

i 'Standard English' is useful in some situations where users of English need to understand each other.

j Non-standard varieties of English prevent people from having a sense of identity.

Language focus

5 Recognising quotes

5.1 ▐C.3▌ **Professor Crystal quotes H. C. Wyld's *A Short History of English*. Choose the best options in italics. Watch and check.**

a He quotes from Wyld *twice / three times.*

b The quotes are *contemporary / historical.*

c The quotes argue *in favour of / against* the idea that dialects are more worthy of study than 'Standard English'.

5.2 ▐C.3▌ **Watch again closely and answer the questions.**

a What background information does he provide before reading the first quote?

b What word does the first quote begin with?

c Does his intonation rise or fall on this word?

d What two words immediately follow the first word?

e Does his intonation rise or fall on these two words?

f How would you describe his tone of voice when reading the quote?

g Why do you think he changes his intonation in this way?

h He uses facial expression and body language to signal the end of the first quote. What does he do exactly? What effect does this have?

i How does he signal that he is about to read a second quote?

j What word introduces the quote itself?

Study tip

Lecturers frequently quote other writers. Sometimes these quotes are projected on a screen, but often they are merely read aloud. There are no specific rules for how quotes are read. For example, there is sometimes a pause between announcing the quote and the actual quotation. The lecturer's tone of voice tone may change and he or she may use facial expressions and body language to signal the beginning and end of a quote. Finally, lecturers will use a variety of reporting verbs such as say, remark, show, point out, etc. to begin quotes.

6 Recognising examples that support key points

6.1 a ▣C.4 Watch the next part of the lecture, where Professor Crystal introduces *The Reeve's Tale* by 14th–century poet Geoffrey Chaucer (about two Cambridge students who have to solve a problem with a flour miller). What does Professor Crystal do?

a   He disagrees with another linguist.
b   He quotes from a literary text.
c   He tells a story.

b **Put the events of the story in order. Watch again to check.**

a   The students manage to get corn for their college. _____
b   A miller has been stealing corn from a Cambridge college. _____
c   The students work out what has been happening at the mill. _____
d   The college sends two students to a mill to discover what's happened to the corn. _____
e   The students decide to trick the miller. _____

6.2 a **Before watching the next part, complete the table below with your predictions.**

sharp   northern   southern   intelligent   inefficient   bright   pompous

A summary of The Reeve's Tale

	Personality type	Dialect
The miller	1 _____ 2 _____	6 _____
The student	3 _____ 4 _____ 5 _____	7 _____

b ▣C.5 **Watch and check your predictions.**

c ▣C.5 **Watch again and answer the questions about the varieties of English Professor Crystal refers to.**

1   How does Professor Crystal know what kinds of accents the students and miller have?
2   Why does he read the students' dialogue / part of the anecdote in northern accents?

6.3 a Professor Crystal begins the final section by saying 'The point of that example is to …'. Work in groups and discuss what you think he will say about the topics below.

    a the key point about English accents

    b the point of the Chaucer example

  b **Watch and check your predictions.**

6.4 **C.7 Answer the questions. Watch and check.**

    a How does Professor Crystal introduce the example?

    b Why do you think he tells the story of The Reeve's Tale before reading excerpts from it?

    c What verb form does he use to tell the story? Why do you think he uses it?

    d How does he signal that he is about to make a key point about the example?

Study tip

Notice how Professor Crystal outlines an example which provides a context and background information in support of the point he is about to make. Background information can include a story or anecdote. If a part of a lecture begins with an example or story of some kind, it is likely that you will need to listen to the key point that follows the example.

Follow up

7 Responding to questions posed in a lecture

At one point in the lecture, Professor Crystal poses the question 'Why do people get so upset about accent and dialect?'.

7.1 a **Work in small groups and prepare a presentation that tries to answer this question. Discuss some of these points.**

    • the difference between accent and dialect

    • possible reasons why accents and dialects have evolved

    • the status of accents and dialects where you are from

    • the reasons why some people get upset about accents and dialects

  b **Take turns to present your ideas to the class. Refer to specific examples to support the points you want to make.**

  c **Discuss whether you think people are justified in getting upset about accents and dialects where you are from.**

7.2 **C.8 Listen to Professor Crystal posing the question** *'Why do people get so upset about accent and dialect?'.* **What are his answers to the points in 7.1a?**

8 Lecture structure

8.1 **C.9 Listen to what Youness says about the structure of a lecture and answer the questions.**

    a What structure does he expect a lecture to have?

    b What is the main difference he notes about undergraduate lectures in the UK compared to Brussels?

Youness

7 Marketing and consumers

Reading

MICHAEL SAREN

THE VIEW FROM THE STREET

➤ *Everything is marketed*
G&V 4, p109

1 Evaluating academic texts: a book review

Book reviews are found in many academic journals. Their purpose is usually both to give information to readers about new books in the subject and to evaluate the work. Students often read book reviews to decide whether a book is worth reading or buying, and to learn about areas of controversy. For research students in many subjects, a book review may be their first academic publication.

1.1 **Your tutor has given you the task of making a short presentation to introduce a book, 'Marketing graffiti: the view from the street', which is to be used as a core text on your Marketing course. Before you read extracts from the book, work in pairs and discuss the questions. Then share ideas with the class.**

    1 What do you understand by the term 'marketing'?

    2 Why do you think the book is called *Marketing graffiti*? Whose view is *the view from the street*?

1.2 **Skim read this description from the beginning of the book. Are any of your ideas mentioned?**

Text 1

About this book

Marketing affects everything – even nothing

Most marketing books discuss the subject as a business discipline, from a managerial point of view. How to 'do' marketing in companies and other organisations. But marketing is not just about being a marketing manager.

Marketing is all encompassing nowadays. Everything is marketed – the church, politics, science, history, celebrities, career, sport, art, fiction, fact. Marketing involves promotion, selling and consumption. However, marketing is more than just an
5 economic activity. It drives the consumer society, a culture of consumption. Marketing affects everybody; as consumers we cannot escape the market, even those who try to live simply.

Consumers are not passive recipients of what marketers do. We re-interpret marketing messages, display their logos; present ourselves through what we consume; make choices; complain; window shop; view celebrities as brands; compete with other consumers. This book explains marketing as consumers experience it, as active participants in it. Marketing may appear to
10 affect more and more of the world nowadays, but its powerful effects are not new. Over the centuries, trade, exchange, and what we now call marketing, influenced how and why empires were built, technologies applied, property law introduced, transport routes constructed, architecture of cities developed, languages grew and spread. It was in order to calculate market exchanges that Europeans imported from the Arabs the mathematical concept of 'nothing'.[1]

The contents

Topics in this book reflect the view of marketing as a social and cultural phenomenon, not just a business function.
15 Therefore, it does not adopt the managerial approach like most textbooks, rather it also seeks to explain how consumers, organisations and society can and do use marketing – for example, in areas of social marketing and the construction of a consumer 'identity'.

The subject is covered from a relational approach. That is, how actors and organisations relate to each other in and through marketing.

20 It takes a critical perspective on the values of marketing, not only 'market value'. Beyond a critique of unethical market practices, it questions and analyses established, traditional marketing theories and the assumptions behind them.

The structure is not organised according to the core marketing functions used in companies – advertising, distribution, strategy, sales, product development, etc. It does, though, introduce how companies and managers think and go about marketing in their businesses, but not in the terms found in traditional textbooks. This book does not explain these using 25 the old concepts and highly gendered, militarised language of traditional marketing – strategy and tactics, campaigns and offensives, intelligence and planning, control and implementation, targeting, market penetration, winning customers, beating competitors.

The contents cover how marketing creates solutions, how marketers build relations with customers, other companies, society, how they build brands, use media, how marketing moves space and time.

30 This book is not written from a single authorial perspective. It includes expert contributors on specific topics from experienced academics and practitioners, which cover a range of views about the subject. These are written in different styles and presented here in different ways, allowing for variety and reflecting the bricolage subject that is marketing.

1 See Rotman, B (1987) *Signifying Nothing: The Semiotics of Zero.* Macmillan: London.

Saren, M. (2006). *Marketing graffiti: the view from the street.* Oxford: Butterworth-Heinemann.

1.3 **a** **Read Text 1 in more detail and use the information to prepare two slides and notes to be used in your presentation. Read the first section, 'Marketing affects everything – even nothing', and prepare the first slide on the view of marketing being taken in the book.**

b **Read the second section, 'The contents', and prepare a second slide outlining the main features of the book.**

c **Work in pairs. Compare slides and notes, and make any necessary changes.**

1.4 **After the tutorial, you find the following review of *Marketing graffiti*. Read it and answer the questions.**

a What are the main differences between *Marketing graffiti* and other Marketing textbooks noted in the review?

b Who do you think the review primarily addresses? Give specific examples that lead you to this view.

c Do you think this is overall a positive or negative review? First, note down features of the book that the reviewer liked and language used to indicate this (e.g. 'immensely readable'). Repeat this for features that the reviewer didn't like.

Text 2

Book review:

Marketing graffiti: the view from the street

This is a readable, appropriately priced, and worthwhile introductory book on marketing written from a non-managerial perspective. It is aimed at advanced undergraduate and postgraduate students who 'want an alternative type of text', and can be seen as part of a gradual change in the way in which the subject of marketing is being presented for study.

5 The 'view from the street' mentioned in the subtitle appears to refer to the fact that the book 'explains marketing from the perspective of the pivotal figure in the process: the consumer'. It 'seeks to explain how consumers, organisations, society can and do use marketing'. This differentiates the book from those that focus on the marketing manager's perspective; it is not organised according to marketing functions, and distances itself from the 'highly gendered, 10 militarised language of traditional marketing'. The book covers a lot of ground in its relatively compact 292 pages; the variety of sub-topics is wide. It encompasses the more interesting thinking from what one might call the interpretive side of consumer studies, with an emphasis on the social and cultural aspects of consumption, as well as some critical handling of mainstream managerial marketing thinking.

15 It would appear that the author and publisher have invested considerable time and thought in the book's design. The colour, layout and font are attractive. There are plenty of (uncaptioned) photographs, graphics, quotation panels, as well as further reading tips, useful lists of references and an index. It does not come with the case studies, internet exercises, and test banks associated with the traditional marketing textbooks. There has also been some effort expended on a sort

20 of content 're-hang'. Turn to the contents page and you will find six topics: marketing contexts, building relations, consuming experiences, creating solutions, brand selection, and moving space. These are printed with a coloured handwritten effect and presented out of sequence – for example, the topic list begins with 'Consuming experience page 93', and 'Marketing contexts page 1' finds itself halfway down the page. This is intended to convey the idea of a web, rather than

25 linear structure. Once the reader gets used to this, it works quite well.

The book includes contributions from 12 other writers – to name them all would take too much space, and to name a few would be invidious. Suffice it to say that this is a pleasing aspect of the book in that it adds diversity of voice. Most of the authors are European-based, and, combined with the non-managerial focus, this seems to make the book less dogmatic or prescriptive. The

30 book is immensely readable, both because of the writing style(s) and the variety of interrelated topics. It can also act as a useful resource or reference to find a quick way into topics, such as value, or identity. It lends itself to a course design that would require students to engage with the journal literature and relate this to contemporary social issues. It is a useful resource for the kind of class where ideas can be discussed and argued about. Its treatment of issues is helpful, as

35 it brings several different ideas to bear on the same question. At times, the book strays from its mission, and spends a little too much time giving the managerial view. However, the overall de-privileging of the marketing manager is very welcome indeed – though whether the consumer's viewpoint is the only appropriate alternative perspective to work from is a matter for debate.

The preface suggests that the book 'can be used as an alternative or supplementary text'. Given

40 conventional business school approaches to marketing, with their expectation of the marketing managerial approach, this seems at first sight a sensibly modest proposal. I think this is a function it performs very well, in practice acting as a useful complement to the functional core textbook. Certainly, it would be difficult to see *Marketing graffiti* as a core text on, e.g. a conventional marketing principles or management module.

45 However, I think the book points the way to something far more worthwhile. It could function as a core text on an introductory marketing module with a substantially different focus, for example, one that dared to look more broadly and critically at marketing and consumption within their socio-cultural-political context, with roughly equal attention being paid to each of these three areas. This kind of module may initially be more likely to occur on leisure, tourism or cultural

50 and creative industries programmes, though there are signs that some management schools are already thinking this way. From this point of view, *Marketing graffiti* already has a considerable contribution to make and ample scope for ongoing development as a text. And, finally, at £19.99, it will encounter a lot less resistance from hard-up students.

O'Reilly, D. (2007). Book review: Marketing graffiti: the view from the street. *European Journal of Marketing*, 41, 704–706.

1.5 Read paragraph 3 of Text 2 again (from line 15). What language would be unusual in more formal academic writing?

Book reviews are often written in a less formal style than in other academic texts such as textbooks, monographs, and research articles. You should avoid this kind of informal language in assignments such as essays and theses.

2 Vocabulary building 1: understanding complex noun phrases

Study tip

When you find a complex noun phrase that is difficult to understand, try explaining aloud to yourself or to a partner what it means. Where possible, use synonyms or brief explanations of some of the words in the noun phrase.

'Core marketing functions' … these are the functions – or purposes – of marketing that are the most basic or most important.

2.1 **Work in pairs and take turns to explain these complex noun phrases from Text 2.**

1 a non-managerial perspective (line 2)
2 mainstream managerial marketing thinking (line 13)
3 contemporary social issues (line 33)
4 introductory marketing module (line 45)

3 Vocabulary building 2: word families

3.1 a **Write the name of a person who matches definitions 1–6. Use a word in the same family as the word in bold. Then check in Text 1.**

1 **consumes** goods (line 7) _____
2 **receives** something (line 7) _____
3 **markets** (= tries to sell) products (line 7) _____
4 **participates** in an activity (line 9) _____
5 **contributes** a paper to a book (line 29) _____
6 **practises** (= works) in a particular profession (line 30) _____

b **Complete the sentences with the correct form of the words in brackets and a preposition. Then check in the texts.**

1 Consumers are not passive recipients of what marketers do … (they also) _____ ___ other consumers. (competition)
(text 1, line 7)
2 … organisations and society can and do use marketing … in areas of social marketing and the _____ ___ a consumer 'identity'. (construct) (text 1, line 16)
3 It questions traditional marketing theories and the _____ ___ them. (assume)
(text 1, line 21)
4 This _____ the book ___ those that focus on the marketing manager's perspective. (difference)
(text 2, line 7)
5 acting as a useful _____ ___ the functional core textbook. (complementary)
(text 2, line 42)
6 It could _____ ___ a core text on an introductory marketing module. (function)
(text 2, line 46)

4 Reading in detail

4.1 a What one-word synonym of *point of view* could be used in this sentence?

> from a managerial **point of view** (text 1, line 1)

> ⊙ *Research shows that in academic writing, other adjectives frequently occur in the structure from a … point of view. What are the adjective forms of these nouns (1–10)?*
>
> **1** manager *managerial* **5** evolution _____ **9** quality _____
> **2** practice _____ **6** computer _____ **10** quantity _____
> **3** theory _____ **7** language _____
> **4** method _____ **8** analysis _____

➤ *Irregular plural nouns*
G&V **1, p108**

b What is the plural form of *phenomenon*?

> a social and cultural **phenomenon** (text 1, line 14)

c Explain the two different meanings of *value* used in this example.

> It takes a critical perspective on the **values of marketing**, not only 'market value'. (text 1, line 20)

d Why does the writer use *appears to* in this sentence beginning?

> The 'view from the street' mentioned in the subtitle **appears to** refer to the fact that … (text 2, line 5)

e Why does the writer include *relatively* here?

> The book covers a lot of ground in its **relatively** compact 292 pages … (text 2, line 10)

Listening and speaking

5 Conclusions and recommendations

As part of a Marketing course, the tutor has given students this project to do.

Marketing – semester 2 group project

Newcraft is a new, small, British company that makes leather wallets, purses and handbags. It wants to increase its exports and has decided to advertise its products in magazines in six countries: China, France, India, Italy, Japan and Russia. Design a relevant questionnaire aimed at finding out consumer attitudes and use it to survey students from these countries at the university. In a group presentation, report what you found, your conclusions and what recommendations you would make to *Newcraft*.

5.1 🔊 **7.1** Listen to part of the presentation given by one of the students, Carmen, and decide which of these two slides she talks about first.

Slide 1

❝ I like products that are not easy to get and that few people have. ❞

(% agree/strongly agree)

China 44% | India 41% | Russia 37%, Japan 27% | Italy 21% | France 17%

Slide 2

❝ A product's design and style are as important as its performance. ❞

(% agree/strongly agree)

Russia 64% | China 63% | India 46%, Japan 35% | Italy 34% | France 27%

5.2 a **Work in pairs and decide what conclusions you would draw from the findings.**

b (◀ᴗ 7.2) **Listen and compare your conclusions with Carmen's.**

5.3 a **Work in pairs and decide what recommendations you would make to *Newcraft*.**

b (◀ᴗ 7.3) **Listen and compare your recommendations with Carmen's.**

6 Presentation practice

6.1 a **Now prepare your part of the presentation, using the two slides below. Find useful phrases in the script on page 161. Structure your talk in a similar way to Carmen's.**

  1 Say what information is in slide 3 and highlight the main findings.
  2 Do the same for slide 4.
  3 Draw conclusions from the findings in both slides.
  4 Make recommendations to *Newcraft* on the basis of your findings.

Slide 3

> **❝ I like to try new products and services. ❞**
> **❝ I prefer to stick with the products and services I have always used. ❞**
> (%)
> **Italy** 70: 30 | **France** 65: 35 | **India** 64: 36
> **China** 59: 41 | **Russia** 54: 46 | **Japan** 43: 57

Slide 4

> **❝ It's best to buy famous brands because you can rely on their quality. ❞**
>
> (% agree/strongly agree)
> (% disagree/strongly disagree)
> **Russia** 66: 15 | **India** 56: 15 | **China** 49: 23
> **France** 34: 28 | **Italy** 33: 30 | **Japan** 15: 48

b **Work in pairs. Take turns to give your talks.**

Writing

7 Organising information in sentences

Although English sentences most typically begin with a subject and then a verb, other sentence elements may be put in an initial position (before the subject of the sentence).

7.1 a **Work in pairs and compare the A and B versions of Text 1 below. In which are the ideas better linked? (Focus on sentence beginnings to help you decide.)**

Text 1

A	B
A brand name is often a product's only distinguishing characteristic. A firm could not differentiate its products without the brand name. A brand name is as fundamental as the product itself to consumers. Many brand names have indeed become synonymous with the product, such as Scotch Tape and Xerox copiers. The owners of these brand names try to protect them from being used as generic names for tape and photocopiers, respectively, through promotional activities.	A brand name is often a product's only distinguishing characteristic. Without the brand name, a firm could not differentiate its products. To consumers, a brand name is as fundamental as the product itself. Indeed, many brand names have become synonymous with the product, such as Scotch Tape and Xerox copiers. Through promotional activities, the owners of these brand names try to protect them from being used as generic names for tape and photocopiers, respectively.

b Now make the same decision for Text 2.

Text 2

A	B
Advertising and sales promotion are the most obvious aspects of the marketing effort. To many people, they are synonymous with marketing itself. Media advertising stares down from posters, enters the home through television, radio and newspapers and is in the workplace through the industrial, trade and technical press. When asked to describe marketing, most consumers would start off with specific advertisements they have seen and offers they have taken up or rejected. This awareness reflects the success of advertising and sales promotion in establishing their presence. It is this access to the buyer or prospective buyer that the firm seeks when considering an investment in advertising or sales promotion.	Advertising and sales promotion are the most obvious aspects of the marketing effort. They are synonymous with marketing itself to many people. Media advertising stares down from posters, enters the home through television, radio and newspapers and is in the workplace through the industrial, trade and technical press. Most consumers would start off with specific advertisements they have seen and offers they have taken up or rejected when asked to describe marketing. This awareness reflects the success of advertising and sales promotion in establishing their presence. The firm seeks this access to the buyer or prospective buyer when considering an investment in advertising or sales promotion.

7.2 a Look at the types of sentence element that can be put in an initial position (1–4). Find examples from Text 1B and Text 2A.

1 Prepositional phrase (e.g. *In the past, ...*) _____
2 Adverb/adverb phrase (e.g. *Unusually, ...*) _____
3 Adverbial clause (e.g. *Despite losing the order, ...*) _____
4 *It*-clause (e.g. *It was the first of these ...*) _____

➤ *Using* it-clauses *to organise information*
G&V **3, p108**

b Why do writers sometimes begin sentences with a sentence element other than the subject? Work in pairs and try to find examples in Texts 1B and 2A to illustrate these possible reasons.

Reasons for sentence element other than subject in initial position	Examples
1 to link ideas in sentences together 2 to move information to the front of the sentence in order to highlight it 3 to emphasise a particular point 4 to avoid repetition	

7.3 Rewrite the following two text extracts by putting sentence elements other than the subject in an initial position, where appropriate. Work individually, and then compare answers in pairs.

Text 1

There have been four eras in the history of marketing according to Boon and Kurtz (1999, p12): the production era, the sales era, the marketing era and the relationship era. Production was the main focus of business up to the mid 1920s, with the view that a good quality product would sell itself. The emphasis changed from then till the early 1950s to focus on effective sales forces to find customers. Personal selling and advertising were seen as the way to convince customers to buy. Increased competition later encouraged the need for marketing to play a part in the full life-cycle of products from the planning through to sales, distribution, and servicing. Relationships with customers and suppliers became the focus in the 1990s.

Based on Sherson, G. W. (2000). *Internet marketing and society.*
Unpublished Master of Communications thesis, Victoria University of Wellington, New Zealand.

According to Boon and Kurtz (1999, p.12), there have been four eras in the history of marketing: the production era, the sales era, the marketing era, and the relationship era. Up to the mid 1920s, production ...

Text 2

Multinational corporations often face a dilemma of 'how to balance the need to leverage global strengths with the need to recognise local differences' (Aaker and Joachimsthaler 1999, 105) in communicating to consumers in different countries. Consumers in different countries have different cultures, values, and lifestyles, as suggested by research literature on cultural differences between countries (e.g. Hofstede 1991, 2001). A marketing strategy that works well in one country may not work in another country because of the cultural differences. However, corporations still want to maintain a consistent brand image and unique identity across the world, even when they adopt a localised approach.

Levitt (1983) sparked the debate on the issue of standardisation versus localisation of international advertising, and according to him standardisation refers to the practice of marketing the same products in the same way in the global market. The localisation approach, on the other hand, focuses on differences among consumers in different countries and uses a tailored marketing strategy for each country, considering its culture, media availability, product life cycle stages, and industry structure (Okazaki and Alonso 2003).

Based on Shin, W. & Huh, J. (2009). Multinational corporate website strategies and influencing factors: A comparison of US and Korean corporate websites. *Journal of Marketing Communications*, 15, 287–310.

 Focus on your subject
Look back at a piece of writing you have done recently on a topic related to your own subject. Could it be improved by moving information to an initial position in any of the sentences?

8 Writing up research: the Methods section

The Methods section is an important section of many theses. In it, the procedures used to answer the research questions are described. In some research areas, Methods sections can be very brief, particularly when the method is quite simple, or a widely accepted method is used. In other research areas, methods may be more complex or may not be so well established, and so Methods sections need a more detailed explanation and justification.

8.1 Match words 1–10, which are commonly found in Methods sections, to definitions a–j.

1 anonymous	**a** a list of questions for people to answer, used to gather information and opinions
2 data	**b** the theory or framework within which research is conducted
3 methodology	**c** done by someone whose name is not made public
4 methods	**d** a group of people or things chosen from a larger group
5 participant (or subject)	**e** information, especially facts or numbers, collected in research
6 procedure	**f** a set of actions for doing something
7 questionnaire	**g** a way of finding information by asking people questions
8 respondent	**h** the techniques and materials used in a piece of research
9 sample	**i** a person who answers a request for information
10 survey	**j** someone who takes part in research

 Focus on your subject
Are any of the words in 8.1 unlikely to be found in Methods sections in theses in your subject?

8.2 a You are going to study the Methods section of a research article with the title 'Chinese children's perceptions of advertising and urban brands – an urban – rural comparison'. Read this summary of the purpose of the research, taken from the abstract, and in pairs discuss what methods might be used to gather the appropriate data.

The purpose of this paper is to examine how perceptions of truthfulness of television advertising and perceptions of brands varies among urban and rural children in mainland China, and also to collect information about the basis of judgement children use to determine whether commercials are true.

b Now read an extract from the Methods section. Did the researcher use any of the methods you suggested in 8.2a? Did she use any additional methods?

➤ were collected
G&V 2, p108

1 Data for the rural sample were collected in July to October 2002 **2** in the counties of seven provinces, including Gansu, Guangdong, Hebei, Jiangsu, Liaoning and Sichuan.

A Provincial per capita GDP of these seven provinces ranged from 54% (Gansu) to 179% (Guangdong) of the national per capita GDP. **3** A national Chinese market research company was hired to conduct the survey. Permission was obtained from school authorities to distribute questionnaires at schools. Questionnaires were administered in classroom settings during normal class periods in 15 elementary schools. The number of students in each school varied from 210 to 700. All the schools were situated in counties with populations of less than 60,000. Researchers read out the questions and possible answers for grades 1 and 2 students and asked respondents to check the most appropriate answers. Respondents in grade 3 to 6 filled in the questionnaires by themselves. All aspects of the research procedure were conducted in Chinese (Mandarin).

[*]

➤ adopted
G&V 5, p109

4 The same questionnaire used in Chan and McNeal's (2004a) study of urban children was adopted. The questionnaire was tested among seven rural children in Guangdong and no

B revisions were made. The questionnaire consisted of close-ended questions about children's perceptions of television advertising and brands, along with four demographic questions. **5** This study focuses on television advertising because a previous study found that rural children were not familiar with other forms of advertising (Chan and McNeal, 2006b).

6 Children's liking of TV commercials was measured by the question "What is your feeling towards TV commercials?" using a five-point scale from "dislike very much" to "like very much". Children's perception of the truthfulness of television commercials was measured by the question: "Do you think what they say in the commercials is true or not?" using a five-point scale from "nearly all are not true" to "nearly all are true". Children's criteria to differentiate true commercials from false ones were measured by the question "How do you know which commercials are true and which are not true?" with a choice of six answers.

Children's perceptions of advertised and non-advertised brands were examined by the question "Suppose there are two different brands of soft drinks (or computer): one advertises on TV and one doesn't advertise. What do you think about them?" Five answers were presented and children were asked to select the most appropriate answer. The two product categories were selected to represent products with low and high involvement.

7 Altogether, 1,559 questionnaires were distributed in the rural sample and 1,481

C questionnaires were returned. **8** Of the respondents, 49% were boys and 51% were girls. Respondents were 6–15 years old. The mean age of the respondents was 10.3 years (SD=2.0 years). The response rate was 95.0%.

[**]

9 Descriptive statistics were compiled to give the perceptions of television advertising and brands of the overall sample, as well as the urban and rural sub-samples. **10** Chi-square

D tests and independent sample t-tests were conducted to examine the urban–rural difference in perceptions of television advertising and brands. The sample was divided into two groups that were of similar size (ages 6–9 and 10–15). Chi-square tests were conducted to examine the age difference in advertising perceptions.

Chan, K. (2008). Chinese children's perceptions of advertising and brands: an urban – rural comparison. *Journal of Consumer Marketing*, 25, 74–84.

c Match labels 1–4, showing the main purpose, to parts A–D of the Methods section above.

1 describe the sample _____
2 describe the data analysis procedures _____
3 describe the materials used for data collection _____
4 describe the data-collection procedures _____

Methods sections often have a number of elements, each of which has a particular function. Note, however, that not all Methods sections contain all of these elements, or order them in the same way.

d Match labels a–j, showing what information is given in each element within the four main parts, to extracts 1–10 in the Methods section.

a details of items in the questionnaire _____
b steps in the data collection _____
c overview of the data-analysis procedure _____
d location of data collection _____
e size of sample _____
f time of data collection _____
g characteristics of sample _____
h steps in data–analysis procedure _____
i justification for the focus of the data collection _____
j overview of the material used in data collection _____

8.3 The methods section in 8.2 is incomplete and needs more information about the urban sample. Expand the notes below into two new paragraphs for sections [*] and [**].

[*]
Urban sample; Dec '01 – March '02; in Beijing (2 schools), Nanjing (2 schools), Chengdu (2 schools) (= high, medium & low levels of advertising expenditure (Fan, 2001)). Biggest school 1,700 students; smallest 800. Appointed local researchers (university staff) to collect data. Same procedure as rural survey. School principals saw questionnaire before & decided whether school would participate. Researchers told students: survey voluntary; could leave questions blank if they wanted to; responses anonymous.

[**]
Urban sample: 1,765 questionnaires distributed & 1,758 returned (= 99.6% response rate); respondents 6–14 years old (mean age 9.6 yrs [SD=1.8 yrs], boys (51%), girls (49%)

8.4 Recall what you learned about word order in section 7. Look again at the paragraphs you wrote in 8.3 and, if necessary, edit them by putting sentence elements other than the subject in an initial position in sentences.

8 Criminology

Reading
· Making predictions
· Vocabulary building 1: adjectives
· Vocabulary building 2: verbs
· Reading in detail
· Understanding plagiarism

Listening and speaking
· Dealing with questions in presentations
· Presentation practice

Writing
· Organising information in texts
· Writing up research: the Results section
· Writing practice

Reading

1   Making predictions

1.1   At the end of a tutorial on criminology (the study of crime and criminals), you were given this handout on how handwriting analysis can help solve crimes. Work through the handout in pairs.

Criminology tutorial – handout 4

a Read an account of a crime, in which handwriting analysis was used to help identify the criminal. Then think of at least two more ways in which analysing the handwriting in a 'questioned document' (i.e. one where there is some dispute about the writer) might help solve a crime.

In March, 1932, Charles Lindbergh Junior, the 20-month-old son of the famous aviator, was kidnapped. Although a ransom of $50,000 was paid, the boy was not returned, and his body was found a few weeks later not far from his home. The notes used in the ransom payment were tracked, which led the police to Bruno Hauptmann. Further evidence was provided by matching his handwriting to that on the ransom note.

b Here are the same words written by two different people. In pairs, both write the same words in the gaps and then compare the four samples of handwriting. What similarities and differences do you notice? Think about: connections between letters, curves, size, slant, spacing, etc.

1 *Crime and society*   3 _____
2 *crime and society*   4 _____

c Read the introduction below from a text on forensic handwriting analysis and answer the questions.
1 What two principles underlie the use of handwriting as a means of individual identification?
2 Is one sample of handwriting usually enough to identify an individual?
3 How does the work of a graphologist differ from that of a forensic document examiner?

Introduction
Generally, the largest part of the work undertaken by forensic document examiners is connected with analysis of handwriting. Fundamental to this analysis is the principle that the writing of each person is unique to them. Further, that each piece of writing from a given individual is in itself unique, but that the writings of that individual vary over a natural range of variation, which is another feature of that person's writing. As a consequence, handwriting can be used as a means of individual identification, provided that sufficient quantities of specimen material (preferably non-request) are available for comparison with the questioned handwriting. It should be noted that the scientific analysis of handwriting undertaken by forensic document examiners is entirely different from the work of graphologists, who scrutinise the handwriting of individuals in an attempt to infer their personality traits. Confusion may arise because graphologists are also often referred to as handwriting experts.

Jackson, A. R. W. & Jackson, J. M. (2008). *Forensic Science (2nd edn)* Harlow: Pearson.

---

d Based on the introductory paragraph, write four questions you expect to be answered in the text extract that follows the introduction.

1.2   a   You are going to read the text extract mentioned in the handout. Before you read it, make sure you understand these key words.

adolescent	distinctive	forensic	infer	scrutinise	specimen	trait

b Read the text extract quickly and find out if it includes answers to your questions from 1.1d.

Forensic handwriting analysis

The development of handwriting

Handwriting is a complex motor task which must be learnt. In the United Kingdom, this process usually begins when the child is about four years of age. In the early stages, the child consciously copies the different letters presented to him or her. As these are usually in a standard form, the handwriting of the child is similar at this stage to that of his or her classmates (and to that of other children taught using the
5   same writing system). Such features in common are known as *class characteristics*. However, as the child increases in skill, the act of handwriting becomes less demanding and his or her construction, and other aspects (such as shape and proportion), of character forms becomes more individualised. Such distinctive features are known as *individual characteristics*, and taken in the context of class characteristics, it is these that are used by document examiners to identify handwriting. The main period during which these
10 individual characteristics are developed is during the adolescent years. After this, the handwriting of a mature individual usually stays basically the same with only minor changes until the lack of pen control associated with advancing years causes it, once again, to alter significantly.

The comparison of handwriting

A number of different basic types of handwriting are recognised. In the United Kingdom, these are designated as *block capitals* (i.e. upper-case unjoined writing), *cursive writing* (i.e. lower-case joined-up
15 writing) and *script* (i.e. lower-case unjoined writing) (Figure 8.1). Two other terms should be mentioned in this context, namely connected writing and disconnected writing. In the United Kingdom, forensic handwriting experts usually consider these terms to be synonymous with cursive writing and script respectively.

(a) THE CASE OF JOHN WHITE   (b) *The case of John white*   (c) The case of John white

Figure 8.1 The three basic types of handwriting recognised in the UK: (a) block capitals, (b) cursive writing, and (c) script

In practice, the normal handwriting of most individuals is somewhere between cursive writing and script.
20 In such cases, handwriting experts will normally use the term 'cursive writing' to denote handwriting in which the letters within words are predominantly joined and, conversely, use the term 'script' for handwriting in which the majority of the letters within words are not joined. Signatures are a specialised form of handwriting.

It is crucial that any comparison between questioned and specimen handwriting is carried out on a 'like
25 for like' basis. This means that in order to make a meaningful comparison, the type of handwriting must be the same in each of the two samples. Furthermore, individual letters that are compared in the two samples must also be the same as each other. For example, the letter 'b' in one document written in cursive style must be compared with the letter 'b' written in cursive style in the other. Groups of letters and words that are compared in the two samples ideally will also be the same as each other. However, this is not always
30 possible in cases where the specimen handwriting used in the comparison is of the non-request variety.

When analysing handwritten questioned documents, the forensic document examiner compares all characters present, deciding on the basis of his or her experience which are those handwriting traits that help make it uniquely identifiable. This examination is best carried out using a low-power stereoscopic microscope. Under magnification, the construction, proportions (both internal and relative to each other)
35 and shape of the individual characters are clearly visible. In the case of the construction of characters, it is necessary to ascertain both the directions in which the constituent pen strokes have been made and the order in which they have been laid down. (The direction of pen movement can also reveal the difference between right- and left-handed individuals. For example, circular pen strokes, as seen in the letter 'o', made in an anticlockwise direction indicate right-handedness, whereas those made in a clockwise direction attest
40 to left-handedness.) Other handwriting features such as the connections between letters (if any) and the slope of the writing may contribute to individualising the content, as can general writing features, such as word and letter spacing, and date style and arrangement.

It is important to realise that the handwriting of an individual shows natural variation. This means that it is never exactly the same on any two occasions. The forensic document examiner is also aware that
45 handwriting may show variation because of other factors. These may be associated with the mental and physical state of the writer, for example, whether a person is ill, stressed or under the influence of alcohol or other drugs, or it may be caused by the writing surface or writing instrument used. In some cases, variation occurs because the writer is attempting to disguise his or her own natural handwriting.

➤ *as can general writing features*

G&V 4, p121

Jackson, A. R. W. & Jackson, J. M. (2008). *Forensic Science (2nd edn)* Harlow: Pearson.

1.3 **Read the text extract again and discuss questions 1–7.**

1 Some characteristics of handwriting are the same in groups of people of the same age and using the same writing system. Why do these 'class characteristics' exist?

2 How is the handwriting of children and adults different?

3 One category of handwriting is 'block capitals'. What others are there?

4 Why is it important to compare 'like-for-like' handwriting samples in forensic analysis?

5 What features of handwriting are analysed by forensic document examiners?

6 What causes variation in handwriting?

7 What are the implications of variation for the analysis of handwriting?

1.4 **Is the method of analysing handwriting in the text objective or subjective? Give reasons.**

2 Vocabulary building 1: adjectives

2.1 **Complete sentences 1–6 with adjectives from the box with a similar meaning to the definitions in brackets.**

complex	fundamental	identifiable	individualised
sufficient	synonymous	unique	

1 Handwriting is a _____ motor skill. (it has many parts and so is difficult to understand)

2 As the child increases in skill, their handwriting becomes more _____ . (increasingly different from that of other people)

3 The forensic document examiner decides which handwriting traits help make it uniquely _____ . (it can be recognised)

4 Document examiners need to have access to _____ quantities of specimen handwriting in order to take natural variation into account. (enough)

5 Connected writing and disconnected writing are _____ with cursive writing and script, respectively. (they have the same meaning)

6 The principle that the writing of each person is _____ is _____ to the analysis of handwriting. (it is different from everyone else's; essential to its success)

3 Vocabulary building 2: verbs

3.1 **Match the sentence beginnings (1–8) and endings (a–h), replacing the phrases in bold with the correct form of verbs from the box.**

ascertain	attest	contribute	denote
designate	disguise	reveal	scrutinise

1 Variation occurs when writers try to **hide**

2 The term *cursive writing* **is used to mean**

3 Connections between letters may **add to**

4 To study the construction of characters, it is necessary to **establish**

5 In the UK, the three basic types of handwriting are **given the names**

6 The direction of pen movement can also **show**

7 Clockwise pen strokes **provide evidence of**

8 Graphologists **examine in detail**

a as block capitals, cursive writing and script.

b to left-handedness.

c handwriting with joined letters.

d their own natural handwriting.

e the handwriting of individuals to identify their personality traits.

f to individualising the content.

g the difference between right- and left-handed individuals.

h both the direction and order of constituent pen strokes.

4 Reading in detail

4.1 **a** Look at these examples from the text on page 111. What do the phrases in bold refer back to?

> **Such distinctive features** are known as … (line 7)

> In **such cases**, handwriting experts… (line 20)

b Look at this example and answer the questions.

1 What function does *namely* have? Can you think of an alternative way of expressing the same meaning?

2 Which word shows that cursive writing refers to connected writing and that script refers to disconnected writing?

> Two other terms should be mentioned in this context, **namely** connected writing and disconnected writing. In the United Kingdom, forensic handwriting experts usually consider these terms to be synonymous with cursive writing and script, respectively. (line 15)

c Which word in this example from the introduction on page 110 means the same as 'particular'?

> … each piece of writing from a given individual is in itself unique, but that the writings of that individual vary over a natural range of variation …

> ⊙ *Look at this example from the introduction.*
> **It should be noted that** the scientific analysis of handwriting…
> *The structure* It should be … that … *is commonly used in academic writing, particularly when the writer wants to draw attention to something important or to remind the reader of some information.*
>
> *Research shows that in the written academic corpus,* noted *is the most common word in this structure, and is used to draw attention or remind. What other phrases are common?*
>
> 1 *noted*   2 reme_____   3 emp_____   4 poi_____ out   5 stre_____
> 6 men_____   7 bo_____ in mind   8 reca_____   9 ke_____ in mind

5 Understanding plagiarism

5.1 Work in pairs. Read the extract below from a university website and discuss the questions.

1 Why do universities disapprove of plagiarism?

2 In your view, is plagiarism a crime?

> Plagiarism is **passing off someone else's work as your own** without acknowledging the source. Some common examples of this are:
>
> - **copying** a portion of text without giving credit to the source (e.g. copying and pasting some text from a website into your assignment);
> - **paraphrasing** text without crediting the source (e.g. changing a few words from an article and including it in your work);
> - **incorrectly citing** a source, **misleading the reader** as to what is yours and what is from the source.

The Open University, United Kingdom. http://library.open.ac.uk/help/howto/plagiar/ retrieved 8 August 2011.

5.2 **Work in pairs. Read the following extracts from published textbooks (A and B) and the five examples of students' writing. Discuss the questions.**

1 Which of the examples of students' writing do think are plagiarised?
2 How would you change the examples?
3 What advice would you give to the students whose work you consider to be plagiarised?

Text A

> With the continuing developments in media technology through the latter half of the 20th century, psychologists, in particular, conducted research and experiments in attempting to find a direct link between exposure to the media and changes in behaviour and attitude. Many of these experiments considered the relationship between media exposure and violent, antisocial behaviour.

Marsh, I. & Melville, G. (2009). *Crime, justice and the media*. Oxford: Routledge.

Text B

> The conclusion from a large number of studies is that although observing violence on television may be a contributory factor to aggressive behaviour, it does not follow automatically. Other factors may be equally, if not more influential.

Clarke, D. (2003). *Pro-social and anti-social behaviour*. Sussex: Routledge.

1 | With the continuing developments in media technology in the second half of the 20th century, psychologists, in particular, conducted research and experiments in attempting to find a connection between exposure to the media and changes in behaviour and attitude. Much of this research considered whether there was a direct link between violent antisocial behaviour and exposure to violence in the media. Most studies came to the conclusion that although observing violence on television may contribute to aggressive behaviour, it does not follow automatically. Other factors may be equally influential, if not more so.

2 | In recent years, psychologists have investigated the potential link between exposure to the media and behavioural and attitudinal changes. Of particular interest has been the relationship between media exposure and violent, anti-social behaviour (Marsh and Melville, 2009). For example, much research has examined whether there is a direct link between watching violence on television and aggressive behaviour. Most studies, however, have found that while it may contribute to aggression, other factors may be equally influential, if not more so (Clarke, 2003).

3 | A large number of studies have investigated the connection between violence on television and aggressive behaviour, and found that: although observing violence on television may be a contributory factor to aggressive behaviour, it does not follow automatically. Other factors may be equally, if not more influential (Clarke, 2003).

9.2 **Work in pairs and answer the questions about the extracts in 9.1.**

   1 What three ways have you seen of directing readers' attention to a figure? Can you think of other ways of doing this?

   2 Results are usually explained cautiously. Why do you think this is? What language is used to indicate this caution in the explanation in Text 1?

   3 Are all the results shown in the figures also mentioned in the texts? If not, can you explain why?

   4 Which usually comes first: giving general or important results, or giving details of results? In which text does this pattern appear?

   5 When is 'per cent' written '%'? Is the same principle applied in your subject?

10 Writing practice

10.1 a **The two figures below show results from a survey of people's attitudes to crime. Work in pairs and discuss what the figures show, the main results and how some of these results might be explained.**

   b **Work alone and write two paragraphs presenting the results from Figures 1 and 2 below.**

   c **Compare your text with your partner's and make any necessary improvements.**

Figure 1: Responses to the question: What makes you think there is more crime now than two years ago?

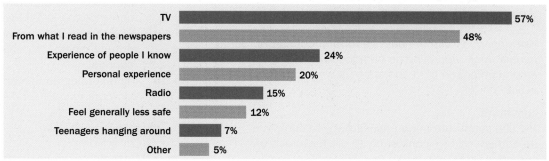

Figure 2: Response to the statement: I agree that I can reduce my risk of being a victim of crime.

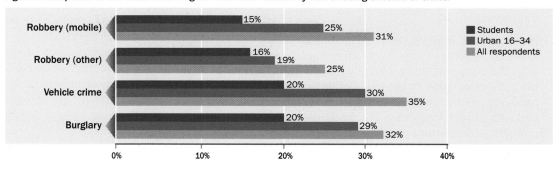

Huntley, A. et al. (2008). *Home Office – Cutting the cost of crime.*
London: Institute of Practitioners in Advertising.

🎓 **Focus on your subject**
Find two research articles from your subject area. Do they have sections that are headed 'Results' or sections that obviously report results? Can you identify elements in these sections which have the same purposes as those listed in 9.1? Do other elements have different purposes?

Grammar and vocabulary

Grammar and vocabulary
· Problem words: *comprise,
be composed of, consist of, constitute,
make up, include*
· Classifying phrases
· Problem–solution phrases
· Word order in *as*-clauses

1 Problem words: *comprise, be composed of, consist of, constitute, make up, include*

These verbs are often used in describing classifications.

1.1 Read the information and decide whether sentences 1–10 from students' writing are right (✓) or wrong (✗). Suggest a correction for wrong sentences.

- **comprise**
  We can say that something comprises *particular things when we mention all of its parts (e.g.* The book comprises eight chapters.*)*

- **be composed of / consist of**
  We can use either is composed of *or* consist of *to say that something is formed from various things (e.g.* Words are composed of / consist of individual sounds.*)*

  Warning: don't use the passive form of consist of. *Some people think that using* be comprised of *in the same way as* be composed of/ consists of *is wrong, so it is best to avoid it.*

- **constitute**
  We use constitute *in an opposite way to* comprise / be composed of / consist of, *to say that parts of something form the whole (e.g.* The factory employees constituted the whole settlement.*) or a fraction of the whole (e.g.* Right-handed people constitute a majority of the population.*).*

- **make up / be made up of**
  Make up *(active) has the same meaning as* constitute *(e.g.* The Bangladeshi community makes up 0.5% of the total population of the UK.*), while* be made up of *(passive) has the same meaning as* be composed of / consists of *(e.g.* Molecules are made up of electrons, protons, and neutrons.*).*

- **include**
  We use include *to say that a thing contains something as a part (e.g.* Table 3.1 includes information about occupation of participants.*).*

  Warning: don't use include *when we mention all the parts of something. Instead, use* comprise.

  Warning: don't use the continuous form of any of these verbs.

1 The sample of patients was consisted of only men between the ages of 40 and 50.
2 This sample was drawn from four locations in the country and comprised 40 families.
3 The European Council of Ministers is consisting of politicians from each member state.
4 Prepositions comprise a closed class of words; that is, no new items can be added.
5 The sales of the company includes 40% domestic and 60% export sales.
6 More than half the audience constituted women.
7 Body cell mass makes up approximately 55% of total body weight.
8 A team of ten people, which consisted of the three authors of the paper, collected the data over a six-month period in 2008.
9 Adjectives in the research articles that indicate attitude include 'thoughtful', 'significant', and 'serious'.
10 My recording equipment is comprised of three web cameras and a microphone.

2 Classifying phrases

2.1 a Match sentence beginnings 1–5 to endings a–e. Add appropriate prepositions. Use a dictionary to help you.

1 Policies designed to influence polluter behaviour can be classified …
2 Among the most common assessment types, a distinction can be made …
3 Survey respondents were divided …
4 Roberts (2010) looks at pensions as distinct …
5 Foraging behaviour in any animal consists …

a … other types of employee benefit.
b … short-answer questions and essays.
c … two main components – food searching and food consumption.
d … three categories: moral persuasion, direct controls and methods that rely on market processes.
e … three groups according to the area of the city they were living in.

b Make a note of any language in the sentences in 2.1a that will be useful to you when you are writing about classifications in your own subject.

3 Problem–solution phrases

3.1 a Do sentences 1–10 present a problem (P), or do they describe a solution to a problem (S)?

1 Blanchet (2005) **raises the question of** how far an ageing labour force calls for additional training opportunities. ____

2 Management **came up with an answer to** the fall in productivity. ____

3 Innovations in hospitals **have mitigated the impact of** the economic recession. ____

4 Many organisations now **face the problem of** which goals to prioritise in the light of increasing competition. ____

5 A number of writers **have pointed to serious weaknesses in** studies showing a relationship between family size and divorce (e.g. Monahan, 1995; Chesner, 2002). ____

6 Countries **have resolved the dilemma of** foreign direct investment in different ways. ____

7 It is important to consider why children **experience difficulties with** writing poetry, in spite of reading and hearing it. ____

8 A number of steps have been taken **to overcome the problem of** inadequate water supplies. ____

9 German metallurgists were the first **to find a solution to** the problem of producing iron from poor-quality ore. ____

10 A number of studies **have revealed shortcomings in** doctor–patient communication. ____

b Using the phrases in bold in 3.1a, add appropriate words to complete sentences a–h.

a Rudel (1996) showed that children with dyslexia often experience difficulties the naming of common objects or colours.

b Ford reduced the length of the working day to the problem a very high turnover of assembly-line workers.

c This raises the of why so few students provide feedback on their courses.

d The company faced the of a decline in its market share.

e Palm trees planted along the coast in the early 2000s significantly mitigated the of the tsunami.

f Our research has shortcomings the quality of the e-learning material available to Marketing students.

g The report to weaknesses the distribution of aid money.

h Union and employer negotiators a solution to the conflict over working hours.

i The company was one of the few that resolved the producing fashionable clothes at low cost.

j The government believe that they have come with an answer public opposition to wind farms.

4 Word order in *as*-clauses

We can use an as-clause to add information in a sentence with the meaning 'in the same way'.

4.1 a Here is an example from the text on page 111. What do you notice about the word order in the *as*-clause in bold?

> Other handwriting features such as the connections between letters may contribute to individualising the content, *as can general writing features*.

(= 'general writing features contribute in the same way as other handwriting features to individualising the content')

b Express the ideas in these sentences more efficiently by writing one sentence for each, using an *as*-clause.

1 Bad weather can reduce turnouts at elections. Turnouts can also be reduced by the day of the week.

_____

2 The total number of lung cancer cases in our work was comparable to the three studies discussed above. The size of the population examined in our work and the three studies was also comparable.

_____

3 TV and radio programmes, especially news broadcasts, have been extensively studied. Newspaper reports have also been extensively studied.

_____

4 The study found a direct relationship between an individual's socio-economic status and their health status. Other studies before have also found this direct relationship.

_____

5 First- and second-born children were more prone to asthma. Children from the southern part of the country were also prone to asthma.

_____

6 Population growth was a cause of increased local housing demand. Increased local housing demand was also caused by rising income.

_____

Lecture skills D

Preparing for lectures
- Thinking about the content of lectures
- Vocabulary for the context

Listening
- Practice in gist and detailed listening 1
- Recogising lecture introductions
- Recognising lecture styles
- Practice in gist and detailed listening 2

Language focus
- Understanding lecture structure

Follow up
- Further listening practice

Preparing for lectures

As part of a course focusing on law, you will hear a lecture on legal interpretations of 'reasonable care' given by Professor John Spencer from the Law Faculty of the University of Cambridge.

John Spencer

1 Thinking about the content of lectures

1.1 **As preparation for a lecture on Law, you have been asked to consider the following scenario. Work in small groups and discuss who you think is responsible: the builder, the company or the employee?**

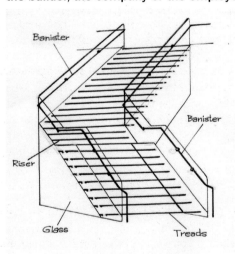

A company has built a new two-storey office. The builder missed the agreed completion deadline for the building, and the company could not stay in its temporary offices because the lease could not be extended. As a result, the company was forced to move into the new office with the building work incomplete, which caused a number of safety hazards. For example, the stairs were unfinished, causing the company to send a warning to their workers that they needed to be careful on the stairs.

One employee was walking down the stairs, reading a text message from his new girlfriend. He slipped on the stairs and fell, injuring his back and causing him to spend time in hospital. Doctors have said that he will experience back pain for the rest of his life, and he now walks with difficulty.

1.2 **Read the questions and check you understand the meanings of the words in bold. Work alone and then discuss your views in small groups.**

1 How **foreseeable** was this accident?
2 Did everyone in the scenario take enough **precautions**?
3 How could people in this scenario have tried to **eliminate** any risk?
4 What could be the **consequences** of everyone's actions in this situation?

2 Vocabulary for the context

2.1 a Read the example sentences and choose the correct options in the definitions.

- They were accused of **negligence** because they did not lock the gate to the swimming pool.
- He denied **liability** for damaging her car and said there was already a scratch on the paintwork.

1 *negligence/liability* is when you are legally responsible for something
2 *negligence/liability* is when you do not give enough care or attention

b Complete the collocation summaries with a noun from 2.1a.

1 to accuse someone of _____
2 to deny/accept _____ for something

c What do you think are the adjective forms of these nouns?

Study tip

Before you go to a lecture, you often have an idea of the content and the kind of terminology that will be used by the lecturer. If this is the case, it's useful to make a note of key words that you think you will hear. You can use a dictionary to double-check the meaning of the words, and also check different forms of the words and possible collocations.

2.2 a The words in bold below are legal terms used in the lecture. Match them to the definitions.

> *A woman brought an **action** for negligence against a hospital because her operation went badly. She **sued** for damages of £25,000 and **alleged** that the **defendant**, the surgeon who performed the operation, wasn't competent and **breached** his professional duty. The case was **tried** before a judge who decided to accept the woman's **claim** for **damages**.*

1 a person in a law case who is accused of having done something illegal
2 money which is paid to someone who has had an injury or loss
3 a legal process decided in a court of law
4 made a claim that someone is guilty of a crime
5 a request for something
6 to take a legal action against someone because they harmed you in some way
7 the act of breaking a law, promise or agreement
8 to judge someone in a court of law and decide if they are guilty or not

b Do you think these words are very technical words or do you think they could be used in newspapers and everyday conversations?

c In the United Kingdom, what do you think is the highest level that you can take a legal complaint to – the House of Lords or the Court of Appeal?

Listening

3 Practice in gist and detailed listening 1

3.1 (▣ D.1) Watch the beginning of the lecture. Professor Spencer talks about a case where the Glasgow Corporation sued Mrs Muir, the owner of a café. It involves a group of children on a Sunday-school outing with an elder of a *kirk* (a church). Correct the information in this summary.

> *A woman takes a group of children on an outing. They try to have cakes and a hot drink in a shelter, but the snow is heavy and they start getting cold. The woman asks the owner of a nearby café if the children can bring their food and drink to have in the café. The woman and the café owner agree on a room and the group of children move to the café. All the children carry an urn (a large metal container) of hot water with them. As they enter the café, they drop the urn and some of the children are scalded by the hot water. The church believed the café owner was to blame because the urn had been carried through a narrow corridor.*

4 Recognising lecture introductions

4.1 **a** (**D.2**) **Watch the beginning of the lecture, that outlines key terms. Complete the notes with one word in each gap.**

Fault – 1_____ 2_____ lawyers 3_____ various other aliases as well; 'carelessness' or 'breach of duty'. And when, as far as lawyers are concerned, is somebody at fault? What is 4_____ 5_____ of it? Lawyers 6_____ 7_____ the 'reasonable man' test: somebody's careless if they fail this, 8_____ that they failed to behave as a reasonable person would in the position in which the defendant found himself or herself.

b Is the style of the language neutral or more formal?

4.2 **a Complete this alternative version of the notes in 4.1a.**

> **talk   that   call   about   shows   mean**

Fault is something lawyers 1_____ 'carelessness' or 'breach of duty'. And when do lawyers think somebody is at fault? What does it 2_____ ? Lawyers 3_____ 4_____ the 'reasonable man' test: somebody's xcareless if they fail the 'reasonable man' test and 5_____ 6_____ they failed to behave as a reasonable person would in the same situation.

b What is the style of the language in the notes in 4.2a?

Study tip
Different lecturers have different language styles. It can help to check with other students on the language style of a particular lecturer so you know what to expect. A more formal style will not prevent you from understanding key information in a lecture, as long as you know to listen for key words associated with the topic.

5 Recognising lecture styles

5.1 (**D.3**) **Listen to what Diana says about the style of different lecturers and answer the questions.**

a Diana notes that some lecturers don't move around a lot. Why doesn't this bother her?
b What becomes a problem during a break in the lecture?
c Does she distinguish between stationary lecturers and those who move around?

6 Practice in gist and detailed listening 2

6.1 (**D.4**) **In a second extract from the lecture, Professor Spencer says:**

> *In deciding whether the defendant has behaved as a reasonable man, the courts ask themselves what a reasonable person would have done in this situation. And approaching the matter on principle, they say this involves weighing up four different factors.*

a How many factors are mentioned in the extract?
b What is the difference between 'likelihood of harm' and 'magnitude of harm'?
c Which of the following scenarios are described in this extract and in which order?

6.2 Watch again and decide if the following statements are true or false. Correct the false statements.

a A person is potentially liable if it is possible to foresee a risk or danger.

b After Mr Hayley fell down the hole, he was no longer able to walk.

c In 1965, there were enough blind people in London to make the hole in the pavement a foreseeable risk.

d The electricity board was the first organisation to use little fences to protect people from holes in the pavement.

e The organisations mentioned in this excerpt are both public bodies.

f Mr Paris thought the council should have given him some protection for his eyes.

g The Court of Appeal agreed that the council was at fault.

Language focus

7 Understanding lecture structure

7.1 (D.5) In the next section, Professor Spencer refers to three different ideas. Choose the correct word in *italics* for the key point, then make notes that summarise the example.

a Idea: Courts having higher or lower standards to judge negligence in different contexts
Key point: Skilful people *should/shouldn't* be judged as equal to skilled people.
Example: The Lady Gwendolen / Guinness beer

b Idea: Ordinary people doing some tasks, but are not considered negligent
Key point: Some small jobs (e.g. DIY) *can/cannot* be done by ordinary people without them being liable.
Example: Wells vs. Cooper / door knob

c Idea: Courts lowering the standards for judging negligence
Key point: Courts *will/won't* lower the standards of liability in some situations.
Example: people who are 'skill-less'

Study tip
A common device used by lecturers is posing a question to which they do not expect an answer because they intend to answer it themselves. This is known as a rhetorical question and it is often used to signal a change in topic or new idea. Lecturers can also use indirect questions such as 'A question was asked …' for the same purpose.

7.2 (D.5) Watch again. Professor Spencer uses both rhetorical and indirect questions in this excerpt. How many can you hear?

Follow up

8 Further listening practice

In this further section from the lecture, Professor Spencer looks at negligence in the context of someone carrying out their job. He considers whether normally accepted professional practice is relevant. He refers to builders in Northern Ireland and doctors who administer ECT (electro-convulsive treatment).

8.1 a (D.6) Watch, and make notes on questions that introduce ideas, topics or key points. Also make notes on the examples Professor Spencer gives and their outcomes.

b Check the script on page 162. As you read, look for examples of more formal language.

9 Families and relationships

Reading
- Understanding the writer's opinion
- Inferring the meaning of words
- Vocabulary building: word families
- Reading in detail
- Understanding figures

Listening and speaking
- Your relationship with your supervisor
- Formality and politeness in arranging meetings

Writing
- Writing a critique
- Writing up research: the Discussion section

Reading

1 Understanding the writer's opinion

1.1 a As part of a Sociology course, you have been given the following essay title: 'The nuclear family has replaced the extended family as the main family unit in industrial societies'.
How far do you agree? Work in pairs. What do you think are the key terms in the essay title? What do you understand by these key terms?

b Look at the percentages below of extended family households in selected countries. Discuss the factors that might influence these figures. Try to use phrases from the box.

childcare	culture	employment opportunities	independence
mobility	property prices	support	tradition

- Venezuela 31.8% (1999)
- Argentina 11.7% (1999)
- South Africa 13% (1998)
- Australia 1.5% (2001)

1.2 a In preparation for the essay, your tutor has given you the textbook extract on page 127. You have read it once and taken the notes below. Read the notes.

b Read the extract and edit your notes. How would you correct, improve and add to them?

1950s argument = nuclear fam in pre-ind society > extended fam in ind soc (a result of 'family privatism')

Some support for argument in 50s & 60s research

Less dense network of fam relationship than pre-ind ('cos pressure of work)

But, less support in more recent research, e.g. families not extended in pre-ind soc (small & not multigenerational)

More important question: how far are indivs & fams involved with close relatives?

Recent research – high level of involvement measured by degree of contact (e.g. 75% adults see mother at least 1/wk)

...1950s argument seems to be accurate

The wider family

One sociological argument of the 1950s ran as follows. Before the industrial revolution in Europe, the predominant family form was extended. That is, people had regular and extensive contact with their wider kin, their grandparents, aunts, uncles and cousins, and they even lived under the same roof. Industrialization, however, changed all that since it entailed substantial migration from the countryside into towns, and as a result people lost contact with their extended family. Families in general shrank to their minimal, nuclear size, consisting of parents and children only. The emotional and personal needs of family members were met within this smaller unit. So, the nuclear family in some sense 'fits' industrial society, while the more extended family is characteristic of pre-industrial society.

The argument is, in many ways, a story of decline and a comparison with a lost golden age – or at least the pessimists would think so. I have already indicated in the last chapter that there is some evidence for the appearance of 'family privatism' – of the shrinking of the family. Research in the 1950s and 1960s certainly seemed to show that families no longer had as dense a network of social relationships involving wider family as they had previously. A number of factors were cited as responsible for lessened contact with wider family. Particularly significant are the pressures of work on both men and women, including shift work and flexitime; a greater frequency of moving house which disrupts local social networks, including family; a more instrumental attitude to work so that men and women try to earn as much as possible by working longer hours; and the emergence of a pattern of domesticity in which interests shift to the home and its decoration and improvement, the children and the conjugal tie.

How then has the argument fared against more recent research? Certainly the historical claims look a little bit more shaky. The family in pre-industrial Britain was not extended but consisted largely of relatively small households which were not multi-generational. Furthermore, the industrial revolution did not produce the nuclear family form. Rather the reverse. During the horrors of that period, extended families were actually created in urban centres and acted as protective mutual-aid devices.

The central issue, however, is the extent to which individuals and families are involved with their more distant relatives. The essential conclusion from recent work is that there is a high degree of involvement as measured by the degree of contact, the flows of support and the emotional importance accorded to wider family, especially on the continuing significance through life of the parent–child tie.

According to one set of recent studies, based on a large sample survey, one-third of adults live within 15 minutes' travel time of their mother, and no less than 65 per cent live within one hour. This geographical proximity does not, of course, necessarily mean that family members actually see one another. However, it turns out that about half do visit their mother at least once a week and almost three-quarters do so each month. Women, manual workers and, perhaps unsurprisingly, those living nearby will see their mothers particularly often.

If the wider family remains a significant source of social contact for many people, it also continues to function as a form of practical and emotional support. For those who had received practical help, say in times of illness, almost half of that help came from parents and less than 10 per cent from friends. The wider kin network is even more significant in the case of money. Parents were the origin of more than 60 per cent of gifts and loans, with other relatives contributing about 20 per cent. When it comes to flows in the other direction, about two in five of people give care. The most common recipients of care are parents or parents-in-law, who are responsible for about one third of all care provided. There are some intriguing differences between men and women in the provision of care, for women seem to spread the care that they give out over a wider range of people.

On the face of it, therefore, the story of decline in kinship relationships seems unconvincing. Levels of contact are high, flows of support are robust and vigorous, and people routinely include members of their wider family when asked about their closest social networks. Interestingly, the importance of these relationships survives the disruptions to family life that have become more common in the 21st century with the rise in divorce rates and the complexities caused by divorce and the creation of step-families. Wider kinship relationships in turn become very complicated. A parent of an adult child who has divorced may have more than one set of grandchildren. A woman who separates from her partner may potentially end up with more than one network of in-laws. The evidence seems to indicate that kinship systems are sufficiently flexible to encompass these more complex relationships. The pool of kin has become wider and is not based so exclusively on blood ties.

Abercrombie, N. (2004). *Sociology*. Cambridge: Polity Press.

1.3 **Discuss these questions in pairs, then report your ideas to the class.**

   1 **Does the writer agree or disagree with the statement in the essay question?**

   2 **What language does the writer use to indicate his views? What evidence does he provide to support them?**

   3 **How far do you agree with the statement in the essay question? Use evidence from the text, and any additional evidence you have, to support your view.**

2 Inferring the meaning of words

> **Study tip**
> *Before you look up a word you don't understand in a dictionary, try to work out its meaning by using the following strategies.*
> · *Read any explanation or example given by the writer.*
> · *Analyse the word's component parts.*
> · *Look for supporting information in the surrounding context.*

2.1 **Work in pairs. Find these words in the extract and try to work out their meanings.**

privatism (line 11)	**flexitime (line 15)**	**disrupts (line 15)**	**instrumental (line 16)**
domesticity (line 17)	**accorded (line 26)**	**proximity (line 30)**	**kinship (line 43)**

> I suppose 'privatism' is to do with 'being private' – perhaps smaller families are more private, concerned with themselves rather than society

3 Vocabulary building: word families

3.1 **a** **One word in each sentence is incorrect. Replace it with a word from the same word family.**

   1 Before the industrial revolution people had regular and extend contact with their wider family.

   2 People migrated to towns as a result of industry.

   3 There is evidence for the appear of family privatism during the industrial revolution.

   4 Pressures of work on both men and women are particularly significance.

   5 Industrial society led to the emerge of different patterns of domestic life.

   6 In the 20th century, family life has been disrupted by the rise in divorce rates and the complex caused by divorce.

   b **Check your answers in the extract.**

4 Reading in detail

4.1 **a** **What are the characteristics of a 'golden age'?**

> ... a comparison with a lost **golden age** ... (line 9)

   b **Look at the third paragraph of the extract on page 127. Can you find any informal language that would be unlikely to appear in a journal article? Try to reword it in more formal language.**

   c **Try to explain what the complex noun phrase means in this extract.**

> ... extended families [...] acted as **protective mutual-aid devices** (line 22)

d Can you think of a phrase with a meaning similar to *say* in this extract?

> For those who had received practical help, **say** in times of illness, ... (line 35)

e Look at this extract. Was the percentage closer to 60% or 90%?

> The family in pre-industrial Britain was not extended
> but consisted **largely** of relatively small households ... (line 20)

> ❷ *Research shows that in academic writing, a number of adverbs are commonly found in the structure* consist ... of, *including:* entirely, exclusively, largely, mainly, mostly, only, predominantly, primarily, simply *and* solely.
> *Divide these words into two groups: 'not consisting of anything else'; and 'consisting to a large degree of'.*

5 Understanding figures

5.1 You have been asked to give a short tutorial talk with the title: 'The impact of changes in working patterns on family life'. As you prepare, you find these figures (1–3). Match them with the titles (a–c).

a The experiences of work/family conflict of parents in the Netherlands, Sweden and the UK, by working hours (% respondents saying *sometimes, often* and *always*).

b Female employment and selected family policies.

c Average weekly hours of total work for men and women with and without children in Australia.

1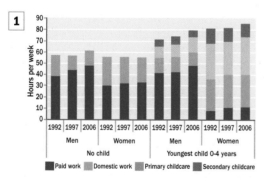

Craig, L., Mullan, K. & Blaxland, M. (2010). Parenthood, policy and work-family time in Australia 1992-2006. *Work, Employment and Society*, 24: 27-45.

2 Table 9

Hours of work per week	Netherlands		Sweden		UK	
	Fathers	Mothers	Fathers	Mothers	Fathers	Mothers
Work makes it difficult for me to do some of the household tasks that need to be done						
< 30	*	44	*	36	*	42
30–39	44	59	44	65	13	52
40–49	53	*	56	64	59	*
50+	72	*	79	*	83	–
Work makes it difficult to fulfil my responsibilities towards my family						
< 30	*	31	*	32	*	32
30–39	42	41	33	59	20	43
40–49	36	*	51	49	43	*
50+	57	*	71	*	70	*
My responsibilities towards my family prevented me from doing my work adequately						
< 30	*	11	*	7	*	15
30–39	12	*	19	18	13	20
40–49	14	*	15	10	24	17
50+	19	*	10	*	37	*
	N = 203	N = 182	N = 234	N = 242	N = 105	N = 185

Note:
* Not included in this table as the numbers are small

Cousins, C. & Tang, N. (2004). Working time and family conflict in the Netherlands, Sweden and the UK. *Work, Employment and Society*, 18: 531-549.

3 Table 2.

	Norway	UK	Portugal
Female employment	76%	69%	71%
	(33% part time)	(40% part time)	(14% part time)
Parental leave	44 weeks 100% or 54 weeks 80% pay (can be shared; first 9 weeks reserved for the mother, 6 weeks reserved for the father) 1 year unpaid parental leave	6 weeks 90% pay + 20 weeks flat rate (mothers only) 2 weeks' paid leave for fathers (flat rate) 13 weeks' unpaid paternity leave	16 weeks (full pay) (first 6 weeks reserved for the mother) 5 (compulsory) + 15 (if required) days' paid leave for fathers 3 months' unpaid parental leave
Dominant solutions for childcare	Public and private (both subsidised) childcare centres	Private nurseries and childminders or relatives	Combination of private, public and family

Sources: Fagnani (2004), OECD in figures (2005), and Ellingsaeter and Leira (2006).

Sümer, S., et al. (2008). Becoming working mothers: Reconciling work and family at three particular workplaces in Norway, the UK, and Portugal. *Community, Work and Family*, 11: 365-384.

Study tip

*When you come across a figure (a table, graph, or chart) in a text, read and try to understand:
1 the title; 2 (in a table) the heading for each row and column; 3 (in a graph) the titles of the two axes and any additional information; 4 any notes below the figure; 5 the main content.*

5.2 a **Work in pairs. Follow the five steps in the Study tip for the three figures in 5.1. Discuss your ideas with the class. Try to use these words.**

➤ *Problem words:*
tendency, tend, trend

G&V **3, p137**

decrease	diversity	increase	substantial
tend	tendency	trend	

b **Decide what information in the figures you would use in your tutorial talk.**

Study tip

Try to understand a figure before reading what the writer says about it. This can help you to understand the text that talks about the figure, and also to evaluate what the writer says.

5.3 **Now that you have tried to understand Figure 1 from 5.1, work in pairs and complete the text that relates to it. Use words from the box.**

greater	height	increased	period	remained
steeply	workloads	70	80	average	shading

Figure 1 shows men and women's **(1)**_____ weekly paid and unpaid work hours in households with and without children in 1992, 1997 and 2006. Total work is represented by the **(2)**_____ of the bars, and the time allocated to paid work, domestic work, primary childcare and secondary childcare is shown by the different **(3)**_____.

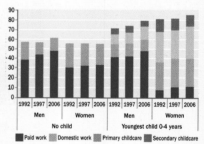

Throughout the **(4)**_____, the total workload of mothers and fathers was **(5)**_____ than that of non-mothers and non-fathers. Moreover, total workloads sharply **(6)**_____ over the period for mothers and fathers, between 1992 and 2006 rising from **(7)**_____.1 to 85.9 hours weekly for mothers and from **(8)**_____.5 to 79.5 hours weekly for fathers. Total **(9)**_____ also increased for men without children, but less **(10)**_____. They rose from 57 to 61.3 hours a week. The total workload of women without children **(11)**_____ level throughout the period at around 55.5 hours a week.

🔾 *Research suggests that* show *is the most common verb in the structure* Figure 1 shows … . *Other verbs often used include:* demonstrate, depict, display, indicate, present, provide, reveal *and* suggest. *Divide these verbs into two groups: verbs that* <u>describe</u> *data; verbs that introduce* <u>implications</u> *of data.*

Listening and speaking

6 Your relationship with your supervisor

When students do a research project, they usually work with one or more supervisors (tutors or advisers). Meetings between student and supervisor are usually referred to as supervisions or tutorials. It is important to develop a good working relationship with your supervisor. This includes establishing what you and your supervisor are each responsible for, and working out how formal or informal your meetings should be.

6.1 Which of these aspects do you think are part of a supervisor's job? Work individually and then compare your ideas in pairs.

1 give a list of all the texts you need to read for your thesis
2 arrange supervisions
3 give detailed feedback on the first draft of your thesis
4 check that the research aims of the thesis can be achieved
5 advise on methods and data collection
6 proofread the final version of your thesis

9780521165211_P138a 7 check that your thesis is within the required word limit
8 check that you are carrying out work to an agreed timetable
9 check that all the references in the text are included in the reference list
10 help you establish the topic of the research

6.2 a (◀) 9.1) Listen to Diana talking about meetings with her supervisor and answer the questions.

1 How many meetings did Diana and her supervisor have in total?
2 What happened in each meeting?
3 Why were the thesis (dissertation) meetings more frequent?

b Which activities from 6.1 did Diana mention?

ana is from Kazakhstan.
...e is studying at a British
...iversity for an MPhil in
...ociology.

7 Formality and politeness in arranging meetings

7.1 a Look at these extracts, in which two students, Karen and Paul, arrange meetings with their supervisors. Reorder the phrases in brackets to form requests to meet.

1
Supervisor: Morning, Karen.
Karen: Hello. Do *you think we could meet* some time soon, please?
(meet / you / we / think / could)
Supervisor: Of course. Later this week? Thursday morning at 11?
Karen: That's great. Thanks

2
Supervisor: Hi, Paul. What can I do for you?
Paul: I _____ today.
(to / need / you / meet)
Supervisor: OK ... Well, I'm busy until four. But after that?
Paul: Yes, that's OK. Thank you.

3
Supervisor: Hello, Karen. How can I help?
Karen: Can _____?
(meet / this / we / morning)
Supervisor: Yes, I should think so. About 11.30?
Karen: Yes, thank you.

4
Supervisor: Afternoon, Paul.
Paul: Hello. Would _____ later this week?
(be / to / possible / meet / you / it)
Supervisor: Yes, of course. Friday, about 11 OK?
Paul: That'll be great. Thanks.

5
Supervisor: Hello, Karen. How can I help?
Karen: I _____ .
(week / to / you / see / want / next)
Supervisor: Right. Is Monday morning OK? About 10?
Karen: Yes, that's right. Thank you.

6
Supervisor: Hi, Paul. What can I do for you?
Paul: I _____ to meet you next week?
(set / I / wonder / a / could / time / if / up)
Supervisor: Sure. How about two on Tuesday?
Paul: That's fine. Thank you.

b (◀) 9.2) Listen and check.

7.2 **Work in pairs. Which requests do you think are polite and appropriate in an academic context? Which do you think are inappropriate?**

7.3 a (◀) **9.3** **Now listen to the beginning of the meetings. How do Paul and Karen address their supervisors?**

1 Hello, Prof ...

b **Work in pairs and discuss the questions.**

1 Which of these forms of address are appropriate and which are inappropriate for a student to use? Share your ideas with the class.

2 From your own experience, do the ways in which students address their supervisors in your country tend to be formal or informal? What factors influence the level of formality?

Writing

8 Writing a critique

Evaluation is an important part of many academic texts. For example, in the extract on page 127, you saw how the writer evaluated ideas on the nuclear and extended family. A text type in which evaluation is of particular importance is the critique. *A critique is a critical evaluation of something you have read, and will often include both a positive evaluation (e.g. that conclusions are valid) and a negative evaluation (e.g. that important information has been left out).*

8.1 **A critique typically has three main sections. Match the common elements of a critique (1–9) to the main sections (a–c).**

a introduction and summary
b evaluation
c conclusion

1 Give a brief statement of your overall evaluation of the work.
2 Are you convinced by the conclusions drawn by the author(s)? Why or why not?
3 Can you see any limitations of the research not mentioned by the author(s)?
4 How good is the evidence (the data and methods) used? How might it have been improved?
5 Briefly restate your overall view of the article, highlighting both strengths and weaknesses of the work (limitations, or areas where further work is needed).
6 Give the name(s) of the author(s), the title and a brief outline of the topic.
7 Report the main findings, conclusions and any implications or recommendations.
8 Are the aims of the research valuable and achievable?
9 Report the aims of the work and the data and methods used.

8.2 *Research is sometimes publicised in a press release issued by a university or funding organisation before it is published in a journal or presented at a conference. An outline of the research is given, highlighting significant findings, so that journalists can report the research in newspapers or magazines, or on radio and television.*

In preparation for writing a critique, you are going to work on a report of some research on nuclear and extended families from a press release. Work in pairs and answer the questions next to the text on page 133.

Are children better off in nuclear or extended families?

Children are worse off living in extended families where their paternal grandfather is head of the household than in nuclear families. But they are better off living in households that include their grandmother.

These are the conclusions of new research by Lena Edlund and Aminur Rahman, which explores household structures and child outcomes in Bangladesh. Their findings will be presented at the Royal Economic Society's Annual Conference this week.

Related research also indicates that the widespread practice of arranged marriages is harmful not only because people cannot marry for 'love', but also because it gives rise to a family structure in which the grandfather has headship, which is bad for children.

The extended family, with the grandfather as the household head, and adult sons and their families under his authority, has traditionally been the prescribed family form in many parts of Asia.

The nuclear family, with its emphasis on the conjugal bond and the emancipation[1] of the prime-aged,[2] has set the European family apart since at least the Middle Ages. While it is accepted that the extended family favours the older generation at the expense of the prime-aged, it is less clear how children fare under the two different family types.

To investigate this subject, the researchers analyse household survey data on Bangladesh, where, as in much of South Asia, there is a strong presumption that adult sons will continue to live in the same household as their father, and that he retains headship. The survey was conducted every four months from June 1996 to September 1997 (four rounds) in 47 villages, where the questionnaire was administered to 5,541 children in 955 rural households in each round. Outcome variables are height-for-age and class completed. Both capture important aspects of a child's current and future well-being and productivity. Height-for-age is a composite measure of the child's nutritional status and morbidity, while education reflects resources intentionally directed to the child.

The fact that children typically outlive their parents means that most extended households eventually convert into nuclear households. This gives rise to variation in household type, which the researchers exploit to investigate their hypothesis that children benefit from having their father rather than their grandfather as head.

They find that children do better in terms of food allocation and education, both important determinants of human capital[3] and future productivity, when they reside in nuclear households.

Interestingly enough, children residing in nuclear households with a grandmother present do best. These are households that arguably combine the beneficial features of both nuclear and extended households: resources are controlled by the father, but there is an extra caregiver, the grandmother. In related work, Edlund (together with Johan Lagerlof) argues that whether extended or nuclear families are the cultural norm depends on who has the right to contract marriage.

This is important from a policy perspective since the practice of arranged marriage is still widespread. The research points to this practice as harmful not only because people cannot marry for 'love' but also because it gives rise to a family structure in which the grandfather has headship, and this has a negative impact on human capital investments in children. (A nuclear family may still support or even co-reside with ageing parents, but unlike the extended family, the elder generation are dependents instead of heads of households.)

1 Why do you think the press release starts with main findings?

2 What is the general aim of the research? What might 'child outcomes' refer to?

3 Is this a controversial conclusion? Is sufficient evidence given below for it?

4 Do you now have a clearer idea of the specific aims of the research? What value might this research have?

5 How useful is this data for achieving the aims of the research? What limitations can you see in either the data–collection method or the type of data collected?

6 What implications arise from this conclusion? Are they realistic?

7 What is your opinion of the findings and conclusions of the research?

[1] emancipation = giving freedom and rights

[2] prime-aged = adults between 45 and 64

[3] human capital = the health, strength, education, training and skills that people bring to their jobs

www.swan.ac.uk/economics/res2004/press/families/edlund.pdf

8.3 **a** **Look at the language frames in bold (1–10), which are useful when writing critiques. Match them with their most likely purpose (a–e).**

1 **Strangely, the authors do not** provide any figures in the results section.
2 **The authors offer a provocative piece of research** on a controversial topic.
3 **I accept that** the Earth cannot support an ever-increasing population. **However,** Smith's solutions are impractical.
4 **It is not clear what evidence the authors have** for their recommendation.
5 **The authors outline / present / discuss** a number of recent approaches.
6 **I fully support the central claim of the authors that** knowledge of the causes of a disease is important for its control.
7 **The authors argue / contend / suggest that** crime victims receive too little support.
8 **In their timely and important work,** Hudson and Charles address the roots of the crisis.
9 **I find persuasive the authors' criticisms of** current European politics.
10 **While I agree that** multicultural education is important, **I think** the authors largely ignore its shortcomings.

a criticise the work
b indicate support for a part of the work
c describe what the authors do
d give an overall evaluation of the work
e indicate support for a part of the work before criticising another part

Note: As critiques present a personal response to a text, in many subject areas it is more common to use 'I' to express opinions in critiques than in other assignments such as essays or theses.

➤ Collocation: evaluative language in critiques
G&V 1, p136

b **Look at these adjectives useful in writing a critique. Are they more likely to be associated with praise or criticism?**

appropriate	comprehensive	convincing	limited	original
restricted	simplistic	small-scale	stimulating	systematic
thorough	thoughtful			

c **Using the outline in 8.1, the answers to your questions in 8.2 and language from 8.3a and 8.3b, write a critique of Edlund and Rahman's work in 400–500 words.**

9 Writing up research: the Discussion section

➤ Comparing results in Discussion sections
G&V 4, p137

9.1 **Compare these extracts from the Results section and the Discussion section of a research report. Which section 'reports' results and which 'interprets' them?**

from the Results section	from the Discussion section
1 Table 1 provides summary statistics for each variable for men, women, and women with dependent children.	3 We also find some evidence that low levels of community trust and reciprocity among men with children may in part be explained by the resource constraints they impose.
2 Our first finding is that marital status is an important predictor of community group membership, trust and reciprocity for men.	4 Our finding is consistent with more recent Australian research by Hughes and Black (2003), which found that community trust was lower among people with children, particularly pre-school and primary-school-age children

9.2 **Read this Discussion section from the same report. Match parts 1–10 with purposes a–g.**

a compare a result with previous research
b report a result
c summarise main results
d suggest further research
e relate a result to theory
f note a limitation of the research
g interpret a result (e.g. by suggesting an explanation)

> **1** In sum, the analyses in this article provide some support for the decline thesis in respect to the role of marriage for men. Overall, however, they provide more evidence that family change is unrelated to community life, or in fact positively related to community life, particularly for women.
>
> **2** Marital status was associated with high levels of community group membership, trust and reciprocity for men, and divorce was associated with low levels. **3** This was in part because marital status is associated with the strength and quality of men's family relationships, as the decline thesis suggests.
>
> **4** In contrast to the decline theory, we found that men with children have lower levels of community trust and reciprocity than men without children. **5** This is also inconsistent with prominent research by Putnam (1996) which found that trust and civic engagement were highest among those who are both married and have children.
>
> **6** We also found that working full time is associated with low levels of community trust and reciprocity among women with dependent children. **7** Long hours in paid work are likely to be a barrier to community engagement and trust where one also has primary or sole responsibility for the care of young children, because of the time constraints associated with combining parenting and full-time work.
>
> **8** It is important to remind the reader that our data are not longitudinal in nature, so we can't determine whether the particular family characteristics we examined caused the community patterns, or vice versa.
>
> **9** Also, the models we estimated explained only some of the variation in levels of community group membership, trust and reciprocity. This means that other factors play an important determining role.
> **10** Research could explore how community group membership, trust and reciprocity relate to personality characteristics and demographic factors, such as cultural background or ethnicity, which the literature suggests may also be important correlates (De Neve & Cooper, 1998; Fukuyama, 1999; Hughes et al., 1999).

Hughes, J. & Stone, W. (2006). Family change and community life: an empirical investigation of the decline thesis in Australia. *Journal of Sociology*, 42, 242–268.

9.3 a **Claims and other ideas in the Discussion section of research reports often include hedging language. Underline the hedges in these extracts.**

1 We also find some evidence that low levels of community trust and reciprocity among men with children may in part be explained by the resource constraints they impose.
2 We would argue that full-time employment is likely to be associated with low levels of community trust and reciprocity among women with dependent children.
3 It is possible that some of these non-family relationships substitute for family relationships.

b **Why do you think hedging is common in Discussion sections? Share your ideas with the class.**

➤ *Hedging*
G&V 2, p136

🎓 **Focus on your subject**
Find two or three Discussion sections from research articles in your subject area. (Note that these sections may not necessarily have the heading 'Discussion'.)
· Identify sections with purposes a–g in 9.2 and note any useful language used to indicate the purpose. Can you find sections that have other purposes?
· Underline all the hedges you can find in these Discussion sections, and suggest a way of grouping them (modal verbs, modal adverbs, etc.).
· Report your observations to the class.

Grammar and vocabulary

Grammar and vocabulary
· Collocation: evaluative language in critiques
· Hedges
· Problem words: *tendency, tend, trend*
· Comparing results in Discussion sections

1 Collocation: evaluative language in critiques

1.1 Express these sentences from critiques more efficiently. Use words from the box with a similar meaning to the sections in bold..

> ~~comprehensive~~ convincing original restricted
> simplistic stimulating systematic thorough

1 This book provides an overview of personal information management (PIM) **that includes everything that is necessary.**

   <u>This book provides a comprehensive overview of personal information management (PIM).</u>

2 The article contains a discussion of Tennyson's use of nature in his poetry **that encourages new ideas.**

3 He takes a view of the role of the media in society **that looks at the topic in a way that makes it seem simpler than it actually is.**

4 She conducted an analysis **that was detailed and careful** of the likely consequences of a proposed reform for the teaching of reading.

5 Harris offers evidence of the need for lifelong learning systems **that makes you believe that he is correct.**

6 Davis uses a definition of 'mental health' **that is limited in what it includes.**

7 She makes a contribution to the debate about the EU's global **role that is different from what has been said before.**

8 Keverne carries out an investigation **that is done carefully and in an organised way** on the role of imprinted genes in the development of the brain.

2 Hedges

Hedges are commonly used in academic language to avoid making statements that are too direct or too confident.

> The argument is, **in many ways**, a story of decline and a comparison with a lost golden age.

2.1 Why do you think the writer includes a hedge?

2.2 Look again at the first paragraph of the text on page 127 and find two hedges. Why are these included?

2.3 a Underline the hedge (a word or phrase) in sentences a below.

   b Decide whether sentences b needs to be made less direct. If so, add the hedge from a in an appropriate place and make any other necessary changes.

1 a Belgium is essentially a bilingual country divided into the Flemish-speaking north and the French-speaking south.
   b Ten percent of the world's population owns 90 percent of its wealth.

2 a Depression on many occasions leads to feelings of suicide.
   b Surveys gather information through written questions and/or oral questioning.

3 a The term 'andragogy' is virtually unknown outside the field of adult education.
   b Construction was halted in many countries during the depression of the 1930s.

4 a Bern's (2002) study appears to be well researched and reaches interesting conclusions.
   b Mercury is the innermost planet in the solar system.

5 a End of course assessment and is most often the form of evaluation used in academic institutions.
   b Long-term unemployment is experienced by older workers who are close to retirement age.

6 a The structure of the noun phrase is relatively neglected in grammars for language learners.
   b As water flows downhill under gravity, it seeks the path of least resistance.

7 a The speed at which business, government and, to a certain extent, the public have begun to use the internet is faster than earlier technology.
   b Everyone's behaviour is determined by their parents.

8 a The results for the males and females in the group were more or less identical.
   b Whereas Asian markets have developed and expanded over the last 50 years, social and cultural values have remained unchanged.

3 Problem words: *tendency, tend, trend*

- *We use* tendency *(of something) to do something to talk about the likelihood of something or someone behaving in a particular way. If there is a tendency for something to happen, it often happens or is likely to happen.*
- *We can use* tend + to-infinitive *to talk about the likelihood of something happening in a particular way, and* tend + to / towards + *noun phrase to say that something increasingly shows a particular characteristic more clearly than others.*
- *A* trend *is a general development or change in a situation. On a graph we may be able to see a trend or line, even though it follows an irregular course.*

3.1 **Complete the sentences with *tendency, tend,* or *trend(s).***

1 Leys (2006) notes the _____ of new governments to increase spending on weapons.

2 It has been observed that stable economies _____ towards lower growth rates (Nixon, 2003).

3 Boys develop the _____ to use direct commands to influence others, whereas girls _____ to use polite suggestions.

4 Chapter 5 looks at recent _____ in family and household composition in Europe.

5 Research conducted by Lamb (1976) indicated that by two years of age, boys _____ to prefer their fathers, while girls prefer their mothers.

6 The upward _____ in official crime rates since 1960 in the US may reflect increases in both the volume and seriousness of offences.

7 Marx claimed that there was a _____ for the rate of profit to fall during the course of history.

8 If prices increase in one industry, this will _____ to raise demand in others.

3.2 **Write a short paragraph reporting the information in each of these figures. First say what is described and then comment briefly on the findings, using *tendency, trend,* or *tend.***

1 *Changes in employment by industry and gender: 1990–2010*

Primary and utilities = agriculture, mining, gas, electricity, etc.
Other services = health, education, etc.

Proportion of men and women in part-/full-time employment by age group

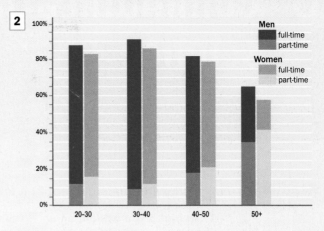

4 Comparing results in Discussion sections

In 9.2, you saw that one of the elements commonly found in the Discussion section of a research report is to compare your results with those of previous researchers.

4.1 **a Decide whether the researcher's results agree (write A) or disagree (D) with those of previous researchers. Underline the phrases that indicate agreement or disagreement.**

1 These findings are in keeping with the pioneering studies of Blume and Friend (1975, 1978) who used data from the 1960s. ____

2 These results contrast with those of Bates et al. (1995), who found that native adult speakers had more difficulty indicating the gender of opaque nouns compared to transparent nouns. ____

3 Our findings accord with earlier research indicating, for example, that divided government influences trade policy. ____

4 The present findings confirm previous reports (McKelvie & Demers, 1979; Phillips, 1978) of no relationship between the VVIQ and recognition memory for faces. ____

5 These results are consistent with the previous studies of the FT-SE 100 by Yadav (1990). ____

6 The results presented here do not support the findings of Lindenberger et al. (1993), who found that 20% of the variance in fluency was accounted for by age among a sample of older adults. ____

7 The findings endorse Lewis's view (1993) that language is made up of lexical chunks. ____

8 The results of this exploratory study differ from those reported by Hughes (2006). ____

b In students' theses, the majority of comparisons with previous research indicate agreement rather than disagreement. Can you suggest why this might be the case?

10 Communicating science

Reading

1 Following the argument in a long article

1.1 In Unit 5 you worked on an essay with the title 'Discuss the influences on the general public's understanding of science and scientists'.

   a Look again at pages 76–78 and remind yourself of some of the points and evidence used in the essay.

   b Work in pairs or small groups. Discuss and write down an outline for the essay title. Make notes on the main points in each section and identify any areas that you need to research further. You will need to refer to these notes later.

1.2 a In preparation for the essay, you are going to read an article with the title 'The Big Bang – a Hot Issue in Science Communication'. Work in pairs and discuss these questions.

   a What do you already know about the 'Big Bang'?
   b Do you know any other theories about how the universe was created?
   c Why do you think it is called a 'hot issue'?
   d The article is from the journal *Communicating Astronomy with the Public*. What is the difference between astronomy and cosmology?

   b Match the words from the article (1–7) with the definitions (a–g).

   1 contentious   **a** an attempt to do something
   2 counter-intuitive **b** being certain that you are right and everyone else is wrong
   3 dogmatic   **c** basing belief on power of luck or magic rather than scientific
   4 endeavour (noun)   knowledge
   5 pseudo-scientific **d** likely to cause disagreement
   6 superstitious   **e** different behaviour, ideas, etc. from what is usual
   7 unorthodox   **f** describing something that doesn't happen as you would expect
                            g claiming to be scientific even though it is not

1.3 Read the article on pages 139–142. To guide you through it, questions are given for each section. Work in pairs and answer the questions.

Introduction

1 The hot Big Bang theory has been extremely successful in correlating the observable properties of our Universe with the known underlying physical laws. However, there are some difficulties associated with the Big Bang theory. These difficulties are not so much errors as mathematical assumptions that are necessary to make some progress, but that do not have, as yet, a fundamental justification. Nevertheless, the Big Bang, taken as a whole, is the most complete and evidence-based explanation that astronomers currently have to account for the origin and evolution of the Universe.

> **1a** Do the writers support the Big Bang theory?
> **b** Do the writers think the public fully understand it?
> **c** According to the writers, how might journalists and scientists contribute to public misunderstanding of the theory?

However, the public understanding of this theory appears to be a somewhat hit-and-miss affair, a situation that is exacerbated not only by the public, but also by journalists and scientists. Most of the issues surrounding the Big Bang can only be understood and resolved with some training in the field. To the outside observer, it would appear that the discipline is riven with dissent. Is this just a case of the public misunderstanding the issues and failing to grasp the connections between disciplines that are necessary to make sense of this theory, or is this misperception one that is due to confusing and contradictory statements issued by the press and scientists alike? This article will examine these issues.

The Big Bang as a scientific theory

2 The Big Bang was named by its strongest critic, Sir Fred Hoyle,[1] during an interview for the programme, *The Nature of Things*, broadcast on BBC Radio in March 1949. As used by cosmologists, the term 'Big Bang' generally refers to the idea that the Universe has expanded from a primordial hot and dense initial condition at some finite time in the past, and continues to expand to this day. It is a cosmological model describing the initial conditions and subsequent development of our Universe, and is supported by comprehensive and accurate explanations based on current scientific evidence and observation, engaging such fields as astronomy, cosmology, chemistry and quantum physics.

> **2a** Did Fred Hoyle support the Big Bang theory?
> **b** What natural phenomenon does the Big Bang theory attempt to explain?

3 From the above, we can already pinpoint a few misconceptions. First of all, contrary to popular belief, a scientific theory is not limited to one area of science; the Big Bang theory is grounded in several scientific disciplines. In addition, a scientific theory continues to be tested repeatedly and the results create a body of evidence supporting the theory. Furthermore, part of the problem with scientific understanding is science education (formal and informal) itself. It usually presents 'the facts', as if everything were already

> **3a** How many 'misconceptions' do the writers give?
> **b** Do they say these are misconceptions of the Big Bang theory, or scientific theory more generally?

➤ *as if*
G&V **2, p149**

known. Science is taught as if it were something complete, a finished endeavour, but science can never be complete as it is constantly being modified and extended by new observations or measurements, which in turn lead to new insights and predictions; and it is this flexibility that makes the 'scientific method' so successful in explaining the world. It does not hold dogmatically to outdated or incorrect information or paradigms as if 'the truth' had been found once and for all, an approach that separates it from religion.

Finally, any gaps in our understanding of a scientific theory do not always bring the overall theory into question – just because we don't fully understand gravity, it doesn't mean that we can't predict what will happen when we jump from the top of a building.

> Science is a work in progress; it is an ongoing human endeavour. It will never be fully complete, otherwise curiosity, and thus part of what it is to be human, would die. The communication of science needs to emphasise this point (Oliveira, 2008).

Communicating the Big Bang

4 Any science communication exercise has to recognise the cultural, educational and social setting of its audience and adjust to this. Communicators often make an assumption that their audience will be reasonably well-educated and aware of some of the fundamental science that will be touched on within the context of the work. These assumptions illustrate the problem of making an

> **4** What main problem of communicating science to the public do the writers identify?

effective interdisciplinary communication. A general audience will be made up of people with different agendas, training, interests and professions. They will, according to Scanlon et al. (1999), probably reflect C. P. Snow's[2] definition of the "two cultures" with the emphasis on the humanities rather than on the sciences. Inevitably something is going to be lost in translation, and few readers or listeners will be able to follow all the arguments or points covered.

5 These are valid points, but communicating the wonder of our understanding of the Big Bang need not be difficult. For instance, take Bill Bryson on cosmic background radiation:

> Tune your television to any channel it doesn't receive, and about one percent of the dancing static you see is accounted for by this ancient remnant of the Big Bang. The next time you complain that there is nothing on, remember that you can always watch the birth of the Universe. (Bryson, 2004)

Science communication of this type is excellent: pithy, entertaining and pointed. Bryson is not a scientist, so his message had to be understood first by him, and then re-written for a public audience. Whilst most journalists follow this approach, they do sometimes fall short – as we shall see later. Occasionally, of course, it is difficult to communicate an idea correctly and scientific simplifications may become oversimplifications and lead to public misconceptions, such as the 'Solar System' model of the atom for example.

Sadly, even the most well-known science writers can fall into the negativity trap and cloud the waters of understanding. Take the following quotes from Terence Dickinson, recipient of the Royal Canadian Institute's Sandford Fleming medal for public communication of science.

- The Big Bang theory is the best explanation we have for the origin and evolution of the Universe. It may be wrong. It may even seem childishly naïve a century from now …
- One concept favoured by researchers in this field offers the fanciful hypothesis that our Universe was created from nothing (Dickinson 1993).

These quotes may seem negative and confusing and, although Dickinson then goes on to attempt an explanation of the underlying theory, he starts two chapters on the intricacies of the Big Bang in this fashion. This form of communication may lead to confusion, as the general reader may get bogged down in the later explanations so that the only part of the discussion that registers are these descriptions of a well-developed theory that is being questioned rather than explained! Here Dickinson is attempting an expression of scientific honesty about the nature and methods of theoretical science as it pertains to the Big Bang. However, such honesty can result in legions of doubters, some of whom then go on to portray the Big Bang theory as problematical, leading to public confusion, with a resultant focus on pseudo-scientific explanations that are presented as fact.

6 This problem can be further illustrated by the writings of astronomer Tom Van Flandern. Van Flandern is notorious for his unorthodox views (human face on Mars, the asteroid belt as an exploded planet) and has written several books on such themes, in addition to forming the Natural Philosophy Alliance and the *Meta Research Bulletin* to propound his unscientific viewpoints. With the rise of alternative explanations, be they religious or pseudo-scientific, what Gregory and Miller (1998) would later call the "anti-science" alliance arose as a form of public communication that supplied positive answers to the doubts of an interested public. In this vein, Van Flandern's views on the Big Bang theory have been received by a wider audience. In public broadcasts and in the pages of the *Meta Research Bulletin*, Van Flandern gives a short list of the leading problems faced by the Big Bang in its struggle for viability as a theory, such as:

- Static Universe models fit the data better than expanding Universe models.
- The microwave background[3] makes more sense as the limiting temperature of space heated by starlight than as the remnants of a fireball. (Van Flandern, 1997)

It is not our intention to answer these points here – and they all have scientific counter-arguments; rather we quote them in full to illuminate the point that the Big Bang theory is in the public domain as a point of argument. It is also an argument that appears to be dressed in scientific clothing, thus compounding the public's problems of perception and choice, muddying the waters of public acceptance and understanding.

7 Van Flandern's views are increasingly being taken up by the pseudo-scientific and religious communities, who not only misunderstand, but misrepresent the Big Bang theory. This sowing of doubt and uncertainty affects the public debate as it gives the false impression that the Big Bang is questionable as an explanation of the Universe's origins. Whilst any scientific theory can certainly be questioned, the methods used should be

---

➤ *Punctuation: colons and semi-colons*

G&V 1, p148

5a The writers identify three weaknesses of many science communicators. What are they?

b What consequences of such weaknesses do they note?

c It is unusual in academic writing to give personal details of the authors whose work they cite ("Terence Dickinson, recipient of [...] communication of science"). Why do you think this information is given here?

d Overall, do the writers seem critical of Terence Dickinson?

6a Do you think the writers are more critical of Van Flandern or Dickinson?

b What do the writers say is the main consequence of writing such as Van Flandern's?

7a What criticisms do the writers have of what they refer to as "the pseudo-scientific and religious communities"?

b What effect do the writers say the actions of these communities have on public understanding of the Big Bang and how scientists view the Big Bang theory?

consistent with scientific methodology. This is not to say that the Big Bang is inviolate; the Big Bang is open to investigation, and is falsifiable according to Popper's definitions,[4] but it must be pointed out to the public that the theory is not under threat within science; some of the interpretations of data are argued over, but the Big Bang as a theory is as solidly founded as Darwinian evolution. How, then, can science communicators face the challenge of informing the public debate?

What now for communication?

8
Perhaps recognising that the public communication of science is a field that is contentious and little understood would be a starting point for communicators. One view of the "dominant" model of science communication (Hilgartner, 1990) sees science as watered down for public consumption and losing some of the flavour and nuances of the rigorous science along the way.

> **8** What main criticism of the dominant model of science communication did the House of Lords Select Committee have?

This model was recently aired and criticised at high levels. In February 2000, the House of Lords Select Committee on Science and Technology[5] reported: "society's relationship with science is in a critical phase" (Hansard, 2000). The report showed that public interest in science was high, yet there was a basic lack of trust in science. The problem was not the amount or quality of the science available for public consumption, but how it was communicated. The committee concluded that:

> There is a condescending assumption that any difficulties in the relationship between science and society are entirely due to ignorance and misunderstanding on the part of the public: and that with enough public understanding activities, the public can be brought to greater knowledge, whereupon all will be well. (Hansard, 2000)

9
It is this assumption of education, science activities and public involvement leading to a more science-oriented society that is at fault. It is obvious from the foregoing examples from our Big Bang case that society is not always attracted to, or even trusts, the answers science gives them. There is no doubt that the public do have more access to information, and thus can be better informed and more educated than ever before. There is no doubt that publications relating to popular science are at an all-time high and the proliferation of Discovery-type TV channels and the plethora of podcasts and radio programmes dedicated to science communication are a testament to the literacy of the public. What is needed is not more public understanding activities, but more acceptance within society of one standard (Odenwald, 1996).

> **9a** Do the writers appear to support the view of the House of Lords Select Committee?
>
> **b** What do the writers suggest (again) is needed to improve public understanding of science?
>
> **c** What advantage do they think 'pseudo-science' has over science in communicating with the public?

The public are not trained scientists and are open to competing claims of knowledge, as seen by the example of Tom Van Flandern given above. What the *Meta Research Bulletin* and other pseudo-scientific sources do well is to transmit certainties about the scientific alternatives which are more ideologically suited to a public audience than the necessary uncertainties of the world of science. The "meaning" in such transmissions already fits with a worldview that is part of the audience's culture and society in a way that the "counterintuitive unnatural nature of science" (Wolpert, 1992) does not.

10
How then can the communication of science answer, or, at least, successfully compete with alternative ideas from such philosophies, pseudo-science or religion? The Big Bang theory strikes at the heart of human philosophical and cultural meaning, uprooting a secure humanity from a known place in the Universe to one of unimaginable smallness, adrift in the unfathomable sea of space. This is the core of its contentious state for those who seek a more comforting and meaningful alternative. It is also a reflection of the place of science and its communication in our society – where does science fit in our culture? It is up to scientists to ensure that we replace one set of meaningful values with one of equal meaning that is deeply rooted in a new culture that addresses an understanding of our place in the cosmos.

> **10 a** According to the writers, what impact does the Big Bang theory have on humans?
>
> **b** What do they think scientists will need to do to find a role for science in our society?
>
> **c** Do they think that the Big Bang theory and creationism are incompatible?

This is not to say that any science communication is going to be perfect. Scientists understand the limitations of models in ways in which the public do not. Simply denying the theory merely because it cannot answer every question or seems to impinge on the power of a creator does not mean that the theory is incorrect. Ultimately, the Big Bang model is about the origin and evolution of the Universe from the Planck time onward (10^{-43} seconds) and can say little about events prior to this. In a broad way then the theory is not 'anti-creationist' and does not negate a spiritual comprehension. A greater understanding of the event leads to a more profound respect for the many facets of our Universe both physical and spiritual.

Conclusion

11 The battleground of public understanding of science is then the open house of a democratic culture. It has taken centuries of cultural, social, economic and political struggle to build and is a continual work in progress. All that scientists can do is to continue to build bridges between experts and the public in such a way that these democratic and scientific ideologies become encapsulated in society. This should not be done within Hilgartner's "dominant" paradigm, but should be an inclusive, open-minded and honest appraisal of the state of science and its uses within politics and society. Science does not stand outside human society; it is an integral part of it. Science therefore should recognise the changes in philosophies and ideologies that it has wrought and should address the idea that science removes "meaning" from life, from philosophies and from cultural institutions. Science not only answers "how and when", but also supplies the "why". If science communication can adequately meet these challenges it will achieve much.

This will be a slow process that will have its share of losses and triumphs along the way, but is an ideological war that is worth the fight. The price of failure is a return to a dark age that may become all the longer and protracted if the superstitious and anti-science alternatives gain the upper hand. As Carl Sagan (1997) once emphasised, "it is far better to grasp the Universe as it really is than to persist in delusion, however satisfying and reassuring".

> **11a** The writers conclude by saying that the dominant paradigm of science communication should be replaced. What do they say it should be replaced with?
>
> **b** Can you think of any other controversies in science that could have been used in the article, instead of the Big Bang theory, to illustrate the problems of science communication?

Notes:

1 Fred Hoyle (1915–2001) was a British astronomer and mathematician.

2 C. P. Snow (1905–1980) was a British physicist and novelist who argued that there is a breakdown of communication between the sciences and the humanities (the 'two cultures' of modern society) and that this prevents the world's problems being solved.

3 'Microwave background' is radiation thought to be left over from the very early stage of development of the universe.

4 Karl Popper (1902–1994) was an Austro-British philosopher of science. He argued that a theory can only be considered scientific if it is falsifiable; that is, if it is false, then this can be shown by experiment or observation.

5 A committee formed by members of the House of Lords, the unelected part of the Parliament of the United Kingdom.

Griffiths, M. & Oliveira, C. F (2010). The Big Bang – a Hot Issue in Science Communication. *Communicating Astronomy with the Public Journal*, 10, 7–11.

1.4 **Sentences a–n summarise the main steps in the writers' argument in the main parts of the article. Put the steps in order.**

The Big Bang as a scientific theory

a For a number of reasons, the public misunderstand aspects of the Big Bang theory specifically, and scientific theory more generally. ___

b The Big Bang theory is a valid one, drawing on evidence from a number of disciplines. _1_

Communicating the Big Bang

c When science communicators point out that a scientific theory may not be true, this can lead to confusion among the public. ___

d Scientific theory is open to question, but the methods of challenging scientific theory should themselves be scientific. ___

e Few general readers or listeners can understand the details of scientific explanation. ___

f Public confusion gives rise to pseudo-scientific explanations, which are presented as fact when they are not. ___

g Science communicators need to adapt what they say to their audience. ___

h It is possible to communicate scientific theory, such as the Big Bang theory, simply and effectively. ___

What now for communication?

i   The public today has access to a great deal of scientific information. ___

j   Science communicators need to consider the place of science in modern society. ___

k   The Big Bang theory is not necessarily incompatible with a spiritual understanding of the universe. ___

l   The dominant model of science communication assumes that the public needs to be given simplified scientific information. ___

m   The public should accept one standard of science. ___

n   The public may prefer the certainties of pseudo-science to the uncertainties of science. ___

1.5 **Work in pairs.**

    a **Discuss how far you agree with each of the main steps in 1.4 (in the order in which they come in the article).**

    b **Overall, how convinced are you by the writers' argument?**

1.6 **Read the article again and make notes to answer the essay question in 1.1. Use these headings.**

- Communicating science to the public
    - What problems do scientists face?

- Pseudo-scientific information
    - How does it differ from scientific information?
    - What impact does it have on the public understanding of science?

Listening and speaking

2 **Working with your supervisor: ending a meeting**

> **Study tip**
>
> *Before you leave a supervision, make sure that you know exactly what you need to do before the next meeting. If your supervisor doesn't write down your next objectives for you, summarise what you think you need to do and ask for confirmation.*

You are going to hear the ending of three supervisions, in which research projects on public attitudes to science are discussed. The endings follow a typical pattern.

2.1 **a** **◀)) 10.1** **Listen to the first conversation and complete the expressions in the table below.**

	Conversation 1	
say what you think you have to do	So can _____ – you _____ should…	
ask for confirmation	Is _____?	
say that you understand	OK, that's _____.	
request another meeting	What _____ good _____ next meeting?	
confirm the time	Fine. That's _____.	
thanks	Thanks _____.	

    b **Work in pairs and complete the last column with other expressions that could be used.**

c (🔊 10.2) (🔊 10.3) Listen to the second and third supervision meetings and add useful expressions in the table below. Had you written any of these in 2.1b?

	Conversation 2	Conversation 3
say what you think you have to do		
ask for confirmation		
say that you understand		
request another meeting		
confirm the time		
thanks		

d Which of the three students you heard do you think is closest to finishing their thesis?

2.2 Work in pairs and take the role of supervisor and student in meetings to discuss what the student should do next on their thesis. Use language from 2.1.

Student

You have written your proposal for research on the understanding of climate change among teenagers, and this has been accepted.

Supervisor

Your student has completed their proposal for research on the understanding of climate change among teenagers. The next step is for them to write an introduction of about 1,000 words. They should briefly review the literature and identify a gap in the research which they are trying to fill. (There has been little research on the understanding of climate change among this age group.) They should also identify two or three specific research questions they are trying to answer. Suggest they write a first draft of the introduction and email it to you in about three weeks, a week before your next meeting. The next meeting should be in a month from today at the same time.

Writing

3 Writing practice

3.1 Using what you wrote on page 78, the notes you took on page 143, and your own knowledge, write an essay of 1,500 words with the title 'Discuss the influences on the general public's understanding of science and scientists'.

4   Editing your work

Developing good editing skills is important for success in academic writing. You should carefully check and improve your assignments before you submit them.

4.1   a   Below is a checklist of questions to ask yourself when editing your work. (Not all the questions will be relevant to each assignment.) Complete the checklist with headings from the box.

Claims and evidence	Organisation	Use of the literature
Style and presentation	**Clarity and relevance**	

Assignment-editing checklist

a _____

1   Does the Introduction tell the reader what is to come?
2   Can the main points of the assignment be clearly identified (e.g. can I underline them)?
3   Do (sub)headings give a clear outline of the organisation of the assignment?

b _____

1   Is every point I make clear?
2   Are all parts of the assignment relevant to the question? If not, can they be omitted?
3   Does the Conclusion sum up what I have said and relate it to the question?

c _____

1   Are the claims I make justifiable?
2   Do I give evidence to support claims where necessary?
3   Do I hedge claims appropriately, or do I overstate them?
4   For an argumentative essay (e.g. *Discuss. ..; To what extent* ...?), is my position on the topic clear (in the Introduction, Conclusion, or both)?

d _____

1   Do I depend too much on one or two sources?
2   Do I use too much quotation?
3   Have I checked that all quotations are accurate?
4   Have I integrated quotations accurately into the text?
5   Have I paraphrased sufficiently to avoid plagiarism?
6   Have I followed conventions in the in-text references and in the reference list?

e _____

1   Do I avoid features of spoken English such as contracted forms (e.g. *it's*) and idiomatic language?
2   Do I use personal pronouns (*I, we*) appropriately?
3   If I refer to other parts of the text, do I do this appropriately (e.g. with *above* and *below*)?
4   Do I use nominalisations where possible?
5   Do I use gender-neutral language?
6   Do I avoid too much repetition?

b   Can you think of any other questions to add the checklist?

c   Work in pairs. Read your partner's essay from 3.1 and note any corrections and improvements using the checklist. Then discuss these with your partner.

5   Writing up research: the Abstract

An Abstract (sometimes referred to as a synopsis) is a brief summary of a thesis or journal article. You will probably be given instructions by your institution or department on how long your thesis Abstract should be. If not, ask your supervisor for advice.

5.1   At the beginning of your thesis, you will probably need to include an Abstract. These typically include some or all of the following elements.

Purpose	Conclusion	Results	Introduction	Methods

a   What is the most likely order of these elements?

b   Although the Abstract will come near the beginning of your thesis, it may be the last section that you write. Why do you think this is?

5.2 **Put the sentences in these Abstracts from journal articles in order. Then identify which elements from 5.1 are included in each abstract. Work individually and then compare answers in pairs.**

Abstract 1

A | Students' pre-instructional ideas were investigated through the use of several student-supplied-response (SSR) surveys, which asked students to describe their ideas about topics such as what is a star, how is starlight created, how are stars formed, are all stars the same, and more.

B | The results from more than 2,200 responses suggest that although students often have some initial knowledge about stars, their knowledge is often incomplete or incorrect in important ways that could negatively impact instructional objectives.

1 Purpose → C | This study investigated the beliefs about stars that students hold when they enter an undergraduate introductory astronomy course for nonscience majors.

Bailey, J. M. et al. (2009). College students' pre-instructional ideas about stars and star formation.
Astronomy Education Review, 8.

Abstract 2

A | Compared to their European counterparts, the American public has been characterized as relatively unknowledgeable and indifferent about genetically modified foods.

B | If these results are any indication, moral and ethical issues will dominate any discussion of foods derived from a mixture of animal and plant genes.

C | However, participants tended to be familiar with debates surrounding benefits, risks and moral issues associated with agricultural biotechnology applications.

D | To evaluate these claims, six focus groups were held in three Arkansas cities to: (1) determine the extent of knowledge the public possesses about genetically modified foods; (2) detail perceived benefits and risks associated with agricultural biotechnology applications; and (3) explore lay perceptions about the genetic modification process itself.

E | Findings also showed that while participants were not overly concerned about combining genes between plants, they were concerned about inserting animal genes into plants.

F | Participants demonstrated partial knowledge, and tended to overestimate the number of genetically modified foods.

Knight, A. J. (2008). Perceptions, knowledge and ethical concerns with GM foods and GM process.
Public Understanding of Science, 18, 177–188.

5.3 a **Complete this Abstract with phrases from the box. The expressions in bold are typical of particular Abstract elements.**

analysis also demonstrated	purpose of this work was to
results showed	these results it may be stated
was conducted	a significant role

The 1 _____ **determine** if public communication of science and technology (PCST) has any influence on people's decision to become dedicated to scientific research.   *Purpose*

For this reason, **a national survey** involving 852 researchers from all disciplines 2 _____ in Argentina.   *Methods*

The 3 _____ **that** the factors affecting scientific vocation are many, and that, regardless of differences in gender, age or discipline, the greatest influence on the decision to go into scientific research is exerted by teachers.   *Results*
The 4 _____ **that** different manifestations of PCST (science books, press articles, audiovisual material, and activities such as visits to science museums) **play 5** _____ **in** awakening the vocation for science.

From 6 _____ **that** PCST – in addition to its function of informing and forming citizens – exerts a significant influence in fostering scientific vocation.   *Conclusions*

Stekolschik, G. et al. (2010). Does the public communication of science influence scientific vocation? Results of a national survey. *Public Understanding of Science*, 19, 625–637.

Study tip
Certain words and expressions are commonly used in particular elements of Abstracts. It can be useful to make a note of these to use in your own Abstracts.

b **Look again at the Abstracts in 5.2 and underline any useful words and expressions associated with particular Abstract elements.**

 Focus on your subject
Take an important journal from your subject and study the Abstracts from a number of recent articles.
· Can you identify the five elements from 5.1? Are there other elements? Do Abstracts in the journal typically have fewer than five elements?
· Underline any language associated with particular elements.

Grammar and vocabulary

Grammar and vocabulary
- Punctuation: colons and semi-colons
- Conditional expressions

1 Punctuation: colons and semi-colons

1.1 Match the examples (a–k) to the rules (1–10).

Colons are used:

1 to introduce lists (e.g. _c_)
2 before a subtitle where the subtitle gives an explanation or paraphrase of the title (e.g. ___)
3 at the beginning of a clause giving a reason or explanation (e.g. ___)
4 to introduce a quotation that does not form a continuous sentence with the previous text (e.g. ___). Note that where it does, no punctuation is needed (e.g. ___)

Semi-colons are used:

5 to join two main clauses that are grammatically separate but linked in meaning (e.g. ___). Note that a full stop can be used instead.
6 before sentence connectors (e.g. ___). Note that a full stop can be used instead.
7 to separate longer items in a list (e.g. ___)
8 to divide items in a list which are themselves divided by commas (e.g. ___)

Note that we use commas rather than semi-colons:

9 to join a clause beginning with a conjunction (e.g. *after*, *in that*) to the main clause (e.g. ___)
10 to connect a finite and non-finite clause in a sentence (e.g. ___)

a Organising a club is a social action, in that it brings people into contact with each other.
b It has been claimed that investment in science is "essential to national success" (Givens, 2005).
c ~~The factors influencing variation in health care provision fall into three key areas: social, political and economic.~~
d Norway has a policy towards parents and children; the UK has a policy towards families.
e A central theme of the discussion of working men is complexity: many workers were both employees and employers, and were engaged in different occupations across the year.
f Older community-dwelling adults value the ability to manage independently their daily tasks (Kutner, 2001; Tanner, 2001; Hinck, 2004).
g The children in Group B had lower reading ability than those in Group A, despite being more than a year older on average.
h The Mental Hygiene Law resulted in a rapid increase in hospitals and patients: in 1954 there were 224 hospitals with a total of 37,849 beds; in 1955 there were 260 hospitals with a total of 44,250 beds; and in 1961 there were 543 hospitals with a total of 106,265 beds.
i Culture has been defined as follows: "a learned system of meaning and behavior that is passed from one generation to the next" (Carter & Qureshi, 1995).
j Cosmology: the science of the universe
k In 1926, the women employed in the factory demanded an increase in wages as well; however, their employer rejected their demand.

1.2 Correct the punctuation in these examples of students' writing.

1 After being interviewed; students were asked to fill in a questionnaire.
2 A conjunction is a word that links two clauses, phrases, or words, a connector links two separate sentences.
3 The computer has changed our lives forever; although many people claim that it wastes people's time.
4 Parents rarely attended meetings, as a result they had little influence on decision-making in the school.
5 Bullying in the workplace has been found to be very common (Carter, 2001, Rose, 2004, Kester, 2006).
6 There are three main types of radiation, Alpha radiation, Beta radiation, and Gamma radiation.
7 Natural disasters; protecting the public's health
8 There are several negative impacts of inflation including; demands for higher wages, to keep up with consumer prices, people buy and store goods, creating shortages, and civil unrest, such as the demonstrations in 2011.
9 The second theory suggests that children; "are positively reinforced when they say something right and negatively reinforced when they say something wrong" (Fromkin & Rodman, 1998: 329).
10 As Norman (2002) asks "What does it mean to be well-educated?"

2 Conditional expressions

It is very common in academic communication to talk about conditions; that is, the circumstances in which a particular event could happen. A variety of expressions are used to talk about conditions.

2.1 **a** **Underline the conditional expressions in these sentences. The meaning of the expression is given in brackets.**

1 Science education usually presents 'the facts', <u>as if</u> everything were already known. (= describing how a situation seems to be)

2 Observations suggest that the universe will continue to expand forever. If so, it will cool and eventually be unable to support life. (= if something is true)

3 Anaerobic digestion produces biogas that can be used for power production, provided that there is a market. (= only if a particular thing is done or happens)

4 Even if there is a risk of side effects of the vaccination, these are tiny in comparison with the risk of catching the disease. (= whether or not)

5 To be effective, teachers must have sufficient knowledge to help students solve problems that arise. Otherwise, both the teacher and the student can become frustrated and learning is impeded. (= if something does not happen, or is not true, something else will happen)

6 Any eight-character password is acceptable, as long as it has both letters and numbers. (= some circumstances must exist before something can happen)

7 Unless students have some understanding of musical theory, they are unlikely to enjoy performing as much as they could. (= if something does not happen, or is not true, something else will happen)

8 The size of the class should be manageable. If not, it may be necessary to divide the class into smaller groups. (= if something is not true)

9 Geographers usually classify climate on the basis of vegetation, assuming that vegetation is mainly a response to climate. (= accepting as true)

10 In the event that the president dies in office, the government as a whole resigns and a general election is called. (= if something happens)

b **Which expressions are connectors and which are conjunctions?**

2.2 **Complete sentences 1–6 with phrases from boxes A and B. (Note the punctuation.)**

A		
in the event that	as if	as long as
even if	if so	otherwise

B
both members of the pair are the same part of speech
the word ended in 'er'
it meant disagreeing with her husband
you may be accused of plagiarism
it would be the first confirmed picture of a world outside our solar system
they are ever found by intelligent life-forms from other planetary systems

1 A daughter in Ancient Rome was expected to remain loyal to her father, _____.

2 Whether you paraphrase material or write it in your own words you should acknowledge the source. _____.

3 In some accents, words ending in the letter 'a' are pronounced _____.

4 A group of European astronomers claim to have photographed a planet orbiting another star. _____.

5 Synonyms can be nouns, verbs, adjectives or adverbs, _____.

6 The Voyager space probes carry audio-visual discs with information about life on Earth, _____.

2.3 **Complete these sentences in any way appropriate.**

1 Many shops will accept goods for return provided that …

2 Doctors should explain treatments simply and clearly. If not, …

3 Total censorship of information on the internet is impossible unless …

4 Assuming that students have access to a computer, …

Lecture skills E

Preparing for lectures
· Discussion on culture
· Vocabulary for the context
· Understanding slides and predicting content

Listening
· Practice in gist and detailed listening

Language focus
· Signposting language
· Referring to diagrams

Follow up
· Further listening
· What happens in lectures

Preparing for lectures

As part of a course focusing on cultural studies, you will hear a lecture called 'The Monocultural Challenge Revisited' given by Professor Guido Rings from the English and Media Department of Anglia Ruskin University, Cambridge.

Guido Rings

1 Discussion on culture

1.1 **a As preparation for the lecture, think of examples that you believe represent your country's culture.**

· a book or story
· a painting or sculpture
· a song or piece of music
· a film
· a sport
· an historical event

b Work in pairs and discuss your ideas. If you come from the same country, give reasons for your choices. If you come from different countries, explain the significance of your choices.

c Work in groups. Decide what you think is a good definition of 'culture'.

Study tip

Academic study often involves working with abstract nouns such as culture, which often have shifting definitions. It is useful to look at different ways these abstract words are used in different contexts. When encountering abstract words in an academic setting, you may need to consider new interpretations of meaning.

2 Vocabulary for the context

2.1 **a Match the adjectives in the box with definitions a–d.**

| monocultural multicultural intercultural transcultural |

a involving a lot of different cultures, but they may not connect
b involving some kind of interaction between people from two different cultures
c involving just one culture
d involving or extending across different cultures

b Now match the underlined prefixes in 2.1a with definitions 1–4.
1 across
2 one
3 between
4 many

3 Understanding slides and predicting content

3.1 Match each set of bullet points (A–D) to the headings (1–4).

1 Methodology   **3** Topic: definition of culture
2 Aims   **4** Research questions

A
- How is cultural difference most commonly expressed and to what extent does this follow traditional concepts of culture?
- How is the interconnectedness of cultures articulated and how does this relate to different notions of interculturality and transculturality?

B
- transcultural theory as developed by Welsch (1999), Huggan (2006), Antor (2006); see also Iljassova-Morger (2009)
- post-colonial discourse theory (Said 1978, 1993; Bhabha 1994; Antor 2006)

C
- raise cultural awareness
- enhance intercultural and transcultural competence

D
- a 'collective programming of the mind' manifested in 'values [...], symbols, heroes, and rituals' (Hofstede 2001: 11, 2ff.)
- an operative concept: 'culture is [...] always a consequence too of our conceptions of culture' (Welsch 1999: 4)

Study tip

Some lecturers organise their lectures around the four headings in 3.1, particularly if the lecture refers to research that the lecturer has carried out. Professor Rings provides headings on his lecture slides. However, this is not always the case and it is useful to identify these key aspects of a lecture from the content and the language used in the slides. For example, it is possible to recognise slide C as the aims because it contains two verbs (raise, enhance).

3.2 Predict the order in which Professor Rings will introduce each heading in the lecture.

Listening

4 Practice in gist and detailed listening

4.1 ▣ E.1 **Watch an early part of the lecture and answer the following questions.**

a Were your predictions about the order of headings correct?
b What is the key focus of this excerpt? Choose the best option.
- to outline the aims of the lecture
- to establish a practical definition of culture for the purposes of the lecture

4.2 ▣ E.2 **Watch the next extract and complete the notes.**

- monoculturality, multiculturality etc. all linked to idea of **1** _____
- human mental programming:

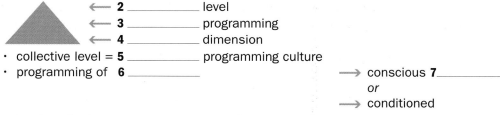

    ← **2** _____ level
    ← **3** _____ programming
    ← **4** _____ dimension

- collective level = **5** _____ programming culture
- programming of **6** _____   → conscious **7** _____
                                        or
                                        → conditioned
- 'reality of culture → our conceptions of culture' = programming families, school, **8** _____ , virtual world (cinema)
- popular films can shape your **9** _____ of culture

Study tip

In this part of the lecture, Professor Rings uses gesture to suggest a diagram. This idea is picked up on and used in the notes. Lecturers will sometimes give visual clues with visuals or slides that can help you decide how to represent your notes.

Language focus

5 Signposting language

5.1 ▐ **E.2** **Watch this part of the lecture again in more detail. Put extracts a–f in order.** ☐

a   What we are interested in, of course, is the collective level. ☐

b   And here comes probably the most important sentence ... ☐

c   But we need a working definition to start from, I think ... ☐

d   ... and that brings us back to the programming of the mind. ☐

e   That brings us already to the monocultural challenge. ☐

f   ... German philosopher Wolfgang Welsch tries to summarise here in the following words. I quote. ☐

5.2 **Think about the context for each extract in 5.1. Match them to functions 1–6.**

1   introduce the next main section of the lecture

2   indicate a specific focus on an idea

3   indicate a specific focus on part of a quote

4   link back to an idea previously mentioned in the lecture

5   define a key word or concept

6   introduce a quotation

Study tip

Many lecturers use language that is similar to Professor Rings' examples in 5.1. This aims to guide the person listening to the lecture, so you know what it coming next or what has been previously mentioned. Learning to listen for this language will help you to understand the overall structure of a lecture and also listen for what are key points.

6 Referring to diagrams

On the right is a diagram called an acculturation curve that is referred to by Professor Rings in the lecture. This illustrates typical reactions when a person encounters a new culture, particularly if they go to live in a new country.

6.1 **Study the diagram and then discuss what you think it represents. Give specific examples of possible behaviour at each stage (for example, during the initial euphoria stage, people might be excitedly seeing and doing as much as they can).**

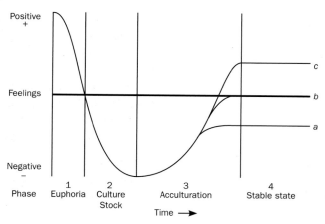

Hofstede 2000

6.2 ▐ **E.3** **Watch Professor Rings explain the acculturation curve. Was his explanation similar to the ideas you discussed in 6.1?**

6.3 a (E.4) **Watch the explanation again. Complete the script with one word in each gap.**

> Whatever you call it, you come usually with relatively high expectations. Some are higher than others, but with positive feelings. That is the **1**_____ **2**_____. There **3**_____ be exceptions to the rule of course but the tendency is that you come with certain high expectations – you wanna go abroad you're looking forward to it. Well the higher your expectations are the more **4**_____ it is that these expectations will be disappointed. You will be frustrated at some stage. It **5**_____ happen after a couple of days. It **6**_____ happen after a couple of weeks.

b **Discuss the questions in pairs.**

a   What kind of language is used in the gaps?

b   How much does Professor Rings refer to and point to the diagram on the screen?

c   Does his use of this language mean he sees the diagram as a very prescriptive model or something that includes the idea of variations?

6.4 a (E.5) **Watch the final part of the explanation of the acculturation curve again. What is the aim of this part? Choose the best answer.**

· to *reiterate/interpret* the information in the diagram

b **Watch again. Make notes on the two key ideas he mentions in this excerpt.**

c **Complete this extract. Watch again to check.**

> So the **1**_____ is – there are two **2**_____ to make. I would **3**_____ that when the culture shock hits you, that is usually the moment when people retreat …

d **Does the language in 6.4c indicate that Professor Rings is expressing an objective point or a subjective point?**

Study tip
When lecturers use diagrams, graphs and charts, they do not always point specifically to the visual information. They may describe and interpret the information in the diagram and use it as a basis for interpretation and putting their own ideas across. Their explanation and ideas are often tentative rather than definite. It is important to listen carefully to the language lecturers use to understand how information in a diagram or graph is being presented.

Follow up

7   Further listening

7.1 a **Before viewing a further part of the lecture, read the information below and think about how Professor Rings will structure his talk, and what vocabulary he will use.**

Mono-cultural features
• characteristic for European colonialism and 19th/early 20th-century nation building
• link to notion of 'the people': homogeneous, essentialist and separatist
• double-sided concept: a culturally/racially 'pure' and superior *Self* versus 'impure' and inferior *Other*
• paradigm of assimilation and exclusion (see Herder 1989 [1784–91]: 45)
• continues after decolonisation

b (E.6) **Watch the lecture and check your predictions.**

c **Watch again and make notes on the monocultural features talked about.**

d **Check your understanding in the script on page 166.**

8   What happens in lectures

8.1 (E.7) **Listen to what Fotis says about what happens in lectures and answers the questions.**

a   What do lecturers assume students have done before lectures?

b   Do they cover one point in detail or many different points quickly?

c   Why do some lecturers not follow a classic lecture structure?

d   What benefit does this have?

Audioscripts

The transcripts of lectures and interviews are from authentic recordings and there may be some slips of the tongue or grammatical errors which are normal for both native and non-native speakers. These are shown as [*].

Academic orientation

🔊 **0.1**

Max: Well, I think the main difference between undergraduate work and postgraduate work is how, how much more structured I think the undergraduate experience is, even when compared to my MPhil, which is unique in some respects in Cambridge because it's entirely untaught. It's purely a research course so the degree comprised pretty much of, of me meeting with my supervisor, meeting various writing deadlines, but it was unstructured in the sense that I didn't have any courses. I didn't formally have to attend any seminars, whereas of course when you're an undergraduate, or when I was an undergraduate, I had a very specific set schedule. I had, uh, a class, a certain number of hours per week. I had, uh, designated times when I had to meet with various professors and, and everything was sort of all planned out for me by the university – and when I came to Cambridge for my MPhil, it was, I was still in, in a, in an MPhil course that did require me to, to meet specific deadlines, and I, and I did have to attend, uh, some, some training sessions and, and some various, erm, some various seminars but, uh, it was pretty much all untaught and, and it's just kind of, the PhD has magnified that. Now it's, it's really on me to figure out what I, I need to be doing, uh, with, with my daily schedule, what I need to be reading and I don't have, uh, even my supervisor is not, uh, overseeing my course of studies, uh, day in and day out. It's, it's really, it's really up to me.

🔊 **0.2**

Youness: So, erm, I'm working on letters that were written by women in the second millennium BC. And I'm working on, erm, their level of literacy compared to the one of their husbands or brothers. And so I would talk about first of all, the fact, well, emphasising the fact that not a lot of scholars worked … well, worked on these letters. They were more focused on the men and since most of them were merchants they were more interested in the, uh, economic history behind it. So then I went on, uh, talking about how many women I would choose and how many men I would choose and how I would compare both of these letters. And then I had another part where I would just, uh, talk about the questions I would ask. Uh, so for each group I had a group with, well I had three different groups of women, and for each group I have two or three questions that I would try to answer in my dissertation, and then I would have the conclusion.

So basically, that's an overview of the research proposal.

Unit 1

🔊 **1.1**

Anna: OK, so Ken found the next graph that we're going to look at. Do you want to tell us what it's about?

Ken: Yeah, sure. Well, most of the information on advertising and consumer behaviour we've looked at so far has been international rather than country-specific. So I thought it might be good to get some data on a particular country, and I found this on China. It's a bit out of date, I'm afraid – 2009 – but I think it's still quite interesting. It shows various product groups – clothing, health and beauty aids, and so on. And then it gives the percentage of people who express a preference for products from countries or regions – China, the US, Europe, and so on …

🔊 **1.2**

1

Anna: There are only a couple of areas where European brands are more popular than US brands – clothing, and furniture, for example.

Barbara: Can I just come in here …? Yeah, I think it's interesting that European brand furniture is a lot more popular than US furniture. Maybe this is because of one furniture store …

2

Ken: … and so Chinese clothes seem to be preferred by a vast majority. If we look at jewellery, we can see a similar pattern …

Dejan: Can I just come back to what you said about clothing? You may be right that Chinese brands are preferred, but it might just be that as they're made locally, they're better value than imported clothes …

3

Anna: … so it's really perhaps not surprising that Japanese electronics are so far ahead.

Barbara: Can I just pick up a point you made a while ago? You said that there wasn't much difference in preferences for health and beauty aids. That's certainly true to some extent, but …

4

Ken: … and I think, in general, the price of many European products is quite high, and that's why they're not preferred in areas like clothing and electronics.

Dejan: Can I say something here? I think that the

situation in electronics is likely to have changed quite a lot since 2009, when these figures were collected. It seems to me that …

5

Anna: … Korean jewellery tends to be quite exclusive, so might be quite popular among the better-off in China.

Barbara: Can I just go back to something you said earlier? You said you weren't surprised that Chinese-brand drinks were so popular. But if you think about the worldwide brands produced by US companies …

6

Ken: … and furniture is something that everyone has to buy. Most of it isn't a luxury like jewellery or electronics.

Dejan: Can I just make a point here? It seems very surprising to me that European furniture's so popular in China given the distances that it has to travel. It must be incredibly expensive …

Unit 2

🔊 **2.1**

A: Well, I suppose the most obvious advantage of credit cards is that they're so convenient. You don't have to carry around lots of cash or a chequebook and identification.

B: That's certainly true. And I think they've encouraged people to shop online. If they didn't have credit cards, it would be more difficult to buy things online – I don't know how you'd do it. It's just so easy with a credit card.

C: Probably too easy, actually. You've only got to hit a button and you've bought something that perhaps you don't really need, or you can't afford. It means that it's very easy for people to get into a lot of debt.

B: Yes, and the credit card companies charge huge rates of interest – a much higher percentage than if you were getting a loan from a bank.

A: If you can get a loan from a bank. One of the advantages of credit cards is that people can get short-term loans quite easily. OK, so they might have to pay high interest rates, but …

🔊 **2.2**

1

A: … and another problem is that everyone pays a bit extra for goods through a credit card supplement, whether they use a credit card or not in a shop. That seems pretty unfair to me, because it puts prices up for everybody.

B: Er, I'm not sure what you mean by credit card supplement.

A: Well, what I mean is that in some shops a bit extra

is added to all the prices because most people pay by credit card, and the shop owners have to pay the credit card company for every purchase. So they can try to get this money back by this credit-card supplement.

2

A: ... and the transaction charge has a big effect on small shopkeepers. A lot of them have gone out of business in the area that I live because they just can't make a profit. It's not the same for the big supermarkets, though. They seem to encourage people to use credit cards.

B: Erm, I didn't quite understand what you said about the impact of credit cards on small shopkeepers.

A: Well, I meant that the transaction charge – the amount the shop has to pay to the credit card company – has a much bigger effect on small shops than on the supermarkets. Small shops have to add it to the price of goods, but supermarkets can absorb the costs elsewhere. So prices in small shops go up in comparison ...

3

B: ... cheap credit, for example, has got both pros and cons. On the one hand, it encourages economic growth because people spend more, but on the other hand, people can get into financial difficulties.

A: Could I just check that I got what you meant by the idea of cheap credit?

B: OK, let me try and explain again. If lenders make it easy for people to borrow money, and also make it available at a relatively low rate of interest, then that's cheap credit. And it's a real danger for some people, particularly people on low incomes...

4

A: ... I know that family budgeting courses for credit card holders have been used in some countries, and these have been quite successful. For the majority of people, though, it's just a question of being sensible and not trying to borrow too much.

B: Sorry, I didn't catch what you said about family budgeting courses for people with credit cards.

A: I was trying to get across that some people need help dealing with money. They may find it difficult to balance what money they've got coming in and the money going out. For these people, some kind of course might be useful ...

5

B: ... it's a problem that hits young people a lot, I think, although lots of other age groups have other kinds of difficulty. Older people, for example, often have problems in keeping track of their income and outgoings.

A: Er, I don't think I understood what you said about the particular problems younger people have with credit cards.

B: What I was trying to say was that when you're not used to having a credit card, it can be difficult to get the hang of making sure you've got enough to pay off the balance at the end of the month. And this is a problem for young people in particular, I think ...

Lecture and seminar skills A

A.1 **A.2**

Lecturer: So that last piece of writing, which was very, very difficult, it- it's quite interesting because it shows a lot of features that are typical of business writing that I'm gonna be talking about today. But, erm, when I'm thinking about business writing I like to think of it in terms of the body. So if writing were a human body, which-, which of these would you like? Who would like this gentleman who's pass- possibly eaten quite a lot over the past few years? Would you like to look like him? Would you, would you like your writing like him? What about our skeletal friend here? Anyone want a skeleton? No. What about our athletic body?

Student A: He's very handsome!

Lecturer: He, he is quite handsome isn't he? Erm, so I'm going to be talking through how language is like the human body. You've already dealt with the fat. That cutting process, trimming the fat, getting rid of flabby writing, that you find in phrases like: 'we are of the opinion of' for, 'we think' or 'in excess of' when we mean 'more than'; 'at the present time' for 'now', er, 'and with the minimum of delay': 'quickly'. Now, one of the things we touched on towards the end of the last session was the question of abstraction. And do you remember I showed you this real life example of bad business language? 'We are a provider of fluid transfer solutions'. Yeah and people thought maybe it was a logistics firm or you know, I don't know ...

Student B: Pipeline.

Lecturer: Pipeline, pipeline, and it sort of was pipelines because it was hoses. Erm, and that's very, very typical that people trying to impress their customers or their clients or their competitors go into sort of very abstract language, erm, and so we talked a bit about abstract nouns. Can you remind me what an abstract noun is?

Student C: Ideas.

Lecturer: Ideas. So, a noun as we-, as we know, is a-, a person, place or thing, so, a bottle, a table, these are all things that we can touch, whereas an abstract noun is a thing but you can't touch it. Erm, so, our official definition, 'a noun denoting an idea' as you say, 'an emotion or a feeling, something that's not physical and can't be touched'. So, 'jealousy', 'advice', 'justice'. Or these businessy words, 'expansion', 'implementation', 'strategy'. Business language seems to attract these types of, er, words. And the thing about abstract nouns is they're quite easy to spot, though people tend to use them too much and don't realise that they're using them, but they're quite easy to spot. Er, they often come from verbs or adjectives. So 'available' gives you the abstract noun 'availability', 'efficient' gives you 'efficiency', another good businessy word that, er, possibly one could get rid of. 'Reduce' becomes 'reduction', 'enhance' becomes 'enhancement', 'expand' becomes 'expansion'. And this is where our human body comes into it. To me, your abstract nouns are like your skeleton. They give your writing structure, they're necessary, often nouns are, you can't write a sentence without using a noun. But if you use too much of them, your language feels very rigid and dead, your writing feels very ossified. Do you know what I mean by ossified? Sort of rigid and bony. When you use verbs, your language automatically has muscle. It's dynamic, it moves your writing forward. And I'll show you some examples. So here's an example, 'The road created a connection between two villages'. So where's the abstract noun in that sentence?

Students: Connection.

Lecturer: Connection. And, as we see, there's a perfectly good verb that you could use instead. So not only do abstract nouns make your language less concise, it also makes it less muscley. Er, 'The road created a connection'. That word, what's wrong with ... the phrase 'created a connection'? Why?

Student C: It's not clear what type of connection it is. Is it road or is it internet connection? Or perhaps it's a phone.

Students: The road-, the road can't create itself.

Lecturer: Exactly, it can't create anything. So this is just a sort of padding verb, it's a filler verb, so your verb in this sentence isn't doing the real work of the sentence. Whereas here – and as you say, that can often introduce ambiguity – whereas here, 'The road connected two villages' is much punchier, as well as being shorter. Abstract nouns are very easy to spot, they often have similar endings. So, er, when I'm talking to business people who use a lot of abstract nouns, I often say you can actually do a search and replace in your computer and look for these common endings, 'ion', observation, 'ity', conformity, 'ment', agreement, 'isms', 'acy' provides immediacy, 'ence', we show patience, 'ability' and 'ness'. All these endings tell you that you're dealing with an abstract noun. And as you can see, it creates- when you use one you always have to have a filler verb to make a sentence, to make it make sense. So, to make an observation, rather than to observe. And you'll find that business people use these sorts of phrases a lot. So, for example, this is a phrase I see a lot, 'driving improvements in the business'. How might that be said in a more muscular way?

Student D: Improving.

Student E: To improve.

Lecturer: To, improving the business, yeah. We're not driving improvements, we're not driving anything. We're improving the business, yeah. 'Delivering change across the firm'.

Students: Changing.

Lecturer: Changing the firm, yeah. 'Our teams are focusing on cooperation'.

Students: Cooperate ... Cooperating.

Lecturer: Coop-, cooperating, yeah- yeah. 'Our firm is committed to growth'.

Students: Growing.

Lecturer: It's growing. And doesn't that sound so much more dynamic? If you say 'we're committed to growth', you're not ...

Student E: It doesn't mean that you are growing.

Lecturer: Exactly, exactly. It means that you're possibly planning to grow at some point, once we've had the meeting and finalised the agenda. 'Supporting business expansion'.

Students: Expanding.

Lecturer: Expanding bus-, yep, yeah. 'Facilitating communication'.

Students: Communicating.

Lecturer: Communicating. Can we think of a less ... do you remember we talked about 'Latinate' versus 'Anglo-Saxon' verbs. Communication, communicating is quite Latinate. Can you think of a less Latinate way of saying 'communicating'? Simpler, shorter?

Student G: Collaborating

Lecturer: Collaborating. That's ... I'm not sure that's shorter! Erm, talking to each other. Talking to each other. 'Achieving success'.

Students: Succeeding.

Lecturer: Succeeding. Yeah.

A.3

Lecturer: OK do you want to, erm, take a look at, erm, the next exercise. Again, some real life examples of business language. It's entitled 'Curing Nounitus'. Do you know what I mean by 'Nounitus'? Nounitus. So, if you have a disease of your tonsils in your throat, you'd call it 'Tonsillitis'. Or your appendix, you have 'Appendicitis'. So, quite a few of us professional writers we- when we see copy writing that has got a lot of nouns in it we- we think of it as diseased. So it's Nounitus. So if you could cure those examples of Nounitus ... That would be great.

A.4 – A.7

Lecturer: So, do you want to have a go at, erm, talking us through number one?

Student B: The first, er, the first phrase here?

Lecturer: Yep, number one.

Student B: OK, number one. Er ...

Lecturer: So do you want to read out the original?

Student B: OK. 'We have the willingness and capacity to close this transaction in the most rapid and effective manner and we are confident in our ability to deliver a solution that will be acceptable to all parties'.

Lecturer: Great, now first of all, can you talk me through the abstract nouns?

Student B: Abstract nouns are the following: willingness, and, er, er, maybe solution ...

Lecturer: Capacity ... transaction ...

Student B: Solution.

Lecturer: Ability ...

Student B: And effective manner.

Lecturer: Manner?

Student B: Manner, yeah.

Lecturer: Yeah, yeah. OK, so how would a human being say that?

Student B: I'll try like a human being to say that. Er, we can quickly close the transaction and we are confident in solving a problem that will be acceptable to both of us.

Lecturer: I think you had far fewer abstract nouns there, yeah. So, 'we have the willingness and capacity', so we're willing and able.

Student C: We have a-, another phrase.

Lecturer: Do you have an alternative?

Student C: We will ban the thing in an effective and acceptable way.

Lecturer: We will do what?

Student C: Ban the thing.

Lecturer: Bend the thing?

Student C: Ban. Ban the thing.

Lecturer: Ban the thing?

Student C: Yeah, ban, you know? Ban ... Yeah when ... there's no such word ban?

Lecturer: Ban? Ban the thing?

Student C: Yeah ban the thing, yeah.

Lecturer: You could - you're trying to do a deal not ban stuff.

Student C: No? Perhaps the word 'ban' is wrong.

Lecturer: The ban, we will ...

Student C: OK, we will cancel the thing, in an effective and acceptable way.

Lecturer: Well I think you are trying to do a deal rather than cancel something. Closing this transaction.

Student G: We also have an alter-alternative.

Lecturer: OK.

Student G: Er, we are close to, er ... to transact rapidly and effectively and this solution will be acceptable for all us.

Lecturer: Close, yeah I mean you're definitely much less abstract. So- though I'm not sure you got ... I mean what, what they're trying to say is that we're not actually close to finishing the deal yet, but we are willing and able to. We're committed to this deal. So we're willing and able to seal the deal ... quickly and we're confident. I've no idea what 'deliver a solution' means, it's such business language.

Student G: Deliver a solution.

Lecturer: Er, we're confident that the deal will, will please everyone, I think is what they're trying to say.

Student G: It will be acceptable for everybody.

Lecturer: Yeah, acceptable to all parties.

A.8

Youness: Mm. Yeah, I think the biggest challenge I had to face, uh, while presenting, uh, a seminar was really to have confidence in, in the fact that I had prepared a lot. That even though I wasn't a, a native speaker, I was able, I, I could contribute in one way or another to the seminar by bringing in new ideas or, you know, come or coming up with questions, interesting questions. Because I think the tutors were not expecting a lot from us, it was really they just left us, they just wanted us to, you know, erm, they just wanted to see how you would prepare a topic and, you know. So they just left us really free. In a way.

Unit 3

3.1

A: I think it's fairly obvious that it's air pollution in the city that's causing the respiratory problems.

B: It looks that way, yeah. I suppose it could be that all the cars are producing pollution and this is damaging people's breathing.

C: Yes, that's a possibility. Maybe also the industry is affecting the air quality. It doesn't say what kind of industry it is, but if it's heavy industry like steel or chemicals, then that's going to be a problem.

A: That could be right, but other cities have a lot of cars and industry without too many difficulties. I think the most likely cause of the problem is the location of the city. If it's surrounded by mountains, then maybe the pollution can't escape – it can't get blown away, so it just builds.

B: Yeah, that sounds reasonable. So what are we going to suggest might be done? The mountains can't be moved.

C: No, obviously the pollution needs to be controlled in some way. I think that a number of steps would need to be taken, but we've got to come up with just one response to start with.

A: Well, one option would be to build better public transport systems to get people away from their cars.

B: That might be difficult, though. It would be really expensive, and it's not easy to put in new tramways or railway lines in a city that already exists. It would mean demolishing a lot of buildings.

C: Yes, maybe that's not the best answer.

A: What about if tighter controls were put on the polluting industries? Perhaps giving them financial incentives to produce less pollution and threatening to fine them if they don't.

B: Certainly a possibility, but if they did that, it might be that the industries would just relocate to other parts of the country or move to other countries completely. That would really hit the economy of the city.

A: Going back to the cars – maybe they could encourage people to buy electric cars for commuting. The prices have come down such a lot recently.

C: I'm not sure that's likely to help much if they keep their petrol engine cars as well.

A: No, but if they only use the petrol cars for less frequent longer trips out of the city, that's going to cut down the pollution a lot.

B: Yes, maybe that's a possibility.

A: OK, so we've got to come up with one recommended response. None of the three we've talked about seems perfect in itself, but it looks like we're in agreement that encouraging the use of electric cars might be a good first step.

B: Yes, that would be best.

C: Fine.

Unit 4

🔊 **4.1**

1

In 1977, Kenneth Olson, the founder of Digital Equipment, said: 'There is no reason for any individual to have a computer in their home.' Well, how wrong he was – with computers found in a growing number of homes, and many homes have a number of computers. This rapid growth in access to computers, and the development of the internet, has had huge implications for how business is conducted. And what I want to talk about today is one aspect of this – shopping for groceries online. I'll divide the talk into two main parts. First, I'd like to talk about some of the experiences of supermarkets over the last ten years, focusing on the problems they've faced and the lessons learned. After that I'll go on to look to the future and try to make some predictions about what online grocery shopping will be like ten years from now.

2

Over the last decade, distance-learning programmes have become increasingly popular, in large part because of advances in information technology. Making material available on DVD or online has created a potentially enormous market for distance education, without geographical boundaries. Furthermore, the use of online discussion forums allows teachers and students to interact in a virtual world, recreating many of the benefits of studying in a traditional university environment.

In my presentation, I'd like to look at the experience of undergraduate business students taking an online course. First of all, I'm going to provide some information about the students and the course they're following. Second, I want to consider whether the students' experience of distance learning is influenced by their age, gender and past experiences. Finally, I'll suggest some implications of what I've found for the design of future distance-learning programmes.

3

It's remarkable to think that, according to the latest estimates, around 20 million people in the United States are telecommuters – by that I mean people who work at home by communicating with their offices through their phones and computers. In the next three years, it is expected that the number will rise by 65% in the public sector and 33% in the private sector, and this trend is being repeated round the world.

Although there are many advantages of telecommuting, as these figures suggest, my presentation today looks at the problems associated with telecommuting. The first thing I want to do is outline some of the economic disadvantages – the high costs of setting up employees for home work, and the hidden administrative expenses, and after that I'll look at the social costs, particularly the lack of interaction between employees. In the last part of the presentation I want to present a case study of a telecommuting friend of mine, and highlight the problems she faced and how these were overcome.

Lecture and seminar skills B

📃 **B.1** 📃 **B.2**

Lecturer: Er, what I'd to do now is get you to look at some more business language, and I'd like to divide you into teams of threes. So, maybe that's a good team. Maybe, four here, and five there. OK, so what you have, there are six extracts. So, three types of writing. One is, er, talking to investors. The other one is, erm, talking to industry experts. And then the final one is talking to bankers, economists, politicians and the general public. So what you've got is two extracts under each. Two different types, two writers with very, very different styles, and I would say that one is better than the other in each case. Erm, what I'd like you to do is, so, if you could do talking to investors. So the two extracts, extract one and extract two. Would you like to do talking to, 'cos I know we have an economist here – so I would like you to do the third one, talking to bankers, economists, politicians. So you're talking to the industry experts.

Student G: Choose which extract is the best?

Lecturer: Have a look, do some analysis, there's some guidelines in the question, don't feel you have to stick completely to the guidelines. But those are some questions to think about: the language, and which one sounds more human? Which one sounds friendlier? Why might they have adopted a certain style? What I'd like you to do is to make some notes as we did in the last session, erm, and then I'd like each group to present their ideas on each the two extracts to the rest of the class. So, erm, have a read. What you might want to do is start off just by giving a, a quick read and squiggling, putting a squiggle, squiggly line, underneath anything that just sounds odd. You might also want to do an exercise where you circle all the abstract nouns, 'cos I guarantee one extract will be more abstract than the other. And then make some notes to present to the rest of the group.

📃 **B.3**

Student G: Let's do it like this. Er, right, fea- first of all features. Pl- er, first extract, second extract, plus and minus, plus and minus.

Student B: We have some questions here. So, the first question, answer the question 'would you prefer', what do we prefer?

Student G: We prefer.

Student B: We choose, we choose, we will choose one of the abstract, and then we will describe the issue. OK?

Student G: We can describe both of them, they say- er, then say because this has more pluses. That's why we prefer it.

Student B: OK, you're the linguist.

Student G: OK, so ...

Lecturer: I mean you don't have to stick rigorously to the questions, but they're a good guideline for things you might want to think about.

Student G: So, erm ...

Student B: The language.

Student G: The features, features ...

📃 **B.4**

Student B: So, we have here, er ...

Student I: Technical.

Student H: Technical.

Student B: Tech- technical.

Student G: Technical and business.

Student B: Technical, 'cos it's – technical and er ...

Student G: And business

Student B: Business. Not business because is also ...

Student J: Jargon

Student B: Technical and difficult. Difficult language. Technically difficult.

Student H: Or complicated.

Student B: Complicated.

Student H: Complicated.

Student B: Yeah. And second is simple and, er–

Student J: Was about complicated language.

Student G: Yes, so write 'C' for complicated and 'A' for, and 'U' for understandab-, it's understanding.

Student B: Understanding. No ...

Student J: No understanding is relative to language.

Student G: To language, yeah he's right.

Student B: So we should write here business, business at first is business language here. Er, first extract.

Student G: Technical, technical and business.

Student J: Technical.

Student B: Technical and business.

Student G: Technical and business.

Student J: Business jargon here.

📃 **B.5**

Student G: Moving to the structure about the advertisement so it's more easier [*] to read when the text is listed because you- you just see the main- yeah you can see that the text has ...

Lecturer: Bullet points, again. Very useful in business writing.

Student G: And its, er, not so difficult to read it, er, as the first one because the first one is just simple text with two extracts and they are quite long. An- and talking again about the length of the sentences, it can be even four lines I counted and it's just really difficult to read it in one breath.

Student H: Five point, er, abstract nouns, er, in the first extract we can find very, very many abstract nouns. Only, er, abstract noun 'solution' we can find five times.

Lecturer: OK, great, yeah.

Student H: Solution, solution, solution, in each- in each, er, sentence.

Lecturer: And in any of those uses do you know what it actually means?

Student H: I've- we don't know. And, er, in exer- number two, we can't- we can't find, er, abstract nouns.

Lecturer: OK.

Student D: So, now we are moving to the second question. Er, does either author, er, assume the witness is as knowledgeable as, er, they are. So, er, this two extracts is, erm, probably, er, some kind of report. Erm, er, speaking about the first, er, ex- extract, er, we can see that, erm, the writer assume that, erm, readers knows, er, are some kind of specialist because, er, there are a lot of, er, abbrevia- er, two, two abbreviates ...

Lecturer: Abbreviations, yeah.

Student D: Abbreviations, sorry.

Lecturer: Yeah. Ca- do you want to tell us what they are?

Student D: Er, one is, er, er, 'FOMC' and the second one is 'JOER'. And the write-, writer say [*] nothing about, erm ...

Student E: Explanation. Explanation

Student D: Explanation of this abbreviate. [*]

Lecturer: And what did the second author do with theirs?

Student D: And, er, the second one- er, the second author, er, explanate, er, their, er, abbreviate [*] 'FOMC', er, it is, er, the 'Federal Open Market Cabinet- er, Committee', and he doesn't use, er, the, the, 'IU- JOER' word.

Lecturer: Instead, what does he or she do? It a, I think that what they do is they actually explain it. Erm, it can lower the interest rate that the Fed pays to banks on the reserves they hold ...

Student D: Yeah, he, he, he use interest rate.

Lecturer: Yeah, yeah. So, explains what it is.

Student D: He explains what's it. So, erm, er, what, er, summarising this question, I can see that probably the, er, extract number one can be used as a parliament report, er, because erm, er, writer, er, the main, er, er, the main theme of writer is to make everybody not to understand this.

Lecturer: Oh, right.

Student K: Number three was, which author would you rather do business with? Er, who would you trust more? For my part, I would trust more the author of the extract two, er, because, er, it's really more easier [*] to understand this extract. Er, because the first extract is overcrowded with special, specific terms, expressions, and some were so, very complicated, Latinised, er, and, er, in the extract two, the same idea, the author could put the same idea but using more common use words. What I ...

Lecturer: Can you give me some examples?

Student K: Erm, for example here simply says that, erm, 'Committee hasn't decided but I will say two things just simply, think number one, think number two'.

Lecturer: Right.

Student K: So it's ... Clear structured.

Lecturer: And the first in the original one, he says 'at this juncture, the committee has not agreed on specific criteria or triggers for further action, but I can make two general observations'. So 'I can say two things', instead of 'I can make two observations'. More- more verby, less abstract. Yeah. So, yeah, good point.

Student K: Yes, and also the extract number one is overcrowded with nouns. And in extract number two there is a balanced quantity of nouns and verbs. Er, so that makes it more concrete.

Lecturer: Great, yeah.

Student K: More relevant to the audience.

Student E: As to the, as to the fourth point I think, er, the author of, er, the first extract is the scientist or maybe the expert in the economic field. Er, because use a lot of specific terms, and without explanation. And, er, from by, from my point of view maybe it is, erm, article or a ... because, erm, the author uses, erm, academic style, academic writing style. There are a lot of complex, formal ... impersonal words, er, for example he often or she often uses words such 'significant', 'considerable', er, instead of 'much', 'a lot of', etc. He use passive, 'be' .... Er, he use observation, divitation [*]

Lecturer: So passive forms of the verb and abstract nouns.

Student E: Yes. Er, I think, er, the second extract is more easy to understand, and if, er, the article was written by a scientist, sh- always should use simple way, because all people should understand what he wants to te- to tell you. That's why we all think that the- the extract number two is better way.

📖 **B.6**

Student F: We just separate our list for four parts. Er ...

Student L: That's the ... we are talking about.

Lecturer: Oh, do you want to introduce the- the two extracts? 'Cos the others haven't read them.

Student C: So we were saying two texts for investors, one was more formal, second was less formal. And we write here ...

Lecturer: You have the texts in front of you on the first ...

Student C: And we have written here their growing contract.

Lecturer: Do you want to ...OK, do you want to just talk us through the situation in each text?

Student C: Each text, oh.

Lecturer: So that ... shall I? T- the situation ...

Student C: The situation.

Lecturer: Is that they're both from annual reports, and in each case the company has been in trouble. It's lost some money. So it's an awkward situation

that the writer, who is the CEO, is having to explain to investors. OK?

Student C: Right, right. So, perhaps maybe we'll start with the first text, in he will speak about pro of the first ...

Lecturer: She will speak.

Student C: She will speak about pro of the text.

Lecturer: So the pros of the first text.

Student F: Er, so some of the advantages of this text, er, the first one it's, it's very detailed because, er, we, er, see the de- details about, er, situation and we, erm, they provide some priorities and it's very clear ...

Lecturer: So the ... for example ...

Student F: In the end, yeah ...

Lecturer: The use of ...

Student F: The end of the text.

Lecturer: The use of bullet points is very- that's very useful in business text to make- make your meaning clear.

Student F: So, it's ... it is well, well structured because we see, er ... Describe it, describe it. Description of this creation, and some- some details and then conclusions and priorities as- as I said and it's formal.

Lecturer: Can you give me some examples?

📖 **B.7**

Karhtik: The process I use for preparing the presentations is basically, uh, it comprises most of the things you have mentioned for instance the language, the PowerPoint presentation and then of course the content ... It's a complete mixture and all of them should be at the right proportion, to make for the readers an interesting and at the same time understandable [*]. Erm, so personally, the way I try to do the presentation are first understand what the, uh, listeners are going to get from my talk and what will make them interested in this talk to come, if they come and what they will be interested in to take it [*] from my seminar talk. So, to make those things really explicit to them, so that they understand why they came and while they leave, I wanted to see them like, whatever the purpose they came in, they got it done by my talk. [*] So the way I address is like putting the objective very clear, making some of the results very explicit, these sorts of things we got and then a small transition. And I use PowerPoint, but it will be driven by me rather than the PowerPoint, so I will be the main person ... and I am the speaker so I will take the first portion and I just use the PowerPoint like some backup where I can just share some figures or something to explain the things in a better way. Erm, and of course the language, the way we deliver the talk and then how we the usage of words, everything comes into fixture so almost all together makes the presentation. So I find it very challenging and I do practise before giving a lec, I mean seminar talk. Uh, I did try to put in the time given so yeah. So I try my best to get prepared in this way.

Unit 5

🔊 5.1

Presenter: OK, I'm going to do the first part of the presentation, and I'd like to talk about the positive effects of globalisation on culture. I want to highlight five things that have been said about this in the literature and give a brief comment on each one. First, though, let me just clarify the topic. We all know about globalisation – the idea that changes in transportation, communications, and technology are producing a single world economy and that this is also affecting culture in every country. And some people see this as a positive thing. I've listed some of the most important literature on this on your handout. Hadleigh, for example, argues that globalisation has spread foreign products and ideas to other countries and other cultures and this is good because it increases people's choices. I tend to agree with this. It's a good thing that people have a variety of choices in what they buy, and good that they're exposed to a wide range of ideas. In a sense I suppose it increases their individual freedom, which can only be positive.

Hadleigh and many others, Salman, for example, writing in 2010, have said that globalisation promotes peace and understanding. It's certainly the case that globalisation allows people in one country to know more about people in other countries and their ways of life, but actually this doesn't necessarily lead to more peaceful relationships. This is a point that Robins makes. Finding out that what is unacceptable in your own culture is acceptable in another can instead lead to negative views about that culture, I think. Globalisation is also said to increase cultural diversity. In other words, if ideas and products are transported to another culture they get adapted and changed in that culture to create something new. An example that Simms uses for this is how African music's been transferred into Western pop music to produce new rhythms and styles. Overall, though, I have my doubts about this. Rather, it seems to me that cultures become less diverse when products from multinationals come into a country. So, for example, food chains like MacDonald's and Starbucks are found pretty well everywhere around the world, and this reduces diversity in a country.

Another point that's made is about English. Wilson has argued that it's a good thing that English has become the main global language. It might be true that this is good for business and for tourism, but in fact it can lead to the loss of local languages and all the surrounding culture – the literature or oral story telling – that goes with those languages. A fifth point is that with advances in communications technology, people can become part of what's sometimes called a 'world culture'. Calman et al. note, for example, that you can easily contact people online in different parts of the world, share photos with them, and play games with them. I think they make a good point here. You can find out a lot in this way about people who have different lifestyles and who are from different cultures. So those are the five points I want to pick out here.

Unit 6

🔊 6.1

Presenter: OK, in the part of the survey that I'm going to focus on, we looked at where students spent their time during their working week. So what you can see on this slide is a pie chart showing the average percentage of time that students spent in a number of different locations. So, for example, 16.7% of time is spent in teaching rooms – lecture theatres and classrooms – you can see that segment down the bottom here. And nearly 7% was spent in computing labs – that's the segment over here.

OK, I want to pick out a few things from this slide that we thought were quite interesting. One is the high percentage of time that students spent at home. Let me just clarify that this is 33% of working time – not time when they're relaxing or sleeping. This means that about a third of study time – quite a high proportion, we thought – is spent at home rather than on campus. A possible explanation for this is that so much information is now available online, that it's no longer necessary for students to spend so much time in libraries. And it may be that it's easier for students to use their own computers at home than having to wait to get on a computer on campus – either in the library or in computing labs – where the demand is quite high. Another thing that we found quite surprising was the relatively small amount of time that students reported they spent in refreshment areas – a little over 4%. By refreshment areas, we mean the various coffee shops and restaurants on campus. Our experience of watching students on campus suggests to us that a lot of students spend a lot of time in these places, so this seems to be a very low figure. One reason for this could be that students underreported the actual time they spent in refreshment areas; perhaps they felt a bit guilty about it, so reported less time than they actually spent there. And a third finding that we thought it was worth highlighting was the amount of travelling time that students do – nearly 20% of their total working week. It may be useful for me to explain that a bit more. The average working week came to about 45 hours. This means that nearly nine hours a week on average is taken up with travelling to and from university. What's particularly surprising about this is that the majority of students live in student residences just a short walk from campus. It must be, then, that the minority of students who live in accommodation away from the campus spend a great deal of time getting to university. Maybe this is because they live a long way away, but we felt that a more likely explanation is that journey time is very slow because of the traffic congestion in the city.

OK, I'd like now to hand over to my colleagues who are going to present other findings from the research …

🔊 6.2

Max: To answer your question in terms of erm quoting or paraphrasing I, I do both. I quote directly both from, from primary sources from letters government documents newspapers tha-, that I've been looking at and also from secondary sources from books from, uh, journal articles that that other scholars have written and I will also paraphrase in, in the sense that I'll refer uh, loosely more or less loosely to what people have written or, to what this source says, but as a historian, you always have to document your sources and, and identify the, the source of your, of your evidence.

Karthik: In sciences, mostly, it goes with using, I would say less quotations because mostly we paraphrase, but at the end we do mention, or we do refer to the real author but, uh, we prefer to paraphrase just because of the reason that we try to explain the concept rather than just attaching bits and pieces saying what someone said.

Fotis: You never use quotations, or quotations is quite rare. You usually paraphrase. You are supposed to reference every single thing that you write or you cite from somebody else. And we are quite free to use whatever system we want. The most, uh, convenient is the Harvard system …

Lecture and seminar skills C

🔊 C.1

Professor Crystal: Well, thanks very much for that. Uh, as you entered Peterhouse this evening you will have noticed that there were two notices, one pointing you in the direction of this lecture, the other pointing you in the direction of Peterhouse Choral Evensong. Erm, I hope the temporary confusion that may have affected you means that nobody here is expecting Evensong here. That's all right then. And also I hope somebody is making a parallel announcement in Choral Evensong because when they get to the psalms and the reading I imagine they could think it was an exercise in the stories of English.

🔊 C.2 🔊 C.3

Professor Crystal: It is the 'stories' of English, of course, that's what I'm talking about this evening not the 'story' of English which some of you may remember was the title of a television series, uh oh, 20 or more years ago. And the story of English that was told in that particular programme and indeed has been told virtually in the same way for the last hundred years or more is the story of one kind of English only – the story of Standard English. And dialects, the non-standard varieties of English have been virtually neglected. And quite consciously so. Here's a quote to illustrate the point. H. C. Wyld. *A Short History of English.* Book I cut my teeth on when I went to read English for the first time. Absolutely standard work. And

159

this is what he says when you open his book and look for dialects. You will find them there at the very back in the very last chapter sort of tucked away at the end somewhere. 'Fortunately,' says Wyld, 'at the present time the great majority of the English dialects are of very little importance as representatives of English speech. And for our present purpose we can afford to let them go. Except in so far as they throw light upon the growth of those forms of our language which are the main objects of our solicitude. Namely the language of literature and Received Standard Spoken English.' 'Quaint and eccentric,' he calls dialects. And those are two of the commonest adjectives for dialects in that particular period of our history. Oh, there's another little quote here you'll love this one. He allows at one point that there may be 'sophisticated valleys' of dialect use, saying 'these certainly differ from the pure old dialect but is it identical with the English heard in, let us say, in an Oxford or Cambridge common room or in an officer's mess? We should probably say that it was not,' says Wyld. Now that captures a whole ethos of attitudes towards dialect in relation to the standard language. Standard English is proper English is correct English. Dialect is inferior English, is low quality, is deficient in some way to be judged against the criterion of the standard language. And the names for the dialect situation are of course many and various and they're all negative in their associations, aren't they? Uh, people talk about thing about these varieties being 'patois' or 'cant' or a lingo of some kind or 'broken English' or 'gutter English' or 'substandard English'. Linguists on the whole have tried to get away from this kind of negative terminology – we talk a lot about non-standard English as the most neutral way of expressing the relationship, but even that is a somewhat, uh, negative way of looking at the situation. Something has gone horribly wrong, that's the point. Standard English is the minority dialect – always has been. Perhaps one percent of the English speakers of the world, um, use Standard English. Or I should say, of course, English writers of the world, because Standard English is essentially the dialect of the written language. Defined, as you know, by its grammar, by its spelling and its punctuation and, to a minor extent, by its vocabulary as well. If people say 'What is Standard English?' we give examples and there are dozens of them – like in Standard English, we don't use double negatives, for example. Nobody in Standard English says 'I haven't got nuffink' or something like that. 'I don't have anything.' So a double negative is in current terms non-standard. Or the use of 'ain't'. 'I ain't got nuffin.' Very much non-standard. Or 'We was sat 'ere'. Very much non-standard. And then of course in spelling and in punctuation there are lots and lots of examples of the standardisation of the language. We have to spell correctly in order to use Standard English well. We have to punctuate correctly, in so far as it's possible, in order to use

Standard English well. But that written language, that written definition of standard is still only a minority of the overall English language used in the world. Nobody's got any real statistics, of course. But how many people speak Standard English in that way? I'm doing my best at the moment. And indeed you will hear Standard English spoken on the most public of occasions, and that's why everybody gets the impression that it's universal but in actual fact perhaps only 5% (at most) of the spoken English around the world is going to be Standard English. Most people around the world use double negatives and say 'ain't' and have various kinds of, uh, irregular verb used in a non-standard sort of way. It's time, it seems to me, to rehabilitate non-standard English. And I've been arguing this for a long time, as have many others in my business of linguistics, especially those of us who are sociolinguists. Very much trying to reverse the priorities. Whereas, traditionally, Standard English is seen as the norm and non-standard English is seen as the deviation from the norm, the correct approach in my view is to see non-standard English as the norm and Standard English as a special case. A very important special case, of course, but a special case, nonetheless. There are two stories to be told, in other words. The story of Standard English, which is the story of the need for an intelligibility model of language we need to understand each other, and a standard guarantees that to a very considerable extent. But intelligibility is not the only force driving language. The other force that drives language is the need for identity. It's not just that we need to understand each other, we need to express who we are and where we are from and identify the community to which we belong. And for that, non-standard English is the primary manifestation.

C.4

Professor Crystal: Who's the first person to actually try and put, uh, some regional dialect into literature? Well, this accolade usually goes to Chaucer. Erm, very appropriately *The Reeve's Tale*, seeing as we're in Cambridge. If you know the story. This is the story of the, uh, the two Cambridge undergraduates who are sent to the miller not far from here, in order to find out what's happened to their corn supply. The miller has been cheating the college. Couldn't happen these days. And the two undergraduates go to the miller's place and establish exactly what's been going on. Now, the story evolves. They discover the nature of the problem. They realise exactly what's happening. They decide to con the miller. They, uh, succeed in getting their corn for their college.

C.5

Professor Crystal: Erm, now the point is that this is a story where the undergraduates are being portrayed as intelligent, bright, sharp guys. The miller is being portrayed as a somewhat, uh, inefficient, pompous ass. And the thing is that the dialect that Chaucer gives the two sets

of characters, he gives the undergraduates a northern dialect and he gives the miller a southern dialect. So here we have a situation which is a dialect, dialects appearing in literature in a kind of controlled way for the first time and the northerners, the northern dialect is the intelligent one. The southern dialect is the stupid one. They're quite the reverse of the situation we find recently here. You see it in the spelling. The s, d, the miller says words like 'go' G-O it's spelt. The students say words like 'go' spelt G-A. A northern spelling. 'No' versus 'na'. 'So' versus 'swa'. Uh, the southern people, the southern miller uses a T-H ending on his verbs 'goeth' 'sayeth' and things like that. The undergraduates use an 's' ending on the verbs. 'Goes', 'says' things like that. And if you read that kind of tale, read the tale, it is important to read it in a way which tries to capture that sort of difference. I mean at one point for example, the, in the dialogue between the two Chaucer writes in Modern English. One of the, uh, undergraduates says to the miller, he's gonna stand right by the hopper to make sure that he isn't gonna con, con us of our corn. 'By God right, by the hopper will I stand said John and see how the corn goes in.' Right, now if we put that into Middle English ' "By God right by the hopur wil I stande" Quod John "and se howgates the corn gas in."' 'Gas in' notice not 'goes in'. But that doesn't capture it. It has to be something much more like: 'Be God right by the "opur will ee stande quod John and see howgates the corn gas in."' I mean, you have to put it into some sort of regional context like a mock Yorkshire, or maybe it was even further north than that, it may have been Northumbria, or somewhere, accent in order to capture the contrast between their way of talking and the way in which the miller talks.

C.6

Professor Crystal: The point of that example is to illustrate the way in which Chaucer doesn't have the attitudes towards accent that we have today. The attitudes towards accent in Britain that we have today, as we all know, is that the southern accent and the southern dialect generally and Standard English as a whole is the correct, proper, respectable honest way of communicating and the regional accents and dialects are somehow or other inferior. When did that rot set in? When did people first start being so negative about regional accents? Chaucer himself evidently wasn't. But already in the 14th century we see the beginnings of people starting to snipe at regional speech. Especially if they're from the south, where the court and everything was, sniping at people and the way, people the way people speak in the north and in Wales and in Scotland and in Ireland and so on.

C.7 audioscript see C.4–C.6

C.8

Professor Crystal: The importance of dialect and accent of course, the distinction being that dialect is a matter of grammar and vocabulary and accent is a matter of pronunciation, the two usually coming together in most occasions. The value of, of dialect and accent is in my view essentially evolutionary. Why do people get so upset about accent and dialect? Why are they so sensitive about it? Why do they worry about it so much? Why do they think negatively about it so much? And I think it probably does go back to the very beginning of the human race when humanity was in its earliest stages of language development whenever that was sometime perhaps between 50,000 and 100,000 years ago. And you're in your cave and you are waiting for something to happen, it's a dangerous world out there. And you hear a noise outside so you say in your primitive Stone-Age vocalisation the equivalent of 'Who's there?'. 'Ugg' or whatever. And out back through the ether comes another 'ugg'. Now if you recognise that 'ugg', if to put it in modern terms it is in the same accent, then probably it's part of your tribe and probably it's safe to go out there. On the other hand, if the 'ugg' that comes back is one you don't recognise, then maybe if you go out there you should take your club with you because it may be somebody from a different tribe who wants to take over your cave. Now that kind of notion of accent, and then by implication dialect as a survival value phenomenon, is not I think entirely unusual even today. There are some cities I believe where you walk down a street and you hear an accent round the corner and you decide not to go down that street because you recognise the accent as being a possible threat. Now the importance of accent and dialect is so essential to our condition as human beings that it wouldn't be surprising then to find it a recurrent theme in the history of English, a, as in any language, and that is of course what we find. There has always been variation in English. Dialect variation. There never hasn't been. The evidence in Old English is of course from the spellings. And it's not surprising to find in the earliest accounts of Old English, the various manuscripts that we have, that they represent different dialect parts of the country. Not surprising because the people who came from across the water came from different parts of across the water. Virtually all the way along the north European coast as far as Denmark, people came towards this country presumably speaking different dialects of Germanic. And as a result, when these dialects started to be written down you get the result of different, uh, spellings illustrating different geographical origins. It's hard to study the history of dialect of course. This is one of the problems. Because very soon after the Old English period, we see the beginnings of the evolution of a standard English, a standard written English. It becomes increasingly difficult

to establish what was happening regionally in the other universe, in the non-standard universe. It's hard to tell because most writing is in Standard English. But increasingly people have been able to find examples of material where there is a, a natural voice, as it were – where it's possible to see through the standard form of the language to the non-standard form that lies behind it: court records, for example, in the Middle Ages and Early Modern English, illustrating a much more natural style of presentation than you'd find in the more formal, uh, examples of written English of the period.

C.9

Youness: Erm, what I expect from a lecture is really, it has to be a story. I mean it needs to have a beginning, middle, y'know, some events and an ending a, conclusion, that really summarises and maybe brings new ideas or emphasises some, I dunno phenomenon or concepts or theories that the lecturer's been talking about during the lecture. But, erm, I have to say at the beginning, the lecture, I mean the style of lectures is really different from what I had in Brussels. So it's less, erm, it's less academic in a way, it's more, compared to in Brussels, since most undergrads have just need to attend lectures and don't have any seminars or, uh, more I dunno how to say it, maybe more personal, uh, kind of a personal relationship with the, the topic. You just need to be there and just take notes and just leave the lecture room and, and that's all. But here you, you engage with the topic in a very different way. So you can't just sit back and just take notes. So that's why having a story something that is, I dunno, a thread, a common thread throughout the lecture is really helpful.

Unit 7

7.1

Carmen: OK, in my section of the talk, I'd like to look at responses to two of the questionnaire items, talk a little about the possible implications of our findings, and then make some recommendations to Newcraft on the basis of what we discovered. In the first of these items, people were asked to respond to the statement "A product's design and style are as important as its performance". And the figures you've got here are the percentage of people who said they agreed with this statement – that's a combination of 'agree' and 'strongly agree' answers. And the figures are given for all six countries.

What we found was there was a big difference in attitudes. Getting on for two thirds of informants from Russia and China agreed, whereas only about a third of informants from Japan, Italy and France agreed. India was somewhere in the middle, with around half agreeing.

If we now look at the second item – the statement's on this slide here: "I like products

that are not easy to get and that few people have". Again, we've got the percentage of people who agree – that's 'agree' or 'strongly agree' – with the statement. Although the percentages aren't as high as with the first question, the findings are broadly similar. The figures for China and Russia are relatively high, joined by India. The figures for Italy and France are the lowest, with Japan somewhere in the middle. So what conclusions can we draw from these findings?

7.2

Carmen: The first thing I need to say is that we need to be careful in drawing conclusions. The samples we took were quite small – just 30 students from each group – and it's impossible to say how representative these students are of the population as a whole. But bearing this in mind, it looks like there might be a split between three countries – Russia, China, India – that are at a similar stage of newly advanced economic development, and the rest. In these three, style and design seems to matter a great deal, and also people like to own 'exclusive' products – things that are expensive and so owned by only a few people. It may be that it's only in recent years that the middle classes have been able to afford stylish or exclusive products, but now they're what everyone wants to have. An alternative explanation is that it's only recently that these kinds of products have been available at all, with previous tight import controls in, for example, China and Russia. In contrast, in countries that have had a long period of advanced economic development – like Japan, Italy and France – the novelty of owning products with stylish design and that cost a great deal has worn off – many people already have them – and it's how well things perform that is of more significance.

So what would this mean for Newcraft's advertising campaign?

7.3

Carmen: On the basis of the findings from these two questions, we have three recommendations for Newcraft.

First of all, in Russia, China and India, Newcraft need to highlight the exclusivity of their products – showing that they are luxury items – and probably keeping their prices quite high, too.

Also, in these countries the advertising should emphasise their style, perhaps including them in advertising with stylish clothing or well-designed computers or cars.

In the other countries, however, the advertising may need to draw attention to the durability of their products: Newcraft products can be dropped, thrown around, go on rough camping trips, and will last a lifetime.

In general, then, their advertising needs to be different in different countries, and it should respond to the different preferences of consumers in each country.

Unit 8

🔊 8.1

1

Presenter: So, any more questions?

Audience member: You talked a lot about the consensus view of crime. But isn't there another important view – the conflict view? Could you say something about that?

Presenter: Right, erm … the conflict view … well, I suppose that means that there might be conflicts between people in society, and that can result in crime? Or maybe that where there are conflicts, like wars, you tend to get more crime? Erm, perhaps there are some other questions …

2

Presenter: … and more recent thinking in criminology takes the victim's role into consideration a lot more. So some of the recent research has looked at measuring the factors that increase a person's chances of becoming a crime victim. There's also …

Audience member: Can I just ask a question? A little while ago you said that media reports of crimes are often inaccurate. Why do you think that is?

Presenter: Well, erm, right. Well, I suppose the media love to sensationalise crime. You've got to remember that the media are in the business of selling newspapers or increasing TV viewership for advertisers. So in a way, the more horrific or unusual a crime the better. But this means that their accounts of crime can be biased or inaccurate. That's what I was trying to get across.

Audience member: OK, thanks.

Presenter: Right, er, so, where was I? Let me just have a look at my notes again. OK, so I was saying that, er, there's an increasing focus on the victims in crime, and, erm, right, so I'd mentioned research looking at a person's likelihood of being a crime victim. Other research has tried to calculate the actual costs of crime for victims …

🔊 8.2

1

Audience member: Do you think the huge rise in bike thefts you mentioned is because there are more of them?

Presenter: Er, I'm sorry, I'm not sure I follow you.

Audience member: I mean could the number of bikes being stolen simply be a result of there being more bikes about?

Presenter: That's a good question. I don't have the figures here, but I seem to remember that the increase in bicycle numbers has risen much more slowly than the increase in bicycle thefts, so that doesn't seem to explain the whole picture. I could certainly send those figures to you later. Is that OK?

Audience member: Yes, fine, thank you.

Presenter: Are there any more questions?

2

Audience member: What's the difference between theft and burglary?

Presenter: OK, so the question was how do theft and burglary differ? Well, that's an interesting question. Essentially, theft is taking another person's property without their permission. Burglary involves breaking into a house or car for the purpose of committing a crime, and very often that crime is theft. A complication, though is that 'theft' is sometimes used as a kind of informal word for things like burglary, robbery, shoplifting, and so on, so it may not be used very precisely. Is that the kind of information you were looking for?

Audience member: Thank you, yes, that's very clear.

Presenter: Any other questions?

3

Audience member: If street crime has fallen so much over the last 10 years, why is the perception of most people that they are less safe on the streets?

Presenter: For those of you that didn't hear, the question was: Why is there a general view that streets are now less safe when the amount of street crime has actually fallen over the last 10 years? That's a very good point. I must confess, though, I really don't know what the answer is. The perception of crime isn't something I've really looked into. Sorry.

Audience member: OK, that's fine.

Presenter: Yes. David?

4

Audience member: I wonder why you didn't include figures for vandalism in the property crime slide you showed us.

Presenter: Sorry, I'm not quite sure what you're getting at …

Audience member: Well, if you'd included vandalism the percentages of the other categories like car theft and burglary would have been lower.

Presenter: I see. Well, it would take some time to answer that fully and the detail may not be of interest to everyone – it's to do with differences in how the data is collected – so maybe we could talk about it later?

Audience member: OK, sure.

Presenter: Does anyone want to ask any other questions?

5

Audience member: Would you like to speculate on why car thefts have risen over the period when – I think I'm right in saying – the figures for Europe as a whole have fallen.

Presenter: Right, so the questioner wants to know why car thefts in England and Wales have risen, while they've gone down for Europe. I think that's a really difficult issue. Would anybody like to comment on that?

Audience member: Well, as far as I understand it, the average age of cars in England and Wales is higher than the European average, so it might be something to do with that – newer cars probably have better security.

Presenter: I see, right. Thank you. Does that answer your question?

Audience member: Yes, that's interesting.

Presenter: OK, anything else anyone wants to ask?

6

Audience member: What about the way crime was recorded over the period?

Presenter: Erm, I wonder if you could expand on that a bit more?

Audience member: Well, I was just wondering whether the way the police record and categorise crime might have changed over the period. That might affect some of the trends that you've been showing us.

Presenter: Right. As I think I said near the beginning of the talk, there was a major change in the way crime is recorded about 15 years ago, but over the 10-year period I've been talking about here, it's remained the same. So the figures shouldn't really be affected by any changes in the recording of crime. Does that help?

Audience member: Oh, yes, right. Thank you.

Presenter: We've got a couple of minutes more for questions.

Lecture and seminar skills D

📖 D.1 📖 D.2

Professor Spencer: The central element in a negligence action, an action for damages by somebody who's been injured by alleged negligence, is fault. Fault is known to lawyers by various other aliases as well – carelessness or breach of duty. And when as far as lawyers are concerned is somebody at fault? What is the essence of it? Lawyers refer to the 'reasonable man test'. Somebody's careless if they've failed the 'reasonable man test', meaning they've failed to behave as a reasonable person would in the position in which the defendant found himself or herself. The reasonable man test as a test of fault is so well-established, you don't have to cite cases to prove it. But the one which lawyers do usually mention, in which it was discussed by the House of Lords many years ago, is that one: Glasgow Corporation against Muir. Glasgow Corporation against Muir was a sad incident which had happened in a park in Glasgow, where there was a Sunday-school outing. And the Sunday-school children of this party were up the hill under a shelter, where you could get boiling water to fill the tea urn and where you could sit around and eat your sandwiches. But there was too much rain and too many other children. And so the elder of the kirk went down to the café at the bottom of the hill and said 'Can I bring the children in here to drink our tea and to eat their sandwiches?' She was a hard woman and there was some negotiation before a price was agreed and eventually they all trouped down there. The elder of the kirk and one of the bigger Sunday school boys carrying between them the urn of boiling water. And they went through the passage into the café part carrying the urn with children milling around and alas, alas they managed to drop the urn as they were going through and six of the children got scalded. And they sued not the elder of the kirk but they sued the woman in charge of the café, saying it was be, negligent of her she was at fault in allowing them to carry this urn of tea there through the crowded corridor. And the claim failed because the House of Lords decided, no it wasn't an unreasonable thing to do, and a Scottish judge Lord Macmillan said that among many pages of other things: 'In Scotland at any rate it has never been a maxim of the law that a man acts at his peril. Legal liability is limited to those consequences of our acts which a reasonable man of ordinary intelligence and experience so acting would have in contemplation.'

D.3

Diana: Erm, there are some professors who don't move at all, who just, sitting and changing their slides [*]. But, erm, I really don't, I mean, like for me there is no difference because if you're coming and you know who's the professor - and usually we have the background - you're just listening and basically everything else just disappears, I don't see people who around me, I don't hear the noises, erm, I just see the professor and his words and then we take notes and everything, and he just becoming part of, what he's saying [*]. And then when you take a break I'm alwa-, I'm usually disappointed because, erm, you kind of, you have to get out of this, I don't know, meditation nirvana process that you're really enjoying. And, erm, there are some professors that, erm, that, that yeah, they, they choose, like, body language and they show some books or whatever. We had a professor who worked on publishing, Dr John, John Thompson and he brought Kindle, that in his opinion would change everything, and he was showing some visual, uh, books that he was talking about, like an as an example, and he was always moving around the class and it didn't distract you, so I, I don't think there is a big difference between the person who's sitting and the person who's moving – at least for me because when you're really concentrating on what he is saying, you don't really pay attention on how he's moving. That's my opinion.

D.4

Professor Spencer: In deciding whether the defendant has behaved as a reasonable man, the courts ask themselves what a reasonable person would have done in this situation. And approaching the matter on principle, they say this involves weighing up four different factors. The first is the likelihood or otherwise of any harm resulting from his behaviour. And by the degree of risk involved,

we talk about potentially somebody being liable if it was foreseeable that somebody might get injured, rather than foreseeable that they would get injured. A fairly low level of foresight is needed as to the risk. And that's illustrated by that well-known case decided by the House of Lords back in the 1960s. London Electricity Board did what public utility bodies do best – that's to say dug a hole in the road and went away and left it for a bit. And uh, it was actually in the pavement and to guard the end of the end of the hole, so people didn't fall in, they took a spade and a punner (one of those rammer things) and they put them crossways across the end of it. Mr Haley, the claimant in this case, was alas a born loser it seems. He'd gone blind as a result of an accident some years before and he was tap, tap, tapping down the pavement with his stick and unfortunately the stick, uh, tapped in the gap between the things blocking the hole and he fell down the hole, and in the falling down the hole he went deaf as well. The question was: were the defendants negligent in not putting some kind of better barrier around the end of the hole? And they said 'How would we have known that a blind man was going to come down this road? We expect people to be able to see where they're going.' But the evidence for the claimant in this case was that in London, about one in 500 people are blind, and even though you don't see them round the place driving buses and things like that, nevertheless you see a lot of them out and about finding their way r-, their way round, and it was certainly foreseeable that there was a risk to a more than negligible minority of the population if some better means of guarding the end of the trench wasn't put in place. And another key factor in the case was that other public utilities used little fence things, which you could easily get. It wasn't as if it was a very extravagant thing to expect them to take a better precaution here, which would have protected against the likelihood of injury to some blind person coming down the street. And the second thing that's weighed up in deciding whether somebody has failed to behave as a reasonable man is the magnitude of harm that is likely to result. Not only whether there's any foreseeable risk of harm, but how bad that harm is if it should happen. Obviously, you're expected to take more precautions if you're transporting around the countryside nuclear waste than if you're transporting around the countryside farm manure, for example. And the case which we traditionally use to illustrate that point is Paris against Stepney Borough Council. Mr Paris was a one-eyed mechanic whose job it was to maintain public utility vehicles run by Stepney Borough Council, in the process of which, he had to crawl round underneath doing adjustments. And he was working underneath this dustcart trying to loosen some rusted up part and hitting it with a hammer, when unfortunately something broke off it and landed in his eye. And as ill luck would have it, it was actually his one good eye, and he suffered

an injury to the sight in his one good eye. And he sued them saying that they were negligent in not providing him with goggles. And he failed further down. A judge in the Court of Appeal saying a celebrated wrong dictum: 'The greater the risk of injury, the greater risk of injury is not the same as a risk of greater injury.' And the House of Lords said that's all wrong. When you're dealing with the safety of an employee you know to have only one eye, obviously you ought to take greater precautions than when you're dealing with the safety of somebody who has two. You can get by quite well in life with only one of lots of bits of you with which nature has kindly given you two, but if you're only got one then you're at bigger risk. It behoves your employer to take greater care for the safety of the one you have, because you have more to lose; there's a greater magnitude of harm which is foreseeable in your case than in the case of somebody who's still got both of what they were born with.

D.5

Professor Spencer: To what extent does the c, do the courts depart from the objective standard of the ordinary person the man in the man on the Clapham omnibus (as some judges have described him) and apply either a higher standard for particular defendants or a lower standard for others? Do they ever raise the standard? Yes they do when dealing with experts or people who claim they're experts. There's a Latin maxim: *Imperitia culpae adnumeratur*. To take something that requires skill on, when you don't have it, counts as blameworthiness. It's no good the man on the Clapham omnibus, oh good, the brain surgeon I mean to say, when he's messed up at brain surgery, his brain surgery, to say 'Well, you should have seen what sort of a mess the man on the Clapham omnibus would have made of that.' Obviously, you judge skilful people by the standards of reasonable skilful people. And if the people are doing some skilled activity, which they don't actually, requiring a skill they don't actually have, though they did the best they could by their limited standards, they're held to be blameworthy for undertaking something which shouldn't be done without proper skill. And there's a real case, a maritime law case, the *Lady Gwendolyn*, which illustrates this. Guinness brew great quantities of that beverage in Dublin, and at least at this point in time, used to ship it across in a tanker to Liverpool where there are many thirsty Irishmen anxious to drink it. And they had their own ship which did this. And they had a captain who was a bit gung-ho and inclined to go fast through fog. And if the directors of Guinness had looked carefully at the records of the ship, they would have seen from the, putting the weather conditions and the times together, that this man was a negligent captain. And the question arose under maritime law whether the directors themselves were negligent in not noticing what was going on. And they said 'But we're not

163

ship owners, we're brewers. I mean you know we know about making beer but we don't know about ships.' And the court said in effect 'Look. If you want to do what Onassis does you better have lessons from Onassis.' If you going into running ships as a sideline you have to equip yourself with the necessary knowledge or else you're negligent if you don't have it. Interesting questions arise as to what sort of activities it's thought reasonable for ordinary people to do, even though skilled people would actually do them better. And the courts say that it's OK for householders to do minor DIY even though professionals might do a better job of it. And this point is illustrated by the case of Wells and Cooper. The back doorknob had come off and the defendant householder had reaffixed it. It was one of those doorknobs where you affixed it to the outside of the door by putting screws through a ferril to which the knob was attached. The householder didn't notice that the wood on the door was cold – you know, not with much grip in it, which a professional carpenter might have done, and he didn't use as a longer screws as somebody who was really wised up to these risks would have done. And there were steps that led down from the back door. The claimant was the milkman who was invited into the kitchen for a nice cup of tea with the householder's wife. And as he was leaving, pulled the door to behind him and the knob came off and he went base over apex down the steps and injured himself. And he sued, he sued Mr Householder. The thought has crossed my mind to wonder what the householder thought about his wife having nice cups of tea with the milkman in the kitchen, let alone being sued for the consequences. And he said 'I'm just a householder, I mean, OK, a professional chippie would have known that you needed longer screws to hold that doorknob on, but I couldn't be expected to know.' And the Court of Appeal said 'No you couldn't and it's perfectly reasonable for a householder to do normal jobs like that, which householders do, and when they do them they're not expected to come up to a higher standard than the reasonable householder, which you'd done.' So they raise the standards when dealing with particularly skilful defendants professionals who belong to a particular group. Do they ever do the opposite? Do they ever allow the defendant to say 'But look. I'm particularly skill-less. I'm a dope. Judge me by the standards of the reasonable dope'? Surprisingly, yes they do in certain cases where the particular defendant in question can't help having a lower standard of skill than other people.

D.6

Professor Spencer: What's the relevance of normal professional practice when you get somebody doing something which professionals regularly do? Are the courts much inclined to follow what the normal practice is? To what extent is it possible for defendants to produce strings

of other people who do the same sort of thing to say: 'Well, we would have done just the same as him. It's normal practice in this trade to do this sort of thing.' Does that get the defendant out of liability if the defendant can show that lots of other people in this position do the same kind of thing? Normally yes, the courts are heavily influenced by what other obviously reasonable people who do this sort of thing will regularly do. And defendants, defending claims of this sort if they can find them, often do produce other people in the same trade or profession to tell the court what they would have done. And of course, claimants try to produce other people from the same trade to say: 'No no no. We'd have done something better. We'd have done something different.' But the courts aren't automatically bound to accept the defendant was properly behaving just because this was the standard practice in the trade at the time. And if it was obviously negligent, the courts are capable of saying: 'You're negligent to do this even if other people do the same thing.' And the striking example of that is that case, Cavanagh against Ulster Weaving Company Limited. The hapless claimant in this case was a builder's labourer who had the job of climbing up onto a glazed roof, or a partially glazed roof, carrying buckets of cement in order to give to a roofer who was repairing the pointing on the ridge tiles on the roof. And he was given to climb the ladder in a pair of wellington boots two sizes too big for him by the employer. And he was sent to climb up a ladder which didn't have a handrail, carrying this heavy bucket of cement. It's hardly surprising that partway up he fell and he managed to fall through the glass and badly cut himself, as a result of which he ended up having to have most of one of his arms amputated. Were the defendants liable? Were they negligent? The defendants, would you believe it, managed to produce a whole row of other Northern Ireland builders to say: 'That's what we do in Northern Ireland.' And the claim failed in the lower courts. But the House of Lords said: 'If that's what you do in Northern Ireland, you shouldn't do it. It's perfectly obvious that it's a negligent way to go about things – you should pull your socks up and adopt a better practice.' There's a particular application of this body of learning to doctors. It's known as the Bolam test of negligence in respect of medical professionals, from that case Bolam against Friern Hospital Management Committee. In the Bolam case, a man was given, a man with depression was given electro-convulsive treatment – ECT. Nobody knows why ECT works – it's black magic so psychiatrists tell me – but it does and years ago they used to give depressed people ECT quite often because it cheered them up no end. Maybe it was so horrible they realised there weren't worse things to worry about, but anyway it tended to have a good effect. And giving somebody a huge electric shock causes them to jerk about quite a bit. And this particular claimant jerked around so much that he

managed to break his hip joint in the course of the convulsions induced by the ECT. And he sued for damages saying it was negligent to give him this ECT without either first of all giving him a muscle relaxant or restraining him tying him down. And the defendant doctor produced evidence to show that there were medical professionals who would have done just the same as him. There was a school dispute amongst psychiatrists as to whether it was advisable and good practice to restrain people before ECT or not. There were some compensating disadvantages. And in that case – which was tried by a jury as such cases were in those days but not now – the judge directed the jury as follows: 'A doctor is not guilty of negligence if he's acted in accordance with a practice accepted as proper by a responsible body of medical men skilled in that particular art.' I'm sorry about the, erm, non-gender-neutral language, it was many years ago, this case. Uh, putting it another way round, a man is not negligent if he's acting in accordance with such a practice merely because there's a body of opinion that would take a contrary view. If there's a respectable body of medical opinion that would have done what the defendant did, then he's not regarded as negligent for following that opinion rather than the other. Those who fight for patients' rights and don't like doctors say this is too generous to doctors. It means that any doctor who's sued for negligence can go out into the highways and byways of the medical profession until they can find some geriatric concrete head who's prepared to say: 'Oh, mm, leeches yes, they're wonderful. What? Antiseptics? No, don't have anything to do with them myself.' Or, whatever it is. But the Bolam test is qualified by the power of the courts to reject accepted professional practice as being visibly and manifestly foolish and there are cases where even though the defendant doctor produced other doctors who said they would have done the same the court's reaction was: 'Well, thanks, we won't go to any of them. It was obviously negligent to do this sort of treatment.'

Unit 9

🔊 9.1

Diana: Usually he would um he would schedule like 30 minutes for every student because he also had PhD students. So you have like this space in his in his day usually in the afternoon. Uh, depending on what the student was asking for for example I needed more help with my essays we had to write four essays so I would see him before the essay like two weeks in advance then I would submit my paper ten days before the deadline. And then he would comment on my first draft and I would change it again. So we were meeting like twice before the essay and with the dissertation it was more, uh, frequent because, basically I needed more guidance from him and also my, my MPhil dissertation was really original so we kind of had to work on a new methodology so we were meeting quite a lot. Uh, we had first two meetings just to define the research question and where are where are we going with that. And he kind of edited my objectives. Uh, then there was one meeting b-, well, two meetings before the fieldwork. Erm, I had to bring two drafts of my questions of what I'm gonna interview how I'm gonna interview people. And then, uh, we met about three times on three different drafts, parts of my dissertation and he also re-edited my final draft.

🔊 9.2

1
Supervisor: Morning, Karen.
Karen: Hello. Do you think we could meet some time soon, please?
Supervisor: Of course. Later this week? Thursday morning at 11?
Karen: That's great. Thanks.

2
Supervisor: Hi, Paul. What can I do for you?
Paul: I need to meet you today.
Supervisor: OK... Well, I'm busy until 4.00. But after that?
Paul: Yes, that's OK. Thank you.

3
Supervisor: Hello, Karen. How can I help?
Karen: Can we meet this morning?
Supervisor: Yes... I should think so. About 11.30?
Karen: Yes, thank you.

4
Supervisor: Afternoon, Paul.
Paul: Hello. Would it be possible to meet you later this week?
Supervisor: Yes, of course. Friday, about 11 OK?
Paul: That'll be great. Thanks.

5
Supervisor: Hello, Karen. How can I help?
Karen: I want to see you next week.
Supervisor: Right ... Is Monday morning OK? About 10?
Karen: Yes, that's OK. Thank you.

6
Supervisor: Hi, Paul. What can I do for you?
Paul: I wonder if I could set up a time to meet you next week?
Supervisor: Sure. How about two on Tuesday?
Paul: That's fine. Thank you.

🔊 9.3

1
Supervisor: Come in.
Karen: Hello, Prof.
Supervisor: Oh, hello, Karen. Come in and have a seat.
Karen: Thanks.

2
Supervisor: Come in. Oh, hello, Paul.
Paul: Hello, Dr. Evans. We've got an appointment.

Supervisor: Yes, of course. Come and sit down.

3
Supervisor: Come in.
Karen: Hi, John.
Supervisor: Hi, Karen. Nice to see you.

4
Supervisor: Come in.
Paul: Good morning, Doctor.
Supervisor: Hello, Paul. Sit down.

5
Supervisor: Come in.
Karen: Hello, Professor.
Supervisor: Morning, Karen. How are you?

6
Supervisor: Come in.
Paul: Hello, Sue.
Supervisor: Hello, Paul. Good to see you.

Unit 10

🔊 10.1

Supervisor: What you need to do first, then, is put together a draft questionnaire that you're going to email out to your informants. I'd suggest it shouldn't be more than 20 questions, trying to get at their attitudes to careers in science. Any more than that and people are put off and you might not get a very high response rate. When you've done that, give it to a few people to pilot it: four or five should be enough. Get them to fill it in and then discuss with them any problems they had, and take any suggestions they might have for improving the questionnaire. Then revise it, and show it to me before you send it out.
Student: Right ... So can I just check – you think I should write a draft of the questionnaire with maximum 20 questions, pilot it with four or five people, revise it, and then show it to you. Is that right?
Supervisor: Yes, that's exactly it.
Student: OK, that's clear.
Supervisor: OK, so that's probably all we need to talk about today, I think.
Student: What would be a good time for the next meeting?
Supervisor: Well, you'll need some time to work on the questionnaire, so shall we say two weeks from today. Same time?
Student: Fine, that's great. Thanks for seeing me.
Supervisor: That's OK. Bye.

🔊 10.2

Supervisor: OK, so you've now got your results and you've set them out in tables and charts – the pie charts work very well, I thought – and you've written up that section. There are some really interesting findings on people's attitudes to scientific discoveries. What you need to do now, then, is think about the implications of your findings. So, for example, can you think of any

explanations of what you've found? You won't be able to saying anything for certain, of course, but just consider the possibilities. Also, look back at your literature review and compare what you found with what you reported. Are there any similarities and differences in your findings and theirs? And also think about the implications of what you've found for science education. This is probably the most difficult part of the thesis to write, so I suggest you begin by writing down some notes and ideas, and then we'll discuss them before you start to write the chapter up. How does that sound?
Student: Right ... What you want me to do, then, is think about my results – try to explain them, compare them with previous findings, and also think about what they mean – what are the implications? And I've got to put that in notes first, and talk to you about them. Is that it?
Supervisor: Yes, that's exactly what you should do.
Student: OK. I think I can do that.
Supervisor: Great.
Student: What about another meeting?
Supervisor: OK, well, you'll need a few days. What about meeting again at the beginning of next week? Monday afternoon? Two o'clock?
Student: That'll be fine. Many thanks for your time.
Supervisor: Fine. See you next week.

🔊 10.3

Supervisor: Right, now that you've sorted out the research questions, you need to spend a while doing some more reading and to write it up into a draft literature review. I've already given you a list of key readings, but you'll want to do quite a lot more. There's a lot that's been written about the public understanding of science. The main things are to think all the time about how what you're reading is relevant to your research questions. And also, look for ways of organising what you're reading. Remember that it's not meant to be just a description of what you've read – you've got to compare and contrast work, and evaluate what you're reading as much as possible. Finding an organising framework to report the literature is probably the key to writing a good review. Try and write a first draft – probably about 4,000 words – and get that to me a few days before we meet again, and then we can go through it at the meeting.
Student: So by the next meeting I need to have sent you a draft of a literature review of about 4,000 words. And that needs to include a report of key readings and other texts. I need to show how I've organised it, and I need to be evaluative, not just descriptive. OK, I'll do my best.
Supervisor: Right, well, good luck with it.
Student: When should we meet again?
Supervisor: I'd guess this is going to take a month or so, so let's meet five weeks today, and get the draft to me about a week before that so that I can read it.
Student: That's brilliant. Thanks very much.
Supervisor: You're welcome.

Lecture and seminar skills E

E.1 | E.2

Professor Rings: Now, the aim of this paper is to raise cultural awareness, er, and in an ideal world, enhance a bit your intercultural and transcultural competence. Er, I have two precise research questions in that context. How is cultural difference most commonly expressed? And to what extent does this follow traditional concepts of culture? And secondly, how is the interconnectedness of cultures articulated and how does this relate to different notions of interculturality and transculturality? Methodology – well, I will base this largely on transcultural theory as developed by Welsch, Hagan and Hunter. Er, but you can have an interesting overview, also a bit more recently by Irya Sova-Morgan. And I will also draw on post-colonial discourse theory, in particular on established authors as Said and Bhabha, but also on more recent, er, contributors like Anton. And that brings us already to the monocultural challenge. And of course if we wanna have a look at those four identity constructs as a basic differentiation of patterns of behaviour, as I said monoculturality, multiculturality, interculturality and transculturality. Then what unites them, en-, obviously in the first instance, is their link to culture and the idea, the definition of culture is, of course, a very complex one. There are thousands of definitions around. But we need a working definition to start from, I think, and I think, a very short and clear working definition has been offered by Hofstede. In 2001 he declares, he summarises better, culture as 'a collective programming of the mind manifested in values, symbols and heroes and rituals.' Now, if you imagine the, er, human, human mental programming, so to speak in the form of a pyramid yeah? Then you have at the top of the pyramid something that you could call the individual level of human mental programming. In the middle, the collective programming and the bottom there is some, there's the universal dimension. Now the individual is obviously, makes you unique, while the universal is more or less what you share with all other humans it's an instin-, it's the instinctive level. That's how it's sometimes called. It's, it's instinctive behaviour like you know, search for food, for drink, for whatever. Erm, but what we are interested in is, of course, the collective level and one common starting point and I think, er, helpful starting point for your stay abroad is national programming so national culture er, s-, the collective construct to start from. Clearly what programming of the mind indicates is that culture in particular at that level is learnt. It's not inherited. But learned, not necessarily always in a conscious and cognitive way. Can be conditioned. Can be programmed as Hofstede says. So that's one assumption to make for culture, for our working definition. And the second one is that culture is not just a descriptive concept. I wouldn't have, er,

written this paper I guess if it is just a descriptive concept, but it is also an operative concept. Now what that is I think, er, German philosopher Wolfgang Welsch, er, tries to summarise here in the following words. I quote: 'Our understanding of culture is an active factor in our cultural life. If one tells us as the old concept of culture did.' And he is referring here to monoculturality and we will be coming to that. 'That culture is to be a homogenic event, then we practise the acquired coercions and exclusions. We seek to satisfy the task we are set and will be successful in doing so.' He continues with regard to a more transcultural approach: 'Whereas if one tells us that culture ought to incorporate the foreign and do justice to transcultural components, then we will set about this task. And then corresponding feeds of integration will belong to the real structure of our culture.' And here comes probably the most important sentence: 'The reality of culture is always a consequence too of our conceptions of culture.' And that brings us back to the programming of the mind – it happens, yes already in your families. It happens in school, preschool, it happens in universities. But of course, it happens in our virtual world also, via cinema.

E.3 | E.5

Professor Rings: What you see here in this slide is a standard acculturation curve. In this case it's comes from Hofstede's *Culture's Consequences* from 2001 but I could have taken something very similar from Yang 2005 and from so many other scholars. Most scholars agree that when people go abroad they usually associate that experience before they go and alre-, also still in the first days, erm, with very positive feelings. There is a phase that Hofstede calls 'euphoria', uh, Yang, would call it 'honeymoon'. Whatever you call it, yeah, you come usually with relatively high expectations. Some higher than others but with positive feelings. That is the general tendencies. tendency. There might be exceptions to the rule of course but the tendency is that you come with certain high expectations, er, you wanna go abroad you, you're looking forward to it. Well, the higher your expectations are the more likely it is that er, these de-, expectation will be, er, disappointed. You will be frustrated at some stage. It can happen after a couple of days. It can happen after a couple of weeks. But that it goes down is a very common phenomena, and if it goes down in that way as the acculturation curve suggests then, yes, you can talk about a culture shock. Now, most people will, erm, try to adapt. Will try their very best to somehow survive, to suc-, somehow succeed in the new environment. And acculturation follows. And then, at the end of the day, you are hopefully, again in a stable state. Once again, it depends on the context. How let's say, monocultural, multicultural or, whatever your context is. And on yourself. How, er, monocultural, multicultural or whatsoever you react. Erm, where the new balance

will be found? It can be at a positive level. It can be at a more or less neutral level. Or you stay in the country, er, with rather negative feelings, getting bitter about your experience. But yeah, hey you have paid your fees for one-year MA course, you don't want to give up on that so you stay. You don't like it but you stay. Yeah? So the point is, the po-, there are two points to make. I would argue that, erm, when the culture shock hits you that is usually the moment when people retreat into either a multicultural scenario, so you go back to coexistence, you don't really want to enhance interaction with the other, any more, erm, but here you are, yeah you stay. I've, I've experienced people who just went home, who gave up on the stay abroad but most a, as I said try to cope and, erm, the reaction, uh, the coping strategy yeah is very often multicultural or it's even monocultural with, so linked to exclusions of the other. Yeah? So that's one thing, where these culture concepts get very interesting. And the other thing is of course, erm, what causes the culture shock in the first instance? Well, I would argue very often that it's either multicultural or monocultural patterns of behaviour from your environment that can very significantly contribute to your culture shock. Let's imagine you're coming as an employee to an office who doesn't understand, uh, the office environment. That of course might trigger the culture shock experience.

E.4

Professor Rings: Whatever you call it, yeah, you come usually with relatively high expectations. Some higher than others but with positive feelings. That is the general tendencies. tendency. There might be exceptions to the rule of course but the tendency is that you come with certain high expectations, er, you wanna go abroad you, you're looking forward to it. Well, the higher your expectations are the more likely it is that er, these de-, expectation will be, er, disappointed. You will be frustrated at some stage. It can happen after a couple of days. It can happen after a couple of weeks.

E.6

Professor Rings: Now and with these remarks, we are already, erm, entering the first concept the first identity construct, the monocultural identity construct. Well, it is a construct that is typical clearly for European colonialism and 19th, even early 20th-century nation building. You could argue in fascism, European fascism in Mussolini's Italy, in Franco's Spain in, er, Hitler's Germany, you saw it very clearly. Er, you saw very clearly there in particular, erm, the key characteristics and they are, er, here listed in bullet point number two. Monoculturality is usually supposed to be homogeneous essentialist and separatist. What does that mean? Erm ... Many scholars argue here with the or present here, the metaphor of culture as an island, which is the metaphor commonly used in monocultural constructs. So on one side,

British culture as an island, on the other side let's say German or French culture as an island. Typical for island, is for islands, is that there are clearly defined boundaries and there is water in the middle. So no overlapping at all. Well, we know in particular, in our globalised society these days, there's an awful lot of overlapping. Maybe after this lecture you wanna go in to Facebook or Twitter and contact your friends abroad. Yeah? Erm, or you just go into some internet pages and they don't have to be British internet pages of course. Erm ... And so on. In food culture, in music culture, you see a constant overlap, you see hybrid products all the time. So that is the reality I think of culture. It is an overlapping. It is a constant exchange and, erm, and blurring of boundaries really in real life experience. But the monocultural construct starts from this imagination that culture is an island, yeah, different cultures behave to each other like one island to the next. Meaning separatist. Erm, if you want a clear idea of how that then, erm, yeah transfers into mind sets, just think a bit about common stereotypes that you see in newspapers. Jokes let's say about the British individualism, er about, uh, German discipline, about French laissez-faire, about Spanish fiesta-style behaviour and so on. Erm, of course there is a clear indication that a German is as follows, a British behaves as follows and that this is so by birth and it's never changing. So here you see the essentialist characteristic, you see the clear boundaries. And you see also of course that British people are summarised here into one homogeneous entity as if no significant differences between those millions of British people would exist. And I think, er, that is clearly out of shape. But nevertheless, the monocultural construct is an attractive one. Erm ... We read these jokes, we laugh about them, we think it's funny. Erm ... Clearly if you go along, er, those lines of argumentation, erm, you can also say monoculturality is a double-sided concept. On the one side, you have to imagine a culturally, racially pure and superior Self versus on the other side, at the bottom, rather an impure and inferior Other. So the separatist notion of the two islands metaphor, er, is here transferred into a hierarchy. And obviously it's the self, it's you on top of the hierarchy in the self construct, and it's the other always, er, at the bottom of the hierarchy. And there's something more worth stressing. It's a paradigm of assimilation and exclusion. Now that sounds very abstract. But I think German philosopher Johann Gottfried Herder has already summarised that in very clear words for us. And I quote him. End of 18th century, of course, we're talking here. 'Everything which is still the same as my nature which can be assimilated therein'. So the paradigm of assimilation of course. 'I envy, strive towards, make my own. Beyond this.' And now we come to the paradigm of exclusion: 'Kind nature has armed me with insensibility. Coldness and blindness. It can even become contempt and disgust.' Now, I wouldn't bother mentioning all this if I were to think that monoculturality ends with let's say European colonialism, with fascism in Europe, and so on. But clearly it continues well after de-nazification, decolonisation, and it continues in particular as subtext in different other constructs like multiculturality.

E.7

Fotis: Because they have to cover a vast amount of topics in a very small amount of time, so what they do is usually rush through the topics they they kind of, think that you have done your reading, so you're pretty much familiar with everything. They try to, to structure it in the usual structure that you have. You know, an introduction a main part and a conclusion. But because they do get engaged with questions and answers from their audience, and they do try to blend in both cases and the actual subject, that is isn't usually the case, you know, that structure isn't strictly followed. And the, the advantages of that is that you can actually be engaged in the whole talk. There, I can't find any disadvantages, I could maybe if I was, you know, studying natural sciences, and I would expect a solid structure, but since I'm more of a theoretical discipline I don't. I ki, kind of prefer the chaos.

Appendices

Appendix 1
In-text references
1 The author–date system

- In an *integral* reference the author's surname is used as an element of the sentence.

Bygate (1987) points out that spoken text is generally grammatically simpler than written text.

- The author's surname is followed by the date of publication in brackets. Integral references focus attention on the author.
- In a *non-integral* reference the author's surname and the date of publication are put in brackets.

75 percent of journeys by men and 52 percent by women were by car (**Oxley 2000**).

- A number of sources by different authors can be listed in non-integral references.

Since 1990, authors of numerous articles have recommended the use of problem-centered instruction in secondary social studies classes (**e.g. Benoit 1998; Gallagher 2000; Maxwell, Bellisimo & Mergendoller 2001; Savoie & Hughes 1994**).

- Items in the list are usually given in alphabetical order.
- Commas can be placed between the surname and date.

... by car (**Oxley, 2000**).

... social studies classes (**e.g. Benoit, 1998; Gallagher, 2000; Maxwell, Bellisimo & Mergendoller, 2001; Savoie & Hughes, 1994**).

- When a publication has more than two authors, only the surname of the first author is given, followed by et al. (et alia = and others).

Owen et al. (2009) found that 45% of patients had home internet access. Although these errors are rare, they occur in spontaneous speech (**Clark et al. 1986**).

- For a quotation, it is usual to give a page number in addition to the date:

Jenkins (1995, p. 121) argues that "customers are individuals whose individual wants and needs can be ascertained and fulfilled".

- When we report one writer mentioned by another writer, 'cited in' or just 'in' is used.

Schools often give conflicting messages about the value of sport in the curriculum (**Barrett 2001, cited in Adams 2008**).

2 The numeric or endnote system

- A number is placed in the text, usually in superscript, or sometimes in square brackets. This links to a source given in the reference list.

A growing number of universities are offering modules in communication skills.[1]

Porter noted that "in choosing among technologies to invest in, a firm must base its decision on a thorough understanding of each important technology in its value chain". **[1]**

Appendix 2
Reference lists

The example reference list on page 169 follows the very common APA (American Psychological Association) style of referencing:

- the list should be headed *References*;
- it should include *all* the sources (books, journal articles, newspaper articles, websites, etc.) you have referred to in your text;
- it should *not* include any sources you have read but not referred to;
- references are normally listed in alphabetical order.

Some different conventions may be used in your subject from those shown here. Your department may give you details of what you need to do. If not, follow the conventions used in a leading journal in your subject or use the conventions shown here.

References

Ball, K., Timperio, A. & Crawford, D. (2009). Neighborhood socioeconomic inequalities in food access and affordability. [Electronic version]. *Health and Place*, p. 578.
· *Article in a journal; originally printed, but found online*

Barnett, C., Cloke, P., Clarke, N. & Malpass, A. (2005). Consuming ethics: Articulating the subjects and spaces of ethical consumption. *Antipode, 37*, 23–45.
· *Article in a journal*

Carrell, K. (2011). *The end of cheap food?* MSc lecture notes, 2011/12, Nottingham City University, Department of Geography.
· *Handout from a lecture*

Castree, N., Demeritt, D. & Liverman, D. (eds) (2009). A *Companion to Environmental Geography.* Oxford: Wiley-Blackwell.
· *Edited book*

DeLind, L. (2003). Considerably more than vegetables, a lot less than community: the dilemma of community-supported agriculture. In J. Adams (ed) *Fighting for the Farm: Rural America transformed*, pp. 192l–206. Philadelphia: University of Pennsylvania Press.
· *Paper in an edited book*

Doubleday, R. (2004). *Political innovation: corporate engagements in the controversy over genetically modified foods.* Unpublished PhD dissertation. London: University College London, Department of Geography.
· *Unpublished dissertation*

Elliott, V. (2009, August 10). Food crisis could force wartime rations and vegetarian diet on Britons, *The Times*, p.31.
· *Article in a newspaper or magazine*

Food and Agriculture Organization. (2006). *The State of Food Insecurity in the World.* Retrieved February 9, 2012 from www.fao.org/docrep/009/a0750e/a0750e00.htm.
· *Information or statistics from a government or other organisation online*

Food Research and Action Center (2007). *State of the States: 2007.* Washington, DC: Food Research and Action Center.
· *Book without a named author*

Geography of food. (n.d.). In *Wikipedia.* Retrieved 21 May 2011 from http://en.wikipedia.org/wiki/Geography_of_food.
· *Article in an online reference source*

Magdoff, F. (2008, May 2008). The world food crisis: sources and solutions, *Monthly Review.* Retrieved May 16, 2011 from http://www.monthlyreview.org/080501magdoff.php.
· *Article in an online publication*

Marsden, T., Flynn, A. & Harrison, M. (2000). *Consuming Interests: The social provision of foods.* London: UCL Press.
· *Book with two or more authors*

Patel, R. (2007). *Stuffed and Starved: Markets, power and the hidden battle for the world food system.* London: Portobello Books.
· *Book with a single author*

Appendix 3
Avoiding gender-specific language

Avoid gender-specific language. Use gender-neutral language.

1 Where both males and females are meant, use words which include both.

- If **a person** fails on a test, does **he** have low ability, or is the test difficult?
  → If **a person** fails on a test, do **they** have low ability…?/ If **people** fail on a test, do **they** have low ability…?/ If **a person** fails on a test does **he or she** have low ability…?
- The eight people who stayed behind **to man** the office were given a special appreciation dinner.
  →… who stayed behind **to staff** the office …

- **Man** is a part of nature and bears responsibility for protecting the diversity of the environment.
  → **Humans** are part of nature and …

- Others: the man in the street; manpower; mankind
  → the average person / people in general; staff / workforce / human resources; people / human beings / humankind

2 Where a job or role might be filled by either males or females, do not use a term that implies the gender of the person.

- From the **businessman's** point of view it is desirable to retain freedom in decision-making so that **he** can maintain the initiative in meeting market and social factors.
  → From **the business person's** point of view it is desirable to retain freedom in decision-making so that **they** (or **he or she**) can maintain … / From **business people's** point of view it is desirable to retain freedom in decision-making so that **they** can maintain …

- The **secretary's** principle loyalty is to **her** boss rather than to the company.
  → The **secretary's** principle tie is to **their** (or **his or her**) boss …

- Others: landlord; chairman; policeman; spokesman
  → owner; chair/chairperson; police officer; spokesperson

A number of online sources give more information. Particularly useful are:

- http://en.wikipedia.org/wiki/Gender_neutrality_in_English
- unesdoc.unesco.org/images/0011/001149/114950mo.pdf

Appendix 4

Writing in an academic style

Points A–D below are some general principles to help you write in a style appropriate for academic writing.

A Use formal rather than informal language

1 Avoid contracted forms:

- *mustn't* > **must not**
- *it's* > **it is**

2 Avoid colloquial language ('spoken' language):

- *The results from ~~a lot of~~ **many of these** recent projects have been ~~pretty good~~ **encouraging**.*

3 Avoid punctuation indicating your attitude:

- *Turnout in the election was less than 20 percent!*
  → ***Disappointingly/Surprisingly**, turnout in the election was less than 20 percent.*

B Be concise and precise

4 In general, use a one-word verb where we might prefer a phrasal verb in speech:

- *The issue was ~~brought up~~ **raised** during the meeting.*

5 Avoid vague words common in speech such as *big (bigger, biggest), good, thing,* and *nice*:

- *Government policy has a ~~big~~ **major/significant/important** impact on the way business is conducted.*

6 Avoid *etc., and so on,* and *and so forth* where it would be better to provide a full list or summarise the features of the items in the list:

- *Elements in the periodic table can be divided into ~~metals, non-metals, etc.~~ **metals, non-metals, and metalloids (semi-metals)**.*

7 Consider nominalisation to express ideas efficiently:

- *The number of cases is increasing and this is causing great concern among health authorities.*
  → *The **increase in the number** of cases is causing great concern among health authorities.*

C Use impersonal language

8 Avoid using *I (me, my, mine)* or *we (our, ours)* (referring to yourself) to express an opinion:

- *~~I think~~ **It is likely** that mobile phone technology will be used increasingly in education.*

Note, that *I* is often used when a writer talks about how they are organising their writing, or the procedures followed in their research:

- *In the next section I will go on to demonstrate that …*
- *I first analysed their ability to solve the problems.*

9 Avoid addressing the reader as *you* or *the reader*:

- *~~You~~ can see the results in Table 3.*
  → ***The results are shown** in Table 3.*

- *~~The reader~~ should note two important assumptions.*
  → *Two important assumptions **should be noted**.*

D Be cautious in what you say

10 Avoid generalisations:

- *Nowadays ~~everyone has~~ **there is widespread** access to the internet.*

11 Avoid words that express your emotion rather than show evidence:

- *It is ~~ridiculous to think that~~ **debatable whether** the problems can be solved by economic means.*

12 Use hedges to qualify your statements:

- *In Australia, beef cattle ~~are found~~ **are mostly found** in Queensland and New South Wales.*
- *The virus ~~is~~ **appears to be** widespread in central Asia.*

Writing an introduction

A   Research article introduction

Introduction

I just want my children to be happy.

(36 year-old mother of 2)
(25 year-old father of 3)
(32 year-old father of 2)

5 Parents want their children to be happy. But, what makes children happy? The answer to this seemingly simple question eludes parents, educators, researchers, and the general public. Although opinion-leaders have clearly voiced their concern about the increase in childhood depression, the answer to
10 the question of what contributes to children's happiness is debatable. With children being constantly bombarded with images suggesting that slim figures, trendy fashions, expensive toys, or other material goods are solutions to finding happiness, it is exceedingly difficult to determine what truly makes
15 children happy. Do children look to material goods to find happiness? Or, do they look to sports? Do they rely on other sources to experience happiness that adults have overlooked? Are there age related changes that need to be accounted for? While anecdotal evidence is abundant, empirical studies focused
20 on investigating the sources that contribute to children's happiness at different ages are missing. Such studies would be beneficial not only because they would allow for a more informed discussion of children's global happiness, but also because they would help opinion-leaders guide children down
25 the path towards happiness.

With the inception of the *Journal of Happiness Studies* in 2000, the prominence of the topic of happiness in today's pop culture, and the inception of conferences on happiness and positive psychology within the past year, the topic of happiness
30 and subjective well-being has clearly become a highly valued matter (Diener 2000; Veenhoven 2000). Surprisingly, researchers have been slow in developing studies that specifically address children's happiness. Although a rapidly developing "positive psychology" movement that emphasizes people's strengths
35 instead of their weaknesses is quickly steering social scientists towards conducting studies on happiness, most of these studies have focused on adults, not children. Studies have primarily used surveys to examine how external correlates of adults' lives (e.g. income, employment, marital status, etc.) affect happiness
40 (Andrews and Withey 1976; Bortner and Hultsch 1970; Campbell et al. 1976; Cohn 1979; Cummins 2000). Studies have also been designed to assess *how* happy people are, as opposed to *what* makes them happy.

Park and Peterson (2006) point out that studies of happiness
45 in children have been neglected. In addition to the conceptual gap in understanding what makes children happy, measures that are more conducive to studying an abstract construct such as happiness in a children's sample are also needed. Questionnaires developed for adults cannot be simply lifted and used with
50 children, whose cognitive abilities are not as sophisticated as those of adults. Thus, not only do current happiness studies fall short of providing meaningful answers to questions related to what makes today's children happy, but they also lack effective measures that are suitable for examining age differences across
55 a wide age range.

Our research responds to Park and Peterson's (2006) urge for more research on children's happiness in two ways. First, we introduce a novel measure that is simple, engaging and appropriate for a broad age range of children and adolescents
60 (ages 8–18) to express what makes them happy – a "collage" measure. Second, we use this new technique in combination with more traditional measures to address critical questions that have remained unanswered - what aspects of life make children happy (e.g. people, hobbies, material things)? Do these sources
65 of happiness vary across ages?

We begin by reviewing research on the topic of happiness. We then discuss two studies designed to explore the question – "What makes children happy?" Study 1 collects information about what general themes (e.g. people and pets, hobbies,
70 material things) contribute to children's happiness, using an open-ended task. Study 2 uses a semi-structured thought listing task and a collage task to test for age differences in children's and adolescents' happiness. We conclude with a discussion of the implications of our findings and future research directions.

Chaplin, L. N. (2009). Please may I have a bike? Better yet, may I have a hug? An examination of children's and adolescents' happiness. *Journal of Happiness Studies*, 10: 541–562.

B Thesis introduction

Background

TecÚology has the potential to enhance the quality of life of people. It is ironic when tecÚology may in fact be having the opposite effect. It is this ironic situation that the people of northern Saskatchewan now find themselves confronting. Skilled employment opportunities are plentiful, yet unemployment is high. As is common across the country, the tecÚology "skills" of the people are not at the level to meet the tecÚology "needs" of industry. Until we understand why this dilemma exists, and more importantly, endeavor to correct it, the situation will persist. This study is a part of that process. It examined one aspect of the tecÚology skills gap dilemma; the role that teachers play in the computer education of students in northern Saskatchewan.

Northern Saskatchewan is the term used to describe the top "half" of the province of Saskatchewan. The socioeconomic status of the region is much lower in many categories than the rest of the province. The rate of unemployed adults over age 25 is three times as high in the north. The overall unemployment rate in the north is 20% compared to 7% provincially (Northern Labour Market Committee, 2002). Although unemployment levels in the north are nearly three times as high as in the rest of the province, the paradox is that employment opportunities in a number of resource sectors exist. These jobs, as part of agreements between government and industry, are targeted for northern Aboriginal people. The jobs are simply not being filled. This paradox can more succinctly be referred to as the "tecÚical skills gap". Jobs in the 21st century require higher skill levels, and northerners are not meeting that skill level to benefit from the jobs.

This then, provides the context for this study. In summary, in order to enhance the quality of life for many disadvantaged northerners, employment has to increase. Job opportunities exist, but northerners are not taking advantage of the opportunities and filling the jobs. Employment opportunities require tecÚically skilled and computer literate people, and currently, many people in the region seeking employment do not have these skills. Arguably, there are a number of reasons why northerners have not been meeting the need for skilled employment. This study looks at one piece of the puzzle by surveying teachers in the provincial and First Nation school systems to determine whether or not they are preparing students for the new reality of a computer literate workforce. In a general sense, the study will provide a snapshot of student computer use.

Rationale and aims

Although pre-existing data specific to the computer use of students in northern Saskatchewan are scarce, general data reveal that our public schools have increased the number of computers in their facilities. In the early part of the decade, most schools had about one computer for every 20 to 25 students. By the end of the decade, these numbers overall in Saskatchewan have dropped to around eight students for every computer (Statistics Canada, 1999). One can anticipate that well before the start of the next decade, a computer for every student will be the norm. Schools have increased the level of tecÚology, or more precisely the number of computers, within their walls, however, this has not necessarily translated into an increased use of computers. Recent data from the Saskatchewan Department of Education show that overall in the province about 70% of grade 5 students, 90% of grade 8 students and 90% of grade 11 students report they use a computer to do school assignments at least once a week (Saskatchewan Education, 2001). At first glance, this looks like a positive indicator, however, further analysis reveals that of the same grades, 65%, 55%, and 50% respectively, report that they use a computer less than one hour per school week. Considering there are 25 instructional hours in a typical school week, we can deduce that the majority of students in grades 5, 8 & 11 in Saskatchewan use a computer less than 4% of the time they are in school. In short, Saskatchewan students are significantly underachieving in meeting the standards of computer usage at school.

Many studies have assessed the computer attitude of both pre-service and inservice teachers (Delcourt and Kinzie, 1993; Francis, 1993; Larson & Smith, 1994; Metu, 1994; Mitra, 1998; Omar, 1992; Pepper, 1999; Reece & Gable, 1982;). Most of these studies also examined the computer ability of the subjects. In the majority of cases, it was found that a positive relationship existed between the computer attitude of respondents and their computer ability. The general consensus seems to be that a higher degree of computer ability translates into a more positive computer attitude. Further, most of these studies examine demographic variables such as age, gender and educational background. Not nearly as numerous as studies into the attitude and ability of teachers, a relatively small number of studies have examined the frequency and type of computer use demonstrated by students in schools. The primary purpose of this study is not a comprehensive examination of what students are doing with computers in schools. The purpose rather, is to determine if a relationship exists between teachers' attitudes towards computer use, the level of their ability to use computers and the computer use of students.

The following research question provides the direction for this study: Are teacher attitudes, computer ability, demographic profile and working environment related to student computer usage? Specifically, the purpose of this study is to show whether teachers' attitudes toward computers and competency in using computers as an effective educational tool (computer ability) are factors that are related to the frequency and type of computer use by students. In addition, this study will determine if the demographic and environmental variables of teachers are related to the frequency and type of computer use of students.

To assess student computer use, the same criteria as those employed in the 1999 *Provincial Learning Assessment in TecÚological Literacy* (Saskatchewan Education, 2001) have been utilized. Three components of student use were examined: The overall frequency of computer use, the frequency of specific types of computer activities and the use of computers in subject areas. A comprehensive and critical assessment of how effectively students are using computers in the classroom is beyond the scope of this study.

This study is of value for many reasons. The study is a snapshot of the use of computers in the teaching and learning process in northern Saskatchewan. The study provides insight into what is going on in schools, and by extension, may be of some use to those who are trying to close the "tecÚical skills gap". The study also provides information to those responsible for the educational system that may be of help to determine the inservice needs of teachers and to assess the level of computer integration across the curriculum.

Outline

Chapter One has provided the context, rationale and purpose of the study. It presents the research question that is answered and definition of terms. Chapter Two reviews the literature relevant to the topic. Chapter Three describes the research methodology, the instrument used and the population studied. Chapter Four presents the data derived from the survey, while Chapter Five examines and discusses the findings. Chapter Six summarizes the study, highlights the significant findings, draws conclusions and makes suggestions for future research

Definition of terms

The following are definition of terms commonly used in this study:
Provincial School refers to a school as defined by the Education Act, 1995 and governed by a board of elected trustees.
First Nation School is a school administered within the Indian Act.
Tribal Council is a term used to describe an association of First Nations.
Survey and *questionnaire* are used synonymously to define the tool used to collect data.

Greschner, K. J. (2003). *The relationship between teacher attitudes and skills and student use of computers in northern schools.* Unpublished Master of Education thesis, University of Saskatchewan, Saskatoon, Canada.

Wordlist

Abbreviations: n = noun / n (pl) = plural noun; v = verb; adj = adjective; adv = adverb; conj = conjunction; phr = phrase; phr v = phrasal verb; T/I = transitive/intransitive; C/U = countable/uncountable. The numbers indicate the page on which the word first appears.

Academic Orientation

abstract *n* [C] (13) a shortened form of a speech, article, book, etc., giving only the most important facts or ideas

conduct research / an investigation *phr* (10) to examine a subject carefully and in detail in order to discover new information

characteristic *n* [C] (10) a typical or obvious quality that makes one person or thing different from others

confirm *v* [T] (11) to say or show that something is true

counter *v* [T] (11) to prevent something or reduce the bad effect that it has

develop good practice *phr* (11) to use a working method which is officially accepted as being the best one to use

fall off *phr v* [I] (11) if the amount, rate, or quality of something falls off, it becomes smaller or lower

fieldwork *n* [U] (13) study which consists of practical activities that are done away from your school, college or place of work

hypothesis *n* [C] (13) a suggested explanation for something which has not yet been proved to be true

independent learner *n* [C] (10) a person who does not need help from other people in order to to get knowledge

oriented *adj* (12) directed towards or interested in something

research proposal *n* [C] (13) a written plan of the research that you intend to do

structured *adj* (10) arranged in an organized way

undertake a project *phr* (12) to do or begin to do a carefully planned piece of work

write up *phr v* [I] (12) to write something in a complete form, usually using notes that you made earlier

Unit 1

back up *phr v* [I] (22) to prove that something is true

break through *phr v* [I] (21) to force yourself through something difficult or that is holding you back

contend *v* [T] (24) to say that something is true

correlate *v* [I/T] (24) to connect two or more things, often one in which one of them causes or influences the other

collaborative *adj* (19) involving two or more people working together for a special purpose

conceptualise *v* [T] (16) to form an idea or principle in your mind

corpus *n* [C] (18) the collection of written and sometimes spoken material collected to show the state of a language, or about a particular subject

critical thinking *phr* (16) giving judgments and opinions on books, plays, films, etc

empirical *adj* (16) based on experience or scientific experiments and not only on ideas

ethical dilemma *phr* [C] (21) a difficult choice relating to what you believe is right or wrong

evaluate *v* [T] (24) to consider something carefully and decide how good or bad it is

go hand in hand *phr* (14) to exist together and be connected with each other

grey area *phr* (21) something which people are not certain about, usually because there are no clear rules for it

ills *n* [C] (14) (usually plural) problems

incontrovertible *adj* (23) certainly true

outline *v* [T] (24) to describe only the most important ideas or facts about something

outright *adj* (21) total, clear, and certain

peer *n* [C] (19) someone who is the same age, or who has the same social position or abilities as other members of a group

per capita *adj* (25) for each person

product placement *n* [C/U] (22) when a company advertises a product by supplying it for use in films or television programmes

qualitative *adj* (24) relating to how good something is and not how much of it there is

quantitative *adj* (24) relating to quantity (= the amount or number of something)

skepticism *n* [U] (16) US spelling of scepticism (= when you doubt that something is true or useful)

supporting evidence *phr* (14) information which helps to show something to be true

target audience *n* [C] (16) the particular group of people to which an advertisement, a product, a website or a television or radio programme is directed

working knowledge *phr* (24) knowledge about something which is good enough to be useful

Unit 2

anaesthetic *n* [C] (28) a drug that makes you unable to feel pain during an operation

breakthrough *n* [C] (26) an important discovery or development that helps solve a problem

commercialisation *n* [U] (26) when something is organised to make a profit

complementary *adj* (27) things which are complementary are good or attractive together

distinguish v [T] (27) to make one person or thing seem different from another

developing country n [C] (33) a country with little industrial and economic activity and where people generally have low incomes

drastic change phr (28) a sudden and extreme change

electron microscope n [C] (32) a device used for looking at very small things which produces pictures by sending electrons through objects

follow v [I/T] (26) to understand something

follow up phr v [I] (26) to discover more about a situation or take further action in connection with it

homogeneous adj (28) consisting of parts or members that are all the same

innovate v [I] (29) to introduce changes and new ideas

market v [T] (27) to try to sell products using advertising or other ways of making people want to buy them

rollout n [C] (33) the act of making something, esp. a product or service, available for the first time

solar cell n [C] (28) a device for producing electrical energy from the sun

support v [T] (36) to help to show that something is true

technological advances n (pl) [C] (27) new discoveries and inventions

Unit 3

application n [C/U] (45) a way in which something can be used for a particular purpose

bedrock n [U] (43) a situation, idea, or principle that provides a strong base for something

biofuel n [U] (42) fuel produced from plant material

biomass n [U] (42) the total amount of living things in a particular area

capital n [U] (50) an amount of money that you can use to start a business or to make more money

critical adj (43) very important for the way things will happen in the future

cutting-edge adj (43) very modern and with all the newest developments

a broader picture/context phr (42) including a wider range of information about a situation

decision-maker n [C] (42) a person who decides things, especially at a high level in an organization

demographic adj (53) relating to the study of changes in the number of births, marriages, deaths, etc. in a particular area during a period of time

food security n [U] (42) a situation in which enough food is produced and available for everyone in a group, country, etc. to have enough to eat

genetic engineering n [U] (50) when scientists change the genes parts of cells which control particular characteristics in the cells of plants or animals

genetically modified/GM adj (49) genetically modified plants or animals have had some of their genes (= parts of cells which control particular characteristics) changed

joined-up thinking phr (42) thinking about a complicated problem in an intelligent and original way, and considering everything that is connected with it

outline n [C] (48) a short description of the most important ideas or facts about something

renewable resource n [C] (42) a form of energy that can be produced as quickly as it is used

spike n [C] (49) a higher price, amount, etc., usually before a fall

sustainable adj (43) causing little or no damage to the environment and therefore able to continue for a long time

Unit 4

annotate v [T] (61) to add a short explanation or opinion to a text or drawing

consumption n [U] (61) the amount of something that someone uses, eats, or drinks

counterproductive adj (61) having the opposite effect from the one you want

detrimental adj (55) causing harm or damage

en masse adv (59) if a group of people do something en masse, they do it together as a group

indicator n [C] (59) a fact, measurement, or condition that shows what something is like or how it is changing

induction n [C/U] (59) when someone is officially accepted into a new job or an organization

materialize v [I] (61) f something does not materialize, it does not happen

mitigate v [T] (56) to reduce the harmful effects of something

multitasking n [U] (56) the ability of a person to do more than one thing at a time

paperless adj (60) relating to a system that keeps information on computers, not on paper

paradoxically adv (61) in a way that seems very strange or impossible because of two opposite qualities or facts

paraphrase v [I/T] (60) to express something that has been said or written in a different way, usually so that it is clearer

pedagogy n [U] (59) the study of the methods and activities of teaching

quantify v [T] (55) to measure or state the amount of something

Unit 5

affiliation n [C/U] (74) a connection with a political party or religion, or with a larger organization

be alive and well phr (77) to continue to be popular or successful

characterisation n [C/U] (77) the particular way in which someone or something is described or shown

confrontational adj (75) intentionally causing fighting or an argument

embedded *adj* (71) a very strong and important attitude or value

eradication *n* [U] (70) when something such as a social problem or a disease is destroyed or completely got rid of

GDP *n* [U] (71) (Gross Domestic Product) the total value of goods and services that a country produces in a year

hyperlink *n* [C] (74) text that you can click on to go between computer documents or pages on the internet

infrastructure *n* [C] (71) the basic systems, such as transport and communication, that a country or organization uses in order to work effectively

marginalise *v* [T] (70) to treat someone or something as if they are not important

misconception *n* [C/U] (77) when your understanding of something is wrong

micro-credit *n* [U] (71) a very small loan to individual people or families, for example in developing countries, especially in order to start a business

parameter *n* [C] (77) a limit that controls the way that you can do something

reconciliation *n* [C/U] (71) when two people or groups become friendly again after they have argued

safeguard *v* [T] (71) to protect something from harm

stewardship *n* [U] (70) the way in which that person controls or organizes it

social cohesion *phr* [U] (70) when the members of a group or society are united and work together effectively

Unit 6

acquisition *n* [U] (84) the process of getting something

beg the question *phr* (83) if a statement or situation begs the question, it causes you to ask a particular question

controversy *n* [C] (88) a lot of disagreement or argument about something, usually because it affects or is important to many people

conversely *adv* (84) in an opposite way

determinant *n* [C] (83) something that decides (determines) how or if something happens or doesn't happen

empirical *adj* (83) based on what is experienced or seen rather than on theory

evaluate *v* [T] (84) to judge or calculate the quality, importance, amount or value of something

freshman *n* [C] (83) a student in the first year of high school, college, or university

grade point average *n* [C] (83) a number which is the average mark received for all the courses a student takes and shows how well the student is doing

median *adj* (83) the middle amount in a set of values arranged in order of size

moderate *v* [T] (84) to (cause to) become less in size, strength, or force; to reduce something

outcome *n* [C] (83) a result or effect of an action, situation, etc.

outside of *phr* (83) except for

phenomenon *n* [U] (84) something that exists and can be seen, felt, tasted, etc., especially something which is unusual or interesting

plausible *adj* (84) seeming likely to be true, or able to be believed

preliminary *adj* (86) (coming before a more important action or event, especially introducing or preparing for it

rule of thumb *phr* (83) a practical and approximate way of doing or measuring something

stakeholder *n* [C] (84) a person who is involved with an organization, society, etc. in a way that they have an interest in its success

small-scale *adj* (83) a small-scale activity or organization is not big and involves few people

Unit 7

brand name *n* [C] (103) the special name that a company gives to a product

core text *n* [C] (98) a book or article that all students on a particular course must read

differentiate *v* [T] (103) to make someone or something different

dogmatic *adj* (100) not willing to accept other ideas or opinions because you think yours are right

encompass *v* [T] (99) to include a lot of things, ideas, places, etc

engage with *phr v* [I] (100) to become interested in something and keep thinking about it

global market *n* [C] (105) all the people in all areas of the world who buy or might want to buy something

invidious *adj* (100) likely to cause unhappiness or be unpleasant, especially because unfair

marketing strategy *phr* [C] (105) a plan that you use when you want to sell something to a large number of people

monograph *n* [C] (100) a long article or a short book on a particular subject

pivotal *adj* (99) having a very important influence on something

prescriptive *adj* (100) saying exactly what must happen

prospective buyer *n* [C] (104) a person who is expected to buy something

respectively *adv* (103) in the same order as the people or things you have just talked about

suffice it to say *phr* (100) it is enough to say

synonymous with *phr* (103) closely connected with

Unit 8

adolescent *n* [C] (110) a young person who is between being a child and an adult

anti-social behaviour *phr* [U] (112) anti-social behaviour harms or upsets the people around you

altruistic *adj* (118) helping other people, even if it results in disadvantage for yourself

contributory factor *n* [C] (114) a fact or situation which helps to cause something

crucial *adj* (112) extremely important or necessary

deviance *n* [U] (116) behaviour that is not usual and is generally considered to be unacceptable

distinctive *adj* (110) something that is distinctive is easy to recognize because it is different from other things

DNA analysis *n* [U] (117) when you examine genetic information

forensic *adj* (110) relating to scientific methods of solving crimes

infer *v* [T] (110) to guess that something is true because of the information that you have

like-for-like *adj* (111) similar to something else

mechanism *n* [C] (117) a way of doing something which is planned or part of a system

motor *adj* (111) relating to muscles that produce movement, or the nerves and parts of the brain that control these muscles

public debate *n* [U] (117) serious discussion of a subject in which many people take part

scrutinise *v* [T] (110) to examine something very carefully in order to discover information

social exclusion *n* [U] (117) a situation in which some people do not feel part of the rest of society

stem from *phr v* [I] (118) to start or develop as the result of something

trait *n* [C] (110) a quality, good or bad, in someone's character

violate *v* [T] (116) to not obey a law, rule, or agreement

Unit 9

civic *adj* (135) relating to a city or town and the people who live there

comprehensive *adj* (134) including everything

constraint *n* [C] (134) something that limits what you can do

entail *v* [T] (127) to involve something

exploit *v* [T] (133) to use or develop something for your advantage

extended family *n* [C] (126) a family unit which includes grandmothers, grandfathers, aunts and uncles, etc. in addition to parents and children

in sum *phr* (135) considered as a whole

nuclear family *n* [C] (126) a family consisting of two parents and their children, but not including aunts, uncles, grandparents, etc.

persuasive *adj* (134) able to make people agree to do something

prescribed *adj* (133) set by a rule or order

press release *n* [C] (132) an official piece of information that is given to newspapers, television, etc

predominant *adj* (127) more important or noticeable than others

provocative *adj* (134) causing an angry reaction, usually intentionally

reciprocity *n* [U] (134) when two people or groups agree to help each other in a similar way

simplistic *adj* (134) making something complicated seem simple by ignoring many of the details

systematic *adj* (134) done using a fixed and organized plan

the industrial revolution *n* [U] (127) the period of time during which work began to be done more by machines in factories than by hand at home

variable *n* [C] (133) a number, amount, or situation which can change

Unit 10

agenda *n* [C] (139) a list of aims or possible future achievements

controversy *n* [C/U] (142) a lot of disagreement and argument about something

counterintuitive *adj* (141) describes something that does not happen in the way you would expect it to

critical phase *phr* [C] (141 an extremely important stage in a series of events

discipline *n* [C] (139) a particular subject of study

exacerbate *v* [T] (139) to make something worse

hit-and-miss *adj* (139) not planned, but happening by chance

ideological *adj* (141) based on or relating to a particular set of ideas or beliefs

impinge on *phr v* [I] (141) to have an effect on something, often causing problems by limiting it in some way

interdisciplinary *adj* (139) involving two or more different subjects or areas of knowledge

justification *n* [C/U] (139) a reason for something

paradigm *n* [C] (140) a typical example or model of something

pertain to sth *v* [I] (140) to be connected with a particular subject, event or situation

a plethora of sth *phr* (141) a very large amount of something, especially a larger amount than you need, want or can deal with

primordial *adj* (139) existing at or since the beginning of the world or the universe

proliferation *n* [U] (141) when something increases in number very quickly

riven with dissent *phr* (139) having very strong differences of opinion on a particular subject

(a) testament to sth *phr* (141) proof of